The Use of Rhyme in Shakespeare's Plays

BY

FREDERIC W. NESS

ARCHON BOOKS
1969

SBN: 208 00027 5
Library of Congress Catalog Card Number: 69-12420
Printed in the United States of America

TO

MY MOTHER AND FATHER

PREFACE

ALTHOUGH rhyme as the principal medium for dramatic dialogue was dealt a mortal blow by Marlowe's *Tamburlaine*, it continued during Shakespeare's lifetime to flourish as an occasional embellishment in the more dignified blank verse. In Shakespeare's early plays it at times assumes major proportions; even in his latest it is present; but between the early and the late there is a pronounced diminution.

This study makes no attempt to defend Shakespeare's use nor to praise his gradual disuse of rhyme. It tries rather to determine the effects attained by the rhyme in its various functions and thereby to discover the conditions which brought about its almost complete abandonment. The ultimate result is, I hope, not solely the elucidation of a minor point of Shakespeare's style, but the casting of some further light on the enigma of his mind as it is revealed through his art.

I wish to express my thanks to Professor C. F. Tucker Brooke for his guidance in this work; to Professor Robert J. Menner for his many suggestions and criticisms; to Professor Hubertis Cummings for his helpful suggestions in the early stages of the work; to Mr. W. K. Wimsatt, Jr., for his painstaking criticism of the first draft; and to Professor B. C. Nangle for his assistance in preparing the manuscript for the press.

For assistance of various other kinds I am grateful to Mr. M. C. Beardsley, Miss A. M. Hanson, Professor S. B. Hemingway, Mr. D. R. Johnson, Mr. D. McCluskey, Mrs. H. Ness, and Mr. R. W. Taylor.

In its original form the material for this book was presented as a dissertation in partial fulfillment of the requirements for the degree of Doctor of Philosophy in Yale University.

F. W. N.

Berkeley College, Yale University,
July 5, 1941.

CONTENTS

ABBREVIATIONS USED FOR THE WORKS OF SHAKESPEARE

1 Hen. VI	*The First Part of King Henry the Sixth*
2 Hen. VI	*The Second Part of King Henry the Sixth*
3 Hen. VI	*The Third Part of King Henry the Sixth*
Rich. III	*King Richard the Third*
T. A.	*Titus Andronicus*
C. E.	*The Comedy of Errors*
T. G.	*The Two Gentlemen of Verona*
L. L. L.	*Love's Labour's Lost*
R. J.	*Romeo and Juliet*
Rich. II	*King Richard the Second*
M. N. D.	*A Midsummer Night's Dream*
John	*King John*
M. V.	*The Merchant of Venice*
T. S.	*The Taming of the Shrew*
1 Hen. IV	*The First Part of King Henry the Fourth*
2 Hen. IV	*The Second Part of King Henry the Fourth*
M. A.	*Much Ado About Nothing*
Hen. V	*King Henry the Fifth*
J. C.	*Julius Caesar*
A. Y. L.	*As You Like It*
T. N.	*Twelfth Night, or What You Will*
Ham.	*Hamlet, Prince of Denmark*
M. W.	*The Merry Wives of Windsor*
T. C.	*Troilus and Cressida*
A. W.	*All's Well that Ends Well*
M. M.	*Measure for Measure*
Oth.	*Othello, the Moor of Venice*
Mac.	*Macbeth*
Lear	*King Lear*
A. C.	*Antony and Cleopatra*
Cor.	*Coriolanus*
Tim.	*Timon of Athens*
Per.	*Pericles, Prince of Tyre*
Cy.	*Cymbeline*
W. T.	*The Winter's Tale*
Tp.	*The Tempest*
Hen. VIII	*King Henry the Eighth*
V. A.	*Venus and Adonis*
L.	*Lucrece*
L. C.	*A Lover's Complaint*
P. P.	*The Passionate Pilgrim*
P. T.	*The Phoenix and the Turtle*

I'll rhyme you so eight years together, dinners and suppers and sleeping-hours excepted.

As You Like It

I

Introduction

A RECOGNITION of the importance of rhyme in Shakespeare's plays preceded by a number of years the first attempts to look at it through the scholar's microscope. Although more than a hint was given by Thomas Edwards,[1] it was Edmond Malone who first envisaged the possibilities of a careful examination of Shakespeare's rhymes when, in 1778, he wrote this much-quoted footnote:

As this circumstance is more than once mentioned, in the course of these observations, it may not be improper to add a few words on the subject of our author's metre. A mixture of rhymes with blank verse, in the same play, and sometimes in the same scene, is found in almost all his pieces, and is not peculiar to Shakspeare, being also found in the works of Jonson, and almost all our ancient dramatick writers. It is not, therefore, merely the use of rhymes, mingled with blank verse, but their *frequency*, that is here urged, as a circumstance which seems to characterize and distinguish our poet's earliest performances. In the whole number of pieces which were written antecedent to the year 1600 . . . more rhyming couplets are found, than in all the plays composed subsequently to that year. . . . Whether in process of time Shakspeare grew weary of the bondage of rhyme, or whether he became convinced of its impropriety in a dramatick dialogue, his neglect of rhyming (for he never wholly disused it) seems to have been *gradual*. As, therefore, most of his early productions are characterized by the multitude of similar terminations which they exhibit, whenever of two early pieces it is doubtful which preceded the other, I am disposed to believe, (other proofs being wanting,) that play in which the greater number of rhymes is found, to have been first composed.[2]

Unchallenged for nearly a century, this footnote came finally to give both guidance and misguidance. Its broad suggestion of the possible use of rhyme as a chronological gauge led finally to the

1. *Canons of Criticism* (London, 1750), p. 27. It will be the practice in this study to offer full bibliographical information for a book or article when first cited. Thereafter the work will be identified by the name of the author. When there is more than one book by the same author, a short title will also be given. A list of books cited appears on pp. 157–64.
2. "Attempt to Ascertain the Order in which the Plays of Shakspeare were Written," reprinted in *The Plays of William Shakspeare* (ed. George Steevens: 4th ed., London, 1793), I, 510.

application of metrical tests to the plays of both Shakespeare and his contemporaries, with some valuable results but also with much short-sighted and erroneous speculation. Although its tentative suggestion of reasons for the gradual disuse of rhyme occasioned some constructive hypotheses, for the most part rhyme as a factor in determining the chronological order of Shakespeare's plays has been preferred by scholars to rhyme as a factor in the poet's artistic development. The preference is probably right, since, if metrical tests are "a path where all is misty and vague,"[3] a treatment of artistic development is equally shadowy and tenuous.

Though anticipated by W. Hertzberg,[4] it was actually F. G. Fleay who first began exploiting the possibilities of metrical tests, and particularly of rhyme, as a means of ascertaining the chronological sequence of Shakespeare's dramas. In 1874, after some years of preparation, his paper "On Metrical Tests as Applied to Dramatic Poetry. Part I. Shakspere"[5] was read before the New Shakspere Society, a group organized primarily to settle the problem of dating the plays. The article and the storm which it stirred up were recorded in the Society's *Transactions*, where even without the subsequent application of Fleay's theories to individual plays various weaknesses were immediately apparent. Not only were his figures unreliable but his conclusions were hasty. Carried away by his enthusiasm he showed a dangerous tendency to ignore external evidence and to achieve results whose absurdities were easily noticed. The primary difficulty, indeed, was at the very core of Fleay's theory, as F. J. Furnivall was quick to point out: "To suppose that any one empirical metrical test, like that of Ryme, can settle the stage or development of a myriad-sided mind like Shakspere's is, to me, a notion never to be entertained. If, after close study, the results of any one such test are found to coincide all through with the results of aesthetic criticism, and external evidence, I shall hold it a happy accident, not a scientific

3. H. H. Furness, *The New Variorum Edition of Shakespeare: The Winter's Tale* (Philadelphia, 1898), p. 317.

4. Introduction to *Cymbeline* (*Ausgabe der deutschen Shakespeare-gesellschaft*, 1871), p. 292. For surveys of the early history of verse tests, principally as a means of determining the chronology of Shakespeare's plays, see the following: John K. Ingram, "On the 'Weak Endings' of Shakspere," *New Shakspere Society's Transactions* I (1874), 442–7; R. Boyle, "Blank Verse and Metrical Tests," *Englische Studien* XVI (1892), 440–8; Eilert Ekwall, "Die Shakespeare-chronologie," *Germanisch-Romanische Monatsschrift* III (1911), 101–05. For a brief view of some of the first notices of Shakespeare's use of rhyme see Julius Heuser, "Der Coupletreim in Shakespeare's dramen," *Jahrbuch der deutschen Shakespeare-gesellschaft* XXVIII (1893), 177–8.

5. *N. S. S. Trans.* I, 1–16.

necessity." He then concluded: "Much as I esteem Mr. Fleay's work, I cannot accept his conclusion as to the infallibility of the ryme-test."[6]

Unabashed by such criticism Fleay continued his verse-test analyses and, with a constant emphasis upon rhyme, made a genuine addition to Shakespearian scholarship. His tables formed the basis for subsequent more reliable tables. His chronological data, though utilized at times in a surprisingly short-sighted manner, made possible a better determination of the succession of the plays. His study of individual pieces contributed to an understanding of their peculiarities of composition. Finally, his labors earned a wide recognition of the potentialities of the metrical approach to Shakespeare's development and, not least, of the function of rhyme in this development.

Some important casual notice was given to Shakespeare's rhymed couplets in Abbott's monumental *Shakespearian Grammar* (1874), important because it called attention not to the number of rhymes but to their function in the dramas.[7] It was Abbott's approach which seemed to combine with the chronological stimulus of Fleay to stir up the interest of the German Shakespearians in the subject of the poet's metrics. Beginning with W. Hertzberg's "Metrisches, grammatisches, chronologisches zu Shakespeare's dramen,"[8] in which rhyme receives but slight consideration, the general analysis of the metre of the dramas became the topic for many individual treatments.

One of the most promising of these nineteenth-century German works is Schipper's *Englische Metrik in historischer und systematischer entwickelung dargestellt* (1881–88); but though the remarks on Shakespeare's versification are valuable,[9] the discussion of his rhyme, probably because of the comprehensive nature of the book, is cursory and for the most part unoriginal. This deficiency, however, was remedied somewhat by the appearance in that same year of Goswin König's "Der Vers in Shakspere's dramen." In this work the author attempted to give a summary of

6. *Ibid.*, p. 32.
7. Sec. 515. Some early notices on the general use of rhyme in the drama of Shakespeare's time are to be found in J. Schipper, *De Versu Marlovii* (Bonn, 1867); Arnold Schröer, "Über die Anfänge des blankverses in England," *Anglia* IV (1881), 1–72; W. Wilke, "Anwendung der rhyme-test und double-endings-test auf Ben Jonson's dramen," *Anglia* X (1888), 512–21; and H. Krumm, *Die Verwendung des reimes in dem blankverse des englischen dramas zur zeit Shakspere's (1561–1616)* (Kiel, 1889).
8. *Jahrbuch* XIII (1878), 248–66.   9. II, 287–314.

the various functions which rhyme performs in the plays;[10] and for several years this remained the most complete discussion of the subject in either Germany or England. But because of its brevity it naturally left much to be desired. It does not even accomplish thoroughly the one task which it avows; that is, the review of the varied functions of rhyme in the drama; still it must be recognized as an advance in the right direction. The important thing is that König is not concerned with rhyme as a means of dating the plays but as a basic ingredient in the dramatic medium.

An article which deserves at least passing mention is W. Wilke's "Anwendung der rhyme-test und double-ending-test auf Ben Jonson's dramen," for in it the author, by applying to Jonson certain of Fleay's theories about Shakespeare, attempts to answer what ultimately must be the most interesting and significant question about Shakespeare's practice—Why did the poet gradually discard rhyme? Wilke's conclusions, as Boyle clearly indicated,[11] are unsatisfactory.

In 1893 appeared a comprehensive German study devoted solely to the use of rhyme in Shakespeare's dramas. Heuser's "Der Coupletreim in Shakespeare's dramen," in fact, remains the only study of its kind. With characteristic thoroughness this work attempts several things: it lists all the couplets except those appearing in songs, it classifies these according to certain general rubrics, and finally it considers individually all the metrical inconsistencies of the lines. It is this last, to be sure, which is Heuser's primary concern and which must be counted his major contribution to Shakespearian scholarship. But even this study, after due evaluation, must be adjudged inadequate.

In the first place, Heuser is interested principally in couplets displaying irregularities, irregularities which he, with a characteristic German passion, forces into conformity to metrical rule. The resultant method is in most cases a sifting of former conjectures and the offer of a further, seemingly more acceptable conjecture. Then too, in listing his couplets, Heuser has been unconsciously guilty of certain errors. He has taken as rhyme word-pairs which cannot be counted as such on the basis either of Elizabethan pronunciation or of position in the dramas.[12] In a few cases—natural in a study of such magnitude—he has overlooked a rhyme com-

10. *Quellen und forschungen,* vols. 61–4 (1888), pp. 122–5.

11. pp. 442–3.

12. For example: *indifferent-friend, T. G.,* III. ii. 44–5. All references to the text of Shakespeare will be to the Cambridge Edition: *The Complete Dramatic and Poetic Works of William Shakespeare* (ed. W. A. Neilson: Boston, 1906).

pletely. And in more than a few cases, because of his failure to branch out from the established classifications, he has registered as unintentional certain couplets which were most assuredly written with a purpose. Such inconsistencies, of course, tend to invalidate the author's tabulations and to make necessary a more accurate survey of the material.

The chief weakness of Heuser's study, however, is not so much in what he has as in what he has not done. First, he has not considered in any but a casual way rhymes other than rhymed couplets, contenting himself with one of the lesser peaks of Parnassus. Secondly, by limiting his attention to classification and metrical alteration, he has failed to appreciate the artistic significance of the rhymes. Thirdly, in the plan of presenting his material, that is, in the order of the discussions of individual plays, he has made it difficult for the reader to get any sort of coherent view of the subject. In other words, the reader who is interested in discovering some kind of chronological development in the works of the poet will be obliged to rearrange Heuser's entire essay.

One is forced to the conclusion, then, that the major virtue of Heuser's work is its value as a foundation upon which to build a structure of more permanent and general implications; it is as such that his essay has been employed in this study. Necessarily, of course, the rhymes have been counted anew and the classifications reconsidered, the results being carefully compared with Heuser in order that this phase of the study might be as accurate as possible and, accordingly, that the ultimate structure might rest upon dependable computations.

It must be noticed here that the counts of Fleay and Heuser of the couplets and other rhymes are by no means the only ones. Fleay's original tables, corrected somewhat and more detailed, appeared in C. M. Ingleby's *Shakespeare the Man and the Book*[13] in 1881. Seven years later König, stating his results in the percentage of rhyme per one hundred lines of iambic pentameter, offered figures which disagreed with Fleay's.[14] And until the appearance, in 1930, of E. K. Chambers' revision of Fleay's tables,[15] the various scholars who had occasion to use such metrical tabulations accepted one or another of these early lists.[16] It becomes readily

---

13. II, 99–141.   14. p. 131.
15. *William Shakespeare: A Study of Facts and Problems* (Oxford, 1930), II, 399.
16. No account is taken here of such studies of individual plays as the following: R. Boyle, "Pericles," *Englische Studien* v (1882), 365–6; D. L. Chambers, *The Metre of Macbeth* (Princeton, 1903), p. 68; and Anna Kerrl, *Die metrischen Unterschiede von Shakespeares King John und Julius Caesar* (Bonn, 1913), pp. 188–9. It

apparent, however, to one who is interested in verifying even the figures of Chambers that the mere statement of percentages or numbers, particularly in the case of the rhymes, is not sufficient. The objections raised by the Tests Committee of the St. Petersburg Shakspeare Circle to Professor Ingram's light and weak ending tabulations[17] are equally applicable to Chambers' figures. Final results alone are insufficient: certain critical canons must be given. What, for example, is to be done with accidental or unintentional rhyme? Indeed, how is one to determine whether a rhyme is intentional or not? Or again, just how is one to evaluate rhyme appearing in prologues, epilogues, or other amphibious rhymed passages? Actually, a mere table of rhymes, even one with sufficient classifications, is not enough to give any but a general concept of the poet's development.

There remains to speak of the one aspect of Shakespeare's rhyme which, though primary in importance, has mostly been relegated to a secondary position: the relationship of rhyme to the dramatist's artistic development, and the vital question of why Shakespeare gradually abandoned rhyme in his plays. A few writers, to be sure, have taken more than a passing glance at the esthetic value of the rhymes. Sidney Lanier, in his *Shakspere and his Forerunners* (1902),[18] attempted to blend the scientific and the esthetic in his discussion of the verse tests; and more recently Richard David[19] very sensitively appraised the effectiveness of the rhyme in its dramatic context. But neither of these men offered a carefully substantiated answer to the question of Shakespeare's gradual discontinuance of rhyme. There have been, to be sure, many conjectural answers, beginning at least as early as Malone's; but because these have not relied upon thorough critical examination they must retain the undignified title of conjecture.

The present study proposes, accordingly, to do several things. In the first place, it will present a re-count of the couplets and other rhymes in Shakespeare's plays and attempt to give the data in such a way as to make easily available the methods pursued in establishing doubtful rhymes. Secondly, it will offer a critical study of the rhymes with the view not of ascertaining the approxi-

is interesting to notice that Fleay, Boyle, Meiners, and others have made similar counts for many of Shakespeare's contemporary playwrights.

17. J. Harrison, J. Goodlet, and R. Boyle, "Report of the Tests Committee of the St. Petersburg Shakspeare Circle," *Englische Studien* III (1880), 473–503.

18. II, 203–51.

19. *The Janus of Poets* (Cambridge, 1935), pp. 89–97.

mate dates of the individual pieces,[20] or even of judging the authenticity of suspect passages, but of tracing the development of Shakespeare the artist. Thirdly, it will examine contemporary drama and opinion to ascertain whether the fluctuations and gradual disappearance in Shakespeare are the result of an inner change or of some concession to current tastes. And, lastly, it will try to offer a more satisfactory explanation of Shakespeare's gradual abandonment of rhyme.

20. The chronology of Shakespeare's plays adopted in this study is in general the one followed by E. K. Chambers. Conclusions concerning Shakespeare's development have been drawn as much as possible from those plays only whose approximate dates of composition have been widely agreed upon.

II

Shakespeare and the Contemporary Attitude toward Rhyme

W HEN searching to discover why the rhyme in Shakespeare's dramas tended to decrease in frequency as the
poet grew older, one thinks at once of Malone's tentative assumption that he merely grew weary of the bondage of
rhyme.[1] Indeed, many critics are in complete agreement with Malone's suggestion, or with its counterpart, that Shakespeare came
to feel, with the approach of his dramatic maturity, the artistic
impropriety of rhyme in pieces designed for the stage. That such
views, moreover, deserve careful consideration is to be seen in the
fact that not only was there a strong feeling among contemporary
critics and poets concerning the dubious position of rhyme, but in
the mouths of certain of his characters the playwright himself
seems to express a decided prejudice against it. This being the
case, it is well to enter a caveat to delay judgment until the evidence can be weighed.

There are two major questions which demand attention. First,
is there anything in the attitudes either of the contestants in the
late Elizabethan rhyme controversy or of the practicing dramatists
which could have fostered in Shakespeare a dislike for rhyme on
the stage? Secondly, assuming that there is in rhyme as a dramatic embellishment something which, on purely esthetic grounds,
might have offended Shakespeare's sensitive genius, just how seriously should one receive the comments upon rhyme given by various of the characters in the dramas?

The new interest in classical poets which attended the Revival
of Learning—or perhaps more directly the influence of such Italian poets as Alberti, Trissino, and others "who had endeavored to
cast out rhyme from vernacular poetry and substitute classical
measures"[2]—resulted in an attempt on the part of certain Tudor

1. Above, p. 1.
2. C. F. Richardson, *A Study of English Rhyme* (Hanover, N.H., 1909), pp.
122–3. In the following pages Richardson gives a detailed description of the rhyme
controversy. For similar discussions see these works: Sidney Lanier, *The Science of
English Verse* (New York, 1880); F. E. Schelling, *Poetic and Verse Criticism of the
Reign of Elizabeth* (Philadelphia, 1891); M. W. Croll, *The Works of Fulke Greville*
(Philadelphia, 1903); G. Saintsbury, *A History of English Prosody* (London, 1908),
vol. II; H. Maynadier, "The Areopagus of Sidney and Spenser," *Modern Language*

writers to discard the traditional English forms in favor of a system of versification sanctified by classical precedent.[3] The ultimate result of the movement was, naturally, failure, but it did succeed in making contemporary poets more attentive to certain fundamental qualities of verse.[4]

From the time of *The Scholemaster* (1570), which marked the actual beginning of the controversy, the attention of the opponents of English metres was centred upon rhyme as the most vulgar of the native forms.[5] As Ascham points out, "This mislikyng of Ryming beginneth not now of any newfangle singularitie, but hath bene long misliked of many, and that of men of greatest learnyng and deepest iudgement. And soch that defend it do so, either for lacke of knowledge what is best, or els of verie enuie that any should performe that in learnyng, whereunto they . . . either for ignorance can not, or for idlenes will not, labor to attaine vnto."[6] That is, since rhyme was not used by the decorous classical writers and since it was used by every Tom, Dick, and Harry, it obviously was "brutish Poetrie . . . tynkerly verse."[7]

The next important voice raised on the issue of rhyme was that of the versatile George Gascoigne who, though he avowedly disapproved of rhyme and attempted to distinguish between "English rhymes" and "English verses,"[8] set about to give a series of rules for the proper composition of rhymed poetry and ended by giving an art of poesy rather than merely of rhyme. Now, the interesting thing is that there seems to exist in Gascoigne's mind an unconscious confusion between "English rhymes" and the "English verses" which he feels he "dare not cal them." In fact the very title of his discourse indicates this confusion: *Certayne Notes of Instruction concerning the making of verse or ryme in English.*

Two other vigorous critics of rhyme who wrote at about the same time as Gascoigne are William Webbe, "graduate," and

Review IV (1909), 289–301; T. S. Omond, *English Metrists* (Oxford, 1921); E. C. Dunn, *Ben Jonson's Art* (Northampton, Mass., 1925). Valuable collections of original material relating to the controversy are J. Haslewood, *Ancient Critical Essays upon English Poets and Poësy* (London, 1811–15), 2 vols., and G. Gregory Smith, *Elizabethan Critical Essays* (Oxford, 1904), 2 vols.

3. George Young, *An English Prosody* (Cambridge, 1928), p. 106.

4. E. F. Pope, "Critical Background of Spenserian Stanza," *Modern Philology* XXIV (1926–27), 34.

5. Actually rhyme was not considered a native invention. Webbe, whose opinions are fairly representative of the reforming faction, writes, "I meane this tynkerly verse which we call ryme: Master Ascham sayth, that it first began to be followed and maintained among the Hunnes and Gothians, and other barbarous Nations" (*A Discourse of English Poetrie*, Haslewood, II, 32).

6. Smith, I, 31–2.   7. Webbe, p. 32.   8. Haslewood, II, 5.

James VI of Scotland. The first of these, though at times as vi-
tuperative as his fellow advocates of classical metres, does admit
grudgingly, "In our English tongue it [rhyme] beareth as good
grace, or rather better, then in any other: and is a faculty whereby
many may and doo deserue great prayse and commendation,
though our spéeche be capable of a farre more learned manner of
versifying."[9] James also, while minimizing the value of rhyme (or
indeed of any embellishment which tended to supplant the sense),
favored its use for certain specific types of subject matter.[10] Both
these men, and assuredly too Sir John Harington, whose *Apologie
of Poetrie* appeared in 1591,[11] were not opposed to rhyme so much
as to the abuses of rhyme in the hands of inferior and insincere
poets.

The best organized opposition to rhyme was the Areopagus, a
group of scholars and poets who entertained themselves throughout much of the last quarter of the sixteenth century with certain
reformations of English verse, specifically with a return to the
classical hexameter. Usually included in this group are such men
as Harvey, Greville, Drant, Dyer, Sidney, and Spenser; but what
they actually did or what unanimity of opinion they enjoyed it is
difficult to ascertain.[12] Harvey, perhaps the least poetical of the
group, seemed, along with Drant, to be the strongest advocate
of the abolishment of rhyme, not so much because it was rhyme,
one cannot help thinking, as because it was not classical. Spenser,
though nominally of the group, certainly shows in neither theory
nor practice any antipathy for rhyme.[13] And Sidney, whose *Apolo-*

9. p. 56.
10. "A treatis of the airt of Scottis Poësie," Haslewood, II, 114–17. One cannot
resist calling attention to J. W. Draper's "King James and Shakespeare's literary
style" (*Archiv für das studium der neueren sprachen*, vol. 171 [1937], p. 39) in
which it is maintained that the diminution of rhyme in the plays is the result of the
artistic views of the new king.
11. Haslewood, II, 144–5.
12. It is impossible here to go into the fascinating problems presented by the so-
called Areopagus: Omond (p. 2) and others accept the existence of a well-organized
society without question, but H. Maynadier maintains with fair credibility that if
there was such a body it was at least not well organized, nor did it meet regularly
to discuss its problems. One must recall, however, the following lines from one of
Spenser's letters to Harvey (Haslewood, II, 260): "I would hartily wish, you would
either send me the Rules and Precepts of Arte, which you obserue in Quantities, or
else followe mine, that M. Philip Sidney gaue me, being the very same which M.
Drant deuised." This seems to imply some conversation in addition to considerable
correspondence.
13. It is true that Spenser seemed slightly self-conscious of his "rude" and
"rugged" rhymes (*Faerie Queene* I. xii. 23. 4; II. x. 50. 7; III. ii. 3. 6; IV. ii. 33. 7);
and "E.K."—sometimes supposed to be Spenser himself—objected to rhyme on the

gie for Poetrie (1583) is the one truly great critical work of the period, seemed on the whole to favor rhyme,[14] even if he did try his hand at some of Harvey's hexameters in the *Arcadia*. In general, then, the Areopagus appears in the campaign against rhyme to have been an ineffectual academic group, since the major poets, who at least lent it the support of their names, were in reality only half-hearted adherents to its principles.

Probably the three loudest voices raised in the controversy were those of Puttenham, Campion, and Daniel, the first two against, and the third for, rhyme. Puttenham in his *Arte of English Poesie* (1589) devoted not a little attention to the matter of rhyme, considering it mainly a device invented to compensate for the monotony of measure in English verse.[15] But like Gascoigne and King James, despite his seeming disapproval, he feels constrained to lay down rules for its use, even admitting that the ear takes "pleasure to heare the like tune reported, and to feele his returne." And so Puttenham also appears more against the abuses of rhyme, that is, against such irregularities as doggerel, than against rhyme proper. In Campion, moreover, there is a striking variation between theory and practice; for though he criticizes rhyme severely in his *Observations in the Art of English Poesie* (1602), in his own poetry he uses it with charming facility. Miss Dunn explains this discrepancy in the following manner:

He [Campion] condemns rhyme as 'vulgar' and makes a plea for the adaptation of classical metres to English. Then one remembers his *Books of Airs* where the pretty conceits are far from moral and the melody springs from a delicate pattern of rhyme. The divergence between theory and practice is too wide to be called inconsistency. The educated gentleman knew the classical theory and modern practice, but they were two distinct things, living apart in his mind and art.[16]

Of these controversialists, finally, Samuel Daniel is the chief advocate of rhyme, and it was his *Defence of Ryme* (1603), directed against the attack of Campion, which put an end to the long debate. Uhland says of him, "As a defender of rhyme, he entered upon his argument in a spirit of national defence, criticizing Campion for seeking to lay reproach on England's native ornaments."[17]

basis that it makes "our English tongue a gallimaufray or hodgepodge of al other speches" (*The Shepherd's Calendar* [ed. W. L. Renwick: London, 1930], p. 6).

14. Smith, I, 160, 196, 205.   15. Haslewood, I, 63–113.
16. p. 85.
17. Maude Uhland, "A Study of Samuel Daniel," *Cornell University Abstracts of Theses* (Ithaca, N.Y., 1938), p. 41.

It must be noticed in addition that Daniel has himself fallen under the influence of the classicists; for in the first place he has come to recognize rhyme chiefly as a musical embellishment,[18] and in the second, he has admitted that "those continuall cadences of couplets vsed in long & continued Poems, are very tyresome, & vnpleasing."[19] Of much more importance to the present study, he has confessed that, in his opinion, "a Tragedie would indeed best comporte with a blancke Verse, and dispence with Ryme, sauing in the Chorus or where a sentence shall require a couplet."[19]

There are three very significant observations to be drawn from this survey of the rhyme controversy. First, both the opponents and upholders of rhyme seem to agree in condemning the abuses and, forgetting for a time at least their classical fetish, in admitting the beauties of rhyme as a proper embellishment in English verse. Secondly, there seems to be some justification for Lanier's statement, "About the last quarter of the 16th century the word 'rhyme' had come to be pretty nearly synonymous with vernacular poetry in England as opposed to the more dignified Greek and Latin verse;"[20] and this suggests that the objections were not so much to rhyme as to vulgar verse in general. Thirdly, for the most part both the upholders and the opponents were not thinking of rhyme in relation to the drama but primarily, if not solely, in relation to non-dramatic poetry. Thus it would seem that, with the exception of Daniel and possibly of Nashe, these contenders in the struggle between rhyme and classical metre did not take the drama into account, probably because they did not consider it literature.

Though the professional drama may not have been held in highest regard in Shakespeare's time, it nevertheless came as strongly under the influence of Tudor classicism as did most of the other types of writing. Accordingly one might expect to find among the dramatists and critics of the drama a certain prevalent attitude toward rhyme closely akin to that of the controversialists.

One of the earliest relevant statements comes from the pen of the most vigorous opponent of the stage in the first years of the Puritan attack—Stephen Gosson. Well launched in his campaign

18. Haslewood, II, 197–8.
19. *Ibid.*, p. 217. This second quotation answers the comment of J. P. Collier (*The History of English Dramatic Poetry* [London, 1831], III, 254): "Although Daniel wrote 'an Apology for Rhyme,' and although his earliest play was composed with strict observance of the jingle, in *Philotas* he has in a degree changed his system, and has at intervals interspersed passages of blank-verse."
20. *English Verse*, p. 293.

to rid England of the terrible scourge of playhouses Gosson, in his *Plays Confuted in Five Actions* (1582), an answer to Lodge's *The Play of Playes*, makes the following comment: "Poets send their verses to the stage upon such feet, as continually are rolled up in rhyme."[21] One of the abominations of the theatre, accordingly, is its use of rhyme; yet this criticism can be granted little worth. For, interested in abolishing all drama, Gosson could have had little concern with the esthetic value of the dramatic medium. Furthermore, at the time he made the statement prose and rhyme were virtually the sole forms used in popular dramatic exhibitions.

Since Thomas Nashe, who was later to try his hand at drama, criticized nearly everything except red herring, it is natural to find him deriding also "the swelling bumbast of bragging blanke verse" in his epistle appended to Greene's *Menaphon* (1587).[22] But it is dangerous to take this as anything other than a passing enthusiasm for rhyme in dramas, because later, in his *Foure Letters Confuted,* he seems to find the traditional rhyme equally despicable.[23]

Consequently, it is to Marlowe's famous *locus classicus* on rhyme that one turns for the first really significant assertion of an attitude on its appropriateness to drama—more specifically, to serious drama. In the prologue to *Tamburlaine the Great* (c. 1587) appear these lines:

> From jigging veins of rhyming mother wits,
> And such conceits as clownage keeps in pay,
> We'll lead you to the stately tent of war.[24]

It was this firm declaration of independence from the crudities of the traditional medium, added to the phenomenal success of Marlowe's blank-verse plays, that permanently abolished rhyme from its ruling position in Tudor drama.

Marlowe's meaning in this passage is perfectly obvious. Rhyme is a "jigging" thing to be used by only the unrefined and appropriate to the jig only, not to dignified drama. Two reservations

---

21. Quoted in Collier, III, 108.

22. *The Works of Thomas Nashe* (ed. R. B. McKerrow: London, 1904–1910), III, 311.

23. "I would trot a false gallop through the rest of his ragged Verses, but that if I should retort his rime dogrell aright, I must make my verses (as he doth his) run hobling like a Brewers Cart vpon the stones, and obserue no length in their feete" (*ibid.,* I, 275).

24. In *English Drama 1580–1642* (ed. C. F. Tucker Brooke and N. B. Paradise: New York, 1933), p. 139. Unless otherwise indicated references to plays by Shakespeare's contemporaries are to this collection.

should be made, however. There is little indication—actually none
—that Marlowe was not thinking of the various types of doggerel
rhyme which constituted the popular medium for the vulgar
drama.[25] Or to put this another way, there is no indication that he
was thinking of the rhymed heroic verse, so effectively employed
by the most skilful poets, which lingered in the drama throughout
the Tudor period, rising finally to its meteoric brilliance in the
heroic tragedy of the Restoration. This suggests the second reser-
vation: Marlowe himself, notwithstanding his stricture against
rhyme, continued to use it in non-dramatic composition and even
with a certain effectiveness in his plays. A conservative conclusion
is, then, that, even though the scattered rhyme did diminish in his
successive plays,[26] Marlowe objected to it as the sole medium for
dramatic communication and not as an occasional embellishment
designed for certain special effects,[27] an opinion which Shakespeare himself must certainly have shared.

Marlowe's successors for the most part were mute adherents to
his cause, nor is there any strong evidence to show that the conclusion concerning Marlowe's theories and practice might not be
equally applicable to the others. Marlowe's posthumous collabo-
rator, Chapman, to be sure, openly acknowledges rhyme in *The
Shadow of Night* (1594), but there can be little question that he is
thinking of non-dramatic verse as he writes.[28] Toward the turn
of the century, moreover, there are several statements to be found
in current plays which would seem to indicate an attitude of hos-
tility. Rose, in *The Shoemaker's Holiday* (1599), declares passion-

25. This is not to say that all the rhyme of the plays prior to Marlowe was actually doggerel, for various highly evolved metrical schemes succeeded one another
in popularity. But the vulgar audience seemed, about the time of Marlowe, to be
responding most eagerly to the doggerel rhythms. For information on the verse
structures of the early Tudor drama see particularly the following: J. P. Collier, vol.
III; Schröer; A. W. Ward, *A History of English Dramatic Literature* (London,
1889), vols. I, II; Saintsbury, vols. I, II; P. Reyher, *Essai sur le doggerel* (Bordeaux,
1909); J. E. Bernard, *The Prosody of the Tudor Interlude* (New Haven, 1939).
26. C. F. Tucker Brooke, "Marlowe's Versification and Style," *Studies in Philology* XIX (1922), 202.
27. Collier (III, 123) suggests that Marlowe's rather generous sprinkling of rhyme
in the first part of *Tamburlaine* was merely to make more gradual the weaning of
"the popular ear from that to which it had been so long accustomed."
28.   Sweet poesy
              Will not be clad in her supremacy
              With those strange garments (Rome's hexameters),
              As she is English; but in right prefers
              Our native robes (put on with skilful hands—
              English heroics) to those antic garlands.
                              Quoted in Richardson, p. 138.

ately, "What, love rhymes, man? Fie on that deadly sin!"[29] Yet her sincerity must be doubted somewhat, since her very disavowal rhymes with the previous speech. It is to be noticed, in addition, that by "rhymes" she is actually referring to sentimental love poetry, for in that way does Hammon use the word a few lines earlier. A more convincing attack upon rhyme occurs in the Second Part of the *Returne from Parnassus* (1601), where a character speaks of "Slymy rimes as thick as flies in the sunne," and continues, "I thinke there be neuer an ale-house in England, not any so base a maypole on a country greene, but sets forth some poets petternels or demilances to the paper warres in Paules Churchyard."[30] This, also, though it appears in a play, does not seem to refer to the drama; and even later when mention is made of the gnomic couplet,[31] innumerable examples of which appeared in the coeval drama, the reference seems to be to conversational rather than dramatic rhymers.

Of all Shakespeare's contemporaries in the theatre Jonson perhaps said the most concerning rhyme, and of course any pronouncement from Jonson bears considerable weight. In general it would seem from his statements that he disliked rhyme, though probably not so much as his own George Downright, to whom a rhyme was "worse than cheese, or a bag-pipe."[32] While he scorns "cream-bowl" rhymers in his *Discoveries*,[33] his most renowned declaration is "A Fit of Rhyme Against Rhyme," in which he offers this wish:

> He that first invented thee
> May his joints tormented be,
> Cramped forever.[34]

Of this poem Lanz wrote, "The whole poem is so amusingly humorous that, if we had no further knowledge concerning the literary idiosyncrasies of its author, we could easily mistake his purpose as implying a subtle defense of rime."[35] And, it might be added, there is reason to suppose that Jonson could have been doing just that! At least, he personally had little quarrel with rhyme. For, as Schelling indicates, the decasyllabic couplet is

29. III. iii. 49. 30. Smith, II, 399.

31. *Ibid.*, p. 370.

32. *Every Man in his Humour* IV. ii. 21–2.

33. *The Works of Ben Jonson* (ed. W. Gifford: London, 1875), IX, 157.

34. *Ibid.*, VIII, 379.

35. Henry Lanz, *The Physical Basis of Rime* (Stanford University, California, 1931), p. 311.

really his characteristic measure in his non-dramatic writings.[36] Further, he himself, like many of his fellows, objects not to rhyme but to "common rhymers," or untutored poets who let the jingle supplant the metre.[37] And though used very sparingly, rhyme is still present in his dramas. Finally, if the words of Drummond are to be granted any credence, Jonson had actually written a discourse in which he proved "couplets to be the bravest sort of verses."[38]

What, then, does all this indicate about the attitude of Shakespeare's contemporaries toward rhyme? In the first place, the rhyme controversy appears to have been mostly an academic discussion in which rhyme seemed almost synonymous with vernacular poetry and in which even most of the opponents granted a certain merit to the undisciplined vagrant while condemning him. The movement toward classicism, though related to the drama through some of its exponents, tended, moreover, to ignore drama altogether, probably because common stage productions could not be mentioned in the same breath with the works of the great masters. And when one turns to the drama itself, or to its creators, there is virtually nothing which would indicate a totally condemnatory attitude. The primary objection was either to "jigging" doggerel or to rhyme as the major dramatic medium, not to rhyme as an embellishment reserved for special purposes.

Though this much of the investigation has produced negative results, one might contend that Shakespeare, more sensitive to the disadvantages of rhyme in the dramatic medium than were his fellows, discarded it because he came to recognize its fundamental inappropriateness. This presupposes, of course, that rhyme is fundamentally inappropriate to poetic drama, a view which one cannot unequivocally accept. Even if one does not agree with Oscar Wilde's glowing definition of rhyme as "that exquisite echo which in the Muse's hollow hill creates and answers its own voice; . . . rhyme, which can turn man's utterance into the speech of gods; rhyme, the one chord we have added to the Greek lyre,"[39] one must recognize that it is the form in which the English-speaking peoples have framed their prayers, meditations, and aspirations since before the time of Chaucer.[40] As a means of expressing emotions and experiences it certainly has its place in poetic drama

---

36. "Ben Jonson and the Classical School," *Publications of the Modern Language Association* XIII (1898), 235.

37. Gifford, *Ben Jonson* IX, 215.   38. *Ibid.*, IX, 365.

39. "The Critic as Artist," *Intentions* (New York, 1907), pp. 102–03.

40. Lanier, *Shakspere*, II, 220.

and, therefore, is not to be considered necessarily Shakespeare's "evil angel."[41]

Since Jonson's famous pronouncement upon Shakespeare's never blotting a line, there has existed, in the minds of many, a conception of the Bard of Avon as a genius whose glorious outpourings were a spontaneous overflow unhampered by any of the labors of composition experienced by lesser poets. In recent years the romantic nonsense of this concept has been contested. Alvin Thaler, for example, in his "Shakespeare on Style, Imagination, and Poetry," takes pains to show that Shakespeare was a very conscious artist, intensely interested in the many ramifications of his art.[42] Nor is this by any means the only study of its kind.[43] Thaler's general approach is, moreover, that one can discover, by looking at certain relevant passages in the dramas, the playwright's personal opinions of his art.

There is still another proposition: Edward Dowden wrote, "A difference between this metrical characteristic [rhyme] and those previously noticed must be borne in mind, namely, that although a poet may unconsciously set down a double ending or a weak ending, or run on a line into that which follows (this unconscious action serving as an index to the general growth of his artistic powers), he cannot rhyme unconsciously."[44] This statement, indeed, is a major assumption in the present study. For, while one might expect the poet to rhyme unintentionally in a play otherwise full of rhyme, certainly a couplet or quatrain in a play not replete with rhyme must be the result usually of a deliberate, conscious effort.

It certainly does not seem too much to accept the idea that Shakespeare was a conscious artist who had to meet and master certain problems of his art. Nor can it be denied that rhyme, by its very nature, must have made particular demands upon his attention. And though one is not ready to admit unreservedly the possibilities of discovering Shakespeare's personal views through the

41. Swinburne. Quoted by Oliver Elton, *Style in Shakespeare* (London, 1936), p. 16.

42. *PMLA* LIII (1938), 1019–36.

43. See especially George Rylands, "The Early and the Mature Shakespearian Manner," in *Shakespeare Criticism* (ed. Anne Bradby: Oxford, 1936), pp. 372–88, and G. D. Willcock, *Shakespeare as Critic of Language* (London, 1934). A parallel study, which the present writer has not seen, is P. Hamelius, *Was dachte Sh. über poesie?* (1889).

44. *Shakspere* (Cincinnati: "Literary Primers," n.d.), p. 44.

statements of his characters,[45] it might be well to examine the attitudes toward rhyme which are so presented in the plays.

There are in the dramas some thirty-eight references to the subject of rhyme, in the poems eight; and for the most part these seem to indicate hardly a high opinion of rhyme. If one were to look at the general run of opinions given by Shakespeare's characters on the whole subject of poetry a similar conclusion would probably be drawn. Mark Van Doren has said, "The habit of Shakespeare's best poets—Hotspur, Mercutio, Hamlet—is to berate poetry."[46] This attitudinizing, however, is not the most striking thing about Shakespeare's statements on rhyme.

The really striking thing is that Shakespeare seems to identify "rhyme" with certain types of non-dramatic poetry in which it is most commonly used. The many appearances of the word in the *Sonnets*, for example, suggest that there the poet is thinking of it almost as if it were a synonym of "poem." To look at just one example, here is the concluding couplet of Sonnet 17:

> But were some child of yours alive that time,
> You should live twice, in it and in my rhyme;

in which, as it often does elsewhere in the poems, the word obviously refers not to the technical device by which it is generally understood but, in a loose way, to the poem in which Shakespeare is commemorating his friend. Indeed, many of the sixteenth-century examples of the term offered in the *New English Dictionary* under *rime* indicate that it was often used, not in its more common modern meaning, but in its original sense to denote accentual in contrast to quantitative verse.

A study of the numerous references to rhyme in the plays reveals an analogous situation. Probably the most famous utterance is in *Much Ado*, a play sufficiently late in Shakespeare's career for an antagonistic attitude to be expected:

Marry, I cannot show it in rhyme. I have tried. I can find out no rhyme to "lady" but "baby," an innocent rhyme; for "scorn," "horn," a hard rhyme; for "school," "fool," a babbling rhyme; very ominous endings.

---

45. Shakespeare was above all a dramatist, putting into the mouths of his *dramatis personae* speeches appropriate to character and situation; and though it is pleasant to think of arriving at the man through the book, about the only certain conclusions to be gained thereby are that here is a mind magnificent in its comprehension and limitless in its facility.

46. Quoted by Thaler (p. 1030) from an essay read before the 1937 meeting of The Modern Language Association.

No, I was not born under a rhyming planet, nor I cannot woo in festival terms.[47]

Poor Benedick! The English language, with its poverty of rhyme, makes his incipient wooing a parlous thing. And it is such use of rhyme which is generally referred to when the word appears in the various dramas. When Rosaline, in *Love's Labour's Lost*,[48] and Touchstone, in *As You Like It*,[49] speak scornfully of spending "prodigal wits in bootless rhymes," they are thinking solely of the love jingles of amorous fools, of rhymers who are "guards on wanton Cupid's hose."[50]

Now, while Shakespeare may be condemning in these passages the absurdities of much love poetry, he certainly was too sensitive a poet (as his own practice shows) to deny at least some musical value to rhyme in love lyrics. For when Julia, in *Two Gentlemen*, says, "Some love of yours hath writ to you in rhyme," Lucetta answers, "That I might sing it, madam, to a tune."[51] Thus one might almost conclude that if these various passages express more than a mere courtly attitude, clever rather than sincere, they are at best condemning, as did King James himself, certain absurdities perpetrated by the untutored in the name of poetry.[52]

It is to be noticed, of course, that the various quotations discussed so far are from Shakespeare's earlier dramas, dramas which, while not all of the first period, at least show still the marked lyrical exuberance of youth. The references which appear in the later dramas add but little. They show a similar attitude toward rhyme and a similar tendency to identify it with poetry other than dramatic.

In *Julius Caesar*, Cassius comments, "How vilely doth this cynic rhyme!"[53] thus seeming to voice a disgust with rhyme. The most that can be said of this is that Shakespeare thought little of North's ability as a poet, since the lines referred to are taken directly from the latter's *Plutarch*. Gower, in *Pericles*, expresses the interesting attitude that rhyme is old and out of fashion:

> If you, born in these latter times,
> When wit's more ripe, accept my rhymes;[54]

47. v. ii. 36–41.   48. v. ii. 64.   49. iii. ii. 101.
50. *L. L. L.* iv. iii. 58.   51. i. ii. 79–80.
52. The many uses of the expression "rhyme without reason" can scarcely be said to have any significance, for it was a commonplace. The writer has noticed it used as early as 1561 in the interlude *Godly Queen Hester*: "All this is out of season, and nothing done by reason, Nor yet by good ryme" (Reprinted in Bernard, p. 190).
53. iv. iii. 133.   54. I Gower 11–12.

but even if such an interpretation is accepted, one must recognize that Gower's lines may not be by Shakespeare and that they actually do seem to be an attempt to imitate an older style, similar to that of the Mouse-trap in *Hamlet*. Again, in *King Henry V* appears the statement that "A rhyme is but a ballad,"[55] and in *Antony and Cleopatra*, "scald rhymers Ballad us out o' tune."[56] Here in these words from Cleopatra one might expect, if ever, an identification of rhyme with the dramatic medium; but as she continues, "The quick comedians Extemporally will stage us," she seems to have forgotten about rhyme, or at least to have made no connection between it and the stage.

There remains to look at a passage in one of Shakespeare's latest plays, the following lines from *Cymbeline:*

> Will you rhyme upon't
> And vent it for a mockery? . . .
> You have put me into a rhyme.[57]

These words, spoken by the angry Posthumus, imply a certain scorn of rhyme, as if it indicated a perverse frame of mind; and after he has testily recited several sententious couplets,[58] it is little wonder his companion leaves the stage with only the comment, "Farewell; you're angry." One can scarcely say it is Shakespeare who is here speaking through a character; the words, situation, and temperament are too closely conceived to make plausible such a detachment.

Accordingly, it must be concluded that, just as there is nothing in the words of the controversialists or in the pages of the contemporary dramatists which would rule occasional rhyme off the stage, so there is nothing in the words of Shakespeare's characters which would show him an antagonist of rhyme on the grounds of artistic impropriety. These results are, to be sure, entirely negative, but they do suggest that the reason for Shakespeare's gradual abandonment of rhyme must lie elsewhere.

55. v. ii. 167.
57. v. iii. 55–63.

56. v. ii. 215–17.
58. *Cf. T. N.* iii. iv. 412–13.

III

Rhyme in the Drama of Shakespeare's Contemporaries

ALTHOUGH little can be deduced from contemporary critical theory to explain Shakespeare's gradual disuse of rhyme, a study of the practice of his fellow playwrights may prove more revealing. If, as Fleay said, there was not only "a gradual disuse of rhyme by every author of the period in question as he grows older, but there was also a growing dislike on the part of the public to the mixture of rhyme and blank in stage plays,"[1] then it might be expected that Shakespeare's writings would be somewhat influenced. But that such a condition actually existed must be questioned.

To begin with, a distinction must be clearly drawn between the shift from rhyme as the primary medium of the drama and possible fluctuations in rhyme as an embellishment reserved for specific effects. Only the latter need be considered here, since the former, by the time Shakespeare began his career as playwright, was virtually a *fait accompli*. Thus B. Nicholson said:

In 1586 *Tamburlaine* had practically conquered ryme, that is, ryming plays. Nashe and Greene, in 1589, speak against the fact, but are obliged to accept it. Greene, once the advocate, because a craftsman of the former order of things, when he wrote in blank verse employed ryme but sparingly. Still, however, it was used, and by all; . . . but it is used only as a subordinate, and only for various more or less defined offices; these offices varying somewhat with the idiosyncrasy of each master. As I read the history, there was no battle when Shakspere began to write, but on the contrary the new system had been established.[2]

The question, then, is whether there was any marked alteration in this "new system," an alteration sufficiently tenable to justify its application to Shakespeare.

Any change, to influence Shakespeare's practice, must have occurred before 1613, the probable date of *Henry VIII*. There is, to be sure, reliable testimony to the effect that an alteration in public taste had taken place by 1637 or 1640. In 1640 the printer of Middleton's *A Mad World My Masters* (1608) felt obliged to apol-

1. "On Metrical Tests," in Ingleby, p. 64.
2. *N. S. S. Trans.* I, 36.

ogize to the reader for the old-fashioned rhymes in the play, saying, "Consider, gentle reader, it is full twenty years [actually
thirty-two] since it was written, at which time metre [rhyme] was
most in use, and showed well upon the conclusion of every act
and scene."[3] Likewise, in Heywood's epilogue to *Royal King and
Loyal Subject*, acted about 1603 but not published until 1637, the
author confesses to his reader that rhyme is out of fashion.[4] Neither
of these, however, indicates a change during the time Shakespeare
was an active playwright.

Because there exists a difference of opinion regarding the use
of rhyme in Elizabethan drama at the time of Shakespeare, some
scholars finding, as did Fleay and Creizenach, a marked diminution during the period when it might have had influence upon
him, others asserting that the facts by no means justify such a
view,[5] I have thought it necessary to ascertain the true situation
by examining a group of representative plays.[6] Included in this
group were not only those of the best-known writers—men whose
genius might exempt them from a servile adherence to passing
modes—but some by lesser men and even some anonymous plays.
Likewise, examples of the principal types popular on the professional stage were chosen to find if variations might have grown
out of the artistic demands peculiar to the type. And last, the
plays were apportioned as evenly as possible among the leading
dramatic companies in order to see if the policies of different man-
agers or the tastes of actor or audience had any effect upon the
use of rhyme. Though far from conclusive, the results of this investigation are significant, for they show that, during the dramatic
career of Shakespeare, there was no fluctuation in the use of
rhyme sufficiently marked to have influenced the gradual disuse
of rhyme in his plays. Although there was a tendency away from

3. *The Works of Thomas Middleton* (ed. A. H. Bullen: London, 1885), III, 251.
4. Thomas Heywood, *The Royall King and Loyall Subject* (ed. K. W. Tibbals:
Philadelphia, 1906), p. 135. Fleay (*A Chronicle History of the London Stage 1559–
1642* [London, 1890], pp. 120–21) and Wilhelm Creizenach (*The English Drama in
the Age of Shakespeare* [London, 1916], p. 321) seemingly interpret this epilogue
as indicating a change in taste prior to the performance of the play in 1603. The
epilogue is specifically addressed to the reader, however, and not to the audience,
and was probably composed for the publication of the play, at which time also
certain textual alterations from rhyme to blank verse may have been made. *Cf.*
Tibbals' Introduction to the play, pp. 6–7, and J. P. Collier's Introduction to
Thomas Heywood, *The Royal King, and Loyal Subject. A Woman Killed with
Kindness* (London, 1850), pp. v-vi.
5. *Cf. N. S. S. Trans.* I, 37; Wilke, p. 514.
6. See Appendix A for this list of plays.

long passages of consecutive rhyme, there was little variation in the "new system" of rhyme.

Arranging this group of plays according to the dramatic companies which produced them, one can detect such slight variation in the amount of rhyme as to invalidate this approach to the problem. It would seem that in general the plays produced by the several children's companies contain a somewhat higher percentage of rhyme than do those of the professionals. An explanation of this might lie in the intrinsic qualities of rhyme and blank verse as dramatic media. Rhyme demands far less subtlety of delivery than the more flexible blank verse; it lends itself well to the type of ranting rôle which seemed popular with the children, at least after 1600; it has an easy lyricism, harmonizing with the voices of the youthful singers and actors;[7] and, most important, it is less difficult to remember than blank verse. Though further investigation might offer some interesting results, the plays examined here scarcely show the dramatist, in the matter of rhyme, concerning himself with the demands of any particular group.

More than the dramatic company, the type of play might be expected to affect the number of rhymes. Otelia Cromwell, writing about Heywood, made the following conjecture:

If You Know Not Me You Know Nobody (2), The Wise Woman of Hogsdon, on the one hand, If You Know Not Me You Know Nobody (1), and A Woman Killed with Kindness on the other, all four written probably within a few years of one another, may be grouped in pairs because of the peculiar variation in the proportion of rhymed to unrhymed lines. Can it be that the poet was influenced by the difference in the tone of the plays—the sustained gaiety of the first two plays causing him to use fewer rhymes? This conclusion is far from satisfying.[8]

Generally speaking, the present investigation does show a somewhat higher percentage of rhyme in the tragedies and tragicomedies than in the comedies. Perhaps Saintsbury's facetious comment on Cyril Tourneur explains this difference: "When the blank verse is highest the couplets are nighest."[9] Less cleverly but just as plausibly, one might contend that the continued influence of the English-Senecan[10] style in tragedy probably maintained the

---

7. It has been suggested that the child actors occasionally sang couplets placed at the ends of scenes or of long speeches.

8. Thomas Heywood: A Study in the Elizabethan Drama of Everyday Life (New Haven, 1928), p. 136.

9. II, 82.

10. The Senecan tragedies of the Pembroke school show a relatively high per-

number of rhymes, while the distaste for doggerel and the tendency toward prose may have given less place to rhyme in comedy. The history plays, finally, despite Gervinus' comment that "histories, with their bald and insipid material, helped especially to banish the jingle of rhyme from the stage,"[11] contain for the most part a generous share of rhyme, except for some of the very early plays wherein is found a great predominance of prose.

Even looking at the plays of the individual authors, one cannot discover any consistent disappearance of rhyme. Differences in percentages, it is true, occur between the different writers, but there is not "a gradual disuse of rhyme by every author of the period in question as he grows older." Marlowe's *Edward II* has but slightly fewer rhymes than the first part of *Tamburlaine;* Jonson's *Volpone* has more rhymes than *Every Man in his Humour;* Heywood's *The Late Lancashire Witches* contains a greater number than *The Wise Woman of Hogsdon.* In Beaumont and Fletcher as well, *The Knight of the Burning Pestle* shows a higher percentage of rhyme than *The Woman Hater,* probably written four or five years earlier. Such men as Heywood, Dekker, Beaumont, and Marston seem fond of rhyme and use it plentifully; others, like Jonson, Massinger, and Fletcher, rhyme with far less frequency. But more important, the plays of the same author show variations in keeping with the demands of the individual piece.[12]

Though a more extensive investigation might qualify these conclusions, it seems fair to assume that, whatever may have been the fate of rhyme after the death of Shakespeare, during his career as a dramatist there was no outside influence sufficiently marked to explain its fluctuations in his dramas.

centage of rhyme. See Croll, pp. 33–4, and Alexander M. Witherspoon, *The Influence of Robert Garnier on Elizabethan Drama* (New Haven, 1924), pp. 161–3.

11. G. G. Gervinus, *Shakespeare Commentaries* (tr. F. E. Bunnètt: London, 1903), p. 76.

12. The following works offer metrical tables for some of Shakespeare's contemporaries: F. G. Fleay, "On Metrical Tests as Applied to Dramatic Poetry. Part II. Fletcher, Beaumont, Massinger," *N. S. S. Trans.* i, 51–66; R. Boyle, "Beaumont, Fletcher and Massinger," *Englische Studien* v (1882), 74–96; W. Wilke, p. 518; M. Meiners, *Metrische Untersuchungen über den dramatiker John Webster* (Halle, 1893), pp. 38–9; E. E. Stoll, *John Webster: The Periods of his Work as Determined by his Relations to the Drama of his Day* (Boston, 1905), p. 190; C. F. T. Brooke, "Marlowe's Versification," p. 202; Otelia Cromwell, p. 132.

IV

The Function of Rhyme in Shakespeare's Dramas

SINCE the explanation of Shakespeare's gradual disuse of rhyme does not seem to lie in outside influences, in either the contemporary attitude or practice, and since the remarks of his *dramatis personae* do not indicate an impatience with rhyme as part of the dramatic medium, it must be concluded that the change, consciously or unconsciously, came as the result of some organic alteration accompanying his dramatic development. Essentially, of course, this is the theory of the critics who have used rhyme as a chronological measurement; but figures alone disclose little. Shakespeare's mind is not to be explained by a numerical chart, his artistic growth by a series of well-tabulated figures; nor is it to be expected that a simple formula, applied with no matter how much ingenuity, will answer such a complex problem as this fluctuation in poetic style. The answer, if one is to be found, must result from a careful analysis of the nature and position of rhyme at the very foundations of the dramatic structure.

In order to make such an analysis it is expedient to divide the rhymes into classifications based upon the position of the rhyme in the context. Metrical distinctions, of course, are also important, but they result primarily from functional considerations, as, for example, the four-stress trochaic line which is normally reserved for the speeches of supernatural beings. That such a division into classifications entails difficulties, moreover, is at once apparent. Rhymes which by position demand separate classifications actually may be performing essentially the same dramatic function and consequently deserve to be treated together. The following general principles, therefore, have been observed in classifying the rhymes:

Of the various isolated positions in which a single rhyme or a pair of rhymes commonly occurs, that of scene- or act-end takes precedence over all others. Though such a rhyme also indicates an exit and frequently marks the conclusion of a long speech, it is listed according to its major function, which is to signal the end of a certain action. Similarly, the fact that a rhyme heralds an entrance or, more frequently, accompanies an exit, is normally considered more important than that it marks a speech-end or a speech-pause, or that it constitutes a single speech. Next in importance is a speech-end rhyme, the rhyme used to conclude a blank-verse passage; but contrary to the practice of Heuser, it is not so classified if it concludes a passage wholly in consecutive rhymes, whether of couplets, quatrains, or some formal stanzaic pattern. Rhyme marking a grammatical or dramatic pause in a long speech, a use hitherto unnoticed in works on Shakespeare's verse, conflicts only rarely with other uses. It does, however, yield to the exit and cue rhymes. And finally, in this classification of isolated rhymes according to position, are those which occur at the beginning of blank-verse passages, which link two consecutive speeches, or which, surrounded by blank verse, constitute a total speech. The first two of these are relatively rare, even in the early plays, and must be held as accidental unless sufficient justification can be found for them.

In addition to these isolated rhymes are the passages of consecutive rhyme. In these continuous passages such positions as speech-end or speech-pause, even scene-end and exit, can scarcely be granted any particular worth, since the rhyme results from the medium used in the context rather than from the demands of the position.

Considered separately is the rhyme in prologues and epilogues, inductions and choruses, masques and plays within plays. It is just as shortsighted to count such external rhyme with the rhyme in the actual dramatic dialogue as to ignore it altogether; for while in some plays these elements are not intimately connected with the body of the piece, in others they constitute an immediate outgrowth of the action. Songs, on the other hand, are not considered at all, except when they are an inextricable part of the dramatic dialogue.

With this brief explanation,[1] an examination of the different classifications will now be made to see what Shakespeare's practice was, to make some estimate of its artistic worth, and to ascertain whether the various usages in the organic development of the plays had anything to do with the disappearance of rhyme.[2]

Speech-End Rhyme

One of the most characteristic uses of rhyme in Elizabethan drama is at the end of a blank-verse speech, a speech varying in

---

1. Further notice of the classifications is given in Appendix B.

2. Fleay apparently discarded this approach: "I thought at one time that the number of 'tag-rhymes' spoken by an actor at the end of a scene or on leaving the stage or at the end of an important speech might help us: but the rhyme-test in its usual shape gives more reliable results" ("On Metrical Tests," in Ingleby, p. 59).

length from three to an indefinite number of lines. Many times this speech occurs at the end of an act or scene or before an entrance or exit, thus giving the rhyme an added justification; but fully as often it appears somewhere within the body of the scene, with seemingly no *raison d'être* other than the whim or caprice of the playwright. Occasionally, as in the regular appearance of rhyme every twelve or sixteen lines in Kyd's *Cornelia*, the dramatist followed some definite plan; but ordinarily if he was fond of rhyme he used it frequently, if not, sparingly; in neither case did he adhere to a fixed design. It is difficult, therefore, to determine why a rhyme was used in one place and not in another where the circumstances surrounding each are similar.

The speech-end rhyme in Shakespeare's plays is no exception. Even in a scene generously filled with rhyme it is very difficult to explain why one speech closes with a couplet while a similar speech does not. The only positive statement which can be made is that when a couplet appears at the end of a blank-verse, or even a prose, speech, it normally bears a certain relationship to what has preceded it. That relationship, though in most respects remaining unchanged throughout Shakespeare's plays, shows some slight but important alteration as the playwright achieves full mastery of his medium.

The connection, moreover, is not always a close one. At times the concluding couplet does not grow out of the speech, is not an organic unit of the thought-content which it follows, but stands alone and performs a separate function. The most obvious example of this is the use of the couplet to bid farewell, as in *Richard II* when the Duchess of Gloster, after finishing her passionate outburst, adds,

> Farewell, old Gaunt! thy sometimes brother's wife
> With her companion grief must end her life.[1]

Though this is in keeping with the general mood of the passage, there is an abrupt pause immediately before it, giving the couplet the same effect of isolation as Gaunt's farewell couplet which follows.[2] Occasionally, also, the rhymed lines are used to accompany a certain action performed by the speaker and seem designed to fit that action rather than to give color to the whole speech.[3] Elsewhere they stress a command for action or a determination of the speaker to perform a certain action, and while both these func-

1. I. ii. 54–5. *Cf. R. J.* II. ii. 123–4.   2. I. ii. 56–7.
3. *M. V.* III. ii. 106–7 and *Per.* II. v. 63–4.

tions may be the logical concomitant of the preceding lines, the rhyme seems primarily intended to accentuate its own content. Such a rhyme is Bertram's in *All's Well That Ends Well:*

> I'll send her straight away. To-morrow
> I'll to the wars, she to her single sorrow.[4]

A somewhat similar dissociation or isolation is to be noticed in speech-end couplets which the speaker himself thinks of as having a separate unity, that is, couplets containing such information as reported speeches, messages, words of a supernatural origin, even prophecies, vows, and prayers. Most of these, of course, appear as a natural outgrowth of the speech which they conclude, but the rhyme often seems justified by the content rather than by the rhetorical relationship to the entire speech. It is not surprising, either, that such material should be couched in rhyme, for in that way it is more memorable. Thus King Henry V angrily delivers his message to the ambassadors of France:

> And tell the Dauphin
> His jest will savour but of shallow wit,
> When thousands weep more than did laugh at it.[5]

The epigrammatic sharpness of the words will insure accurate delivery. Also, the prophecies which appear at the ends of speeches seem naturally to resort to rhyme to make their impression on the hearers more indelible. Thus the Earl of Warwick, in *1 Henry VI*, prophesies the outcome of a quarrel in a garden:

> This brawl to-day . . .
> Shall send between the red rose and the white
> A thousand souls to death and deadly night.[6]

Or again, the solemn vow reported by the First Watchman in *3 Henry VI*[7] gains in dramatic intensity by means of its accompanying rhyme.

There is still another way in which a rhyme at the end of a speech might be considered as having a separate identity, or at least as performing a function not related solely to its position. This is when the rhyme, although at the end of a speech, bears a marked relation either to nearby speeches or to the scene as a

---

4. II. iii. 312–13. See also v. iii. 69–70.
5. *Hen. V* I. ii. 295–6.   6. II. iv. 124–7.
7. IV. iii. 5–6.

whole. Sometimes it begins an extended passage of rhyme, and thus seemingly introduces a heightening in the general tone of the scene;[8] but it is not necessary to have such a change of the poetic medium, for in *Romeo and Juliet* two couplets, the first at the end of a speech and the other following immediately, shift the mood of the scene from hatred and violence to love and lyricism, without changing the medium from blank verse to rhyme.[9] Occasionally it serves a function similar to that of the scene-end couplet by bringing to an effective close one part of the action before the beginning of the next, where there is no marked change of the poetic tone.[10] In somewhat the same manner is the couplet used to conclude a formal narrative, after which the interrupted dramatic action again takes the attention of the audience. Thus Aegeon, in *The Comedy of Errors,* breaks off the sad account of his experiences with this couplet:

> O, let me say no more!
> Gather the sequel by that went before.[11]

Normally, however, the rhyme which appears at the end of a speech has a very close association with the speech as a whole. This, of course, is to be expected. Also to be expected is the fact that rhyme, when thus reserved for the most important position in the speech, is used for one main purpose—emphasis. Indeed, even the rhymes which are not intimately connected with the thought of the speech seem usually to emphasize or to call particular attention to something; and the same might be said of the various other classifications to be discussed later, except, of course, the passages of consecutive rhyme. For the one characteristic which nearly all Shakespeare's isolated rhymed lines have in common is that they stand out from the rest of the dialogue to attract special notice to themselves or to what they signalize.

In accomplishing its major design the speech-end couplet which is closely linked with its context is related in one of three ways: it either expresses a contrast, marks a climax, or forms a conclusion.

For the first of these relationships Shakespeare had ample practice. The English, or Shakespearian, sonnet, with its pattern of three quatrains and a couplet, displayed very clearly the ability of the couplet to give a sudden epigrammatic twist to the preceding thought. If example were needed one might refer to Sonnet 30

8. See for example *T. N.* iv. i. 62–3 and v. i. 133–4.
9. i. i. 121–4.   10. See 2 *Hen. VI* iii. i. 325–6.
11. i. i. 95–6. *Cf. Per.* i. iv. 48–9; ii. i. 137–40.

wherein the poet, after bemoaning for twelve lines his "dear time's waste," concludes with this graceful shift in attitude:

> But if the while I think on thee, dear friend,
> All losses are restor'd and sorrows end.

The same thought-pattern appears in many of the dramatic speeches which end with rhyme. Sometimes it is used in a serious speech charged with emotion. Pericles, having easily solved the riddle of Antiochus, addresses the daughter of the king with these words:

> You are a fair viol, and your sense the strings;
> Who, finger'd to make man his lawful music,
> Would draw heaven down, and all the gods, to hearken;
> But being play'd upon before your time,
> Hell only danceth at so harsh a chime.[12]

The rhyme here sharpens the contrast between what the girl could have been and what she actually was, thus making more forceful Pericles' denunciation of her. Even in less dramatic situations one finds this use of rhyme. In *The Two Gentlemen of Verona,* for example, it differentiates merely between two courses of action, as Valentine, after criticizing his friend's determination to live in sluggardly idleness at home instead of going abroad to see the wonders of the world, admits in a couplet that Proteus' love is sufficient excuse for his actions.[13] Still another variation is the legalistic couplet in *Love's Labour's Lost,* a play in which Shakespeare seems particularly interested in formal rhetoric. After a long conditional passage, the Princess concludes with a contrary supposition:

> If this thou do deny, let our hands part,
> Neither intitled in the other's heart.[14]

This use of rhyme for contrast, though effective in serious or semi-serious passages, enjoys its greatest success where the effect desired is a comic one. Its natural tendency toward the epigrammatic twist gives it a peculiar appropriateness, a fact which Shakespeare took advantage of even in his mature pieces. The speeches of the Bastard in *King John* are particularly rich in this use of the couplet, gaining a strong satiro-comic effect.[15] In one of his rhymes

12. *Per.* I. i. 81–5. *Cf. 3 Hen. VI* IV. iv. 14–15; IV. vi. 30–1.
13. I. i. 9–10.   14. V. ii. 821–2.
15. See particularly II. i. 145–6.

the contrast is even within the couplet itself, but since the speech which it concludes is a short one the effect is in no way lessened by the compression:

> Your face hath got five hundred pound a year,
> Yet sell your face for five pence and 't is dear.[16]

Several of the speeches of Apemantus, a blood-brother of the Bastard in manner and attitude, have a similar scoffing tone, heightened somewhat by the greater contrast between a rhymed couplet and the prose which precedes it.[17] One of the most interesting and amusing examples of this use of rhyme for comic contrast, finally, is in a speech of Dromio of Ephesus where the couplet deftly dispatches an elaborate figure which Puttenham called Clymax, or the marching figure:[18]

> She is so hot because the meat is cold;
> The meat is cold because you come not home;
> You come not home because you have no stomach;
> You have no stomach having broke your fast;
> But we that know what 't is to fast and pray
> Are penitent for your default to-day.[19]

This type of construction, however, is characteristic of Shakespeare's early period only.

More common than the use of the speech-end couplet for contrast or for an epigrammatic thrust is its use as an emphatic climax. Because of its natural ability to attract attention to itself and to heighten the effect by means of its position and construction, Shakespeare employs it frequently to "round off a speech of some length with a high-flown sentiment."[20] It is true that this use, particularly in early plays where it is most common, has a tendency toward the bombastic. Thus Bedford, in *1 Henry VI*, rises to a shouting climax,

> Ten thousand soldiers with me I will take,
> Whose bloody deeds shall make all Europe quake.[21]

It is this same tendency, however, which makes the couplet particularly well adapted to a speech of high patriotic fervor; consequently one finds many such rhymes in the history plays. Nearly

16. I. i. 152–3.   17. *Tim.* I. ii. 52–3 and I. ii. 61–2.
18. p. 173.   19. *C. E.* I. ii. 47–52.
20. D. L. Chambers, p. 18.
21. I. i. 155–6. *Cf.* IV. iii. 28–9; IV. iv. 8–9.

every time God and Saint George are coupled in a patriotic cry
the poet uses rhyme.[22] It is probably this tendency, also, which
kept the couplet alive as a climax for the long Senecan soliloquies
of Shakespeare's villains. Thus, even as late as *Othello,* in a speech
which by then had far outgrown in dramatic ease its earlier counterpart in *Richard III,*[23] the arch-villain Iago finishes his first soliloquy with these mouth-filling lines:

> I have 't. It is engend'red. Hell and night
> Must bring this monstrous birth to the world's light.[24]

Elsewhere the couplet is used for a much less bombastic climax,
though usually it conveys a similar emotional heightening. Of all
the plays of Shakespeare, *Romeo and Juliet* and *Richard II* are
probably the most abounding in this use of the couplet for an
emotional climax. Indeed, there is a striking similarity in the poetic mood of the two plays, a similarity which is made more noticeable by the high percentage of rhyme in both.[25] Richard's cry
of anguish,

> Cry woe, destruction, ruin, loss, decay;
> The worst is death, and death will have his day,[26]

reminds one of Juliet's lines,

> There is no end, no limit, measure, bound,
> In that word's death; no words can that woe sound.[27]

Both speeches, it is to be noticed, employ Brachiologa, or the
cutted comma,[28] in order to get a further stylistic heightening,
that is, they give a list of similar words which do not change the
meaning but which add to the weight of the expression. The emphasis is thus doubly enforced.

Curses, vows, and prayers, when closely related to the speech
both in the grammatical construction and in the thought-develop-

---

22. See 2 *Hen. VI* II. iii. 30–1.   23. I. i. 1–40.

24. I. iii. 409–10. This couplet also closes the act.

25. Hardin Craig (*Shakespeare: A Historical and Critical Study with Annotated
Texts of Twenty-one Plays* [New York, 1935], p. 313) said the following of *Richard II:* "The play has a disproportionately large amount of rhyme for a date so late
as 1595; but this may possibly be accounted for on the ground that rhyme, being a
conscious feature of composition, may be due to reaction or to some passing
literary influence." A safer conjecture would be that the rhyme is abundant because Shakespeare felt it best brought out the poetic atmosphere which he had
conceived for the play.

26. III. ii. 103–04.   27. III. ii. 125–6.

28. Puttenham, p. 178.

ment, produce this same effect of climax. King Henry's passionate cry to God for forgiveness in 2 *Henry IV*, though an emotional climax in his long account to Hal of his seizure of the throne, seems almost an afterthought;[29] but when Queen Isabel, in *Henry V*, prays for a blessing on the new alliance between two great kingdoms, her final words form a well-prepared climax:

> That English may as French, French Englishmen,
> Receive each other. God speak this Amen![30]

In a like manner the couplet occasionally brings to its oratorical zenith a passage of curses, such as Timon's bitter invective against mankind which concludes:

> Let prisons swallow 'em,
> Debts wither 'em to nothing; be men like blasted woods,
> And may diseases lick up their false bloods![31]

Finally in this category should be mentioned a use of rhyme which, though not emotional in content, nevertheless gives a sense of climax to a speech: that is the rhyme which closes a formal, graceful address. Cupid, for example, in the early part of *Timon* and before the tone of the play turns to one of bitterness, rounds off a formal compliment to Timon with these words:

> The ear,
> Taste, touch, and smell, pleas'd from thy table rise;
> They only now come but to feast thine eyes.[32]

This same use is particularly effective in speeches of graceful welcome, as in Portia's greeting to Bassanio's friends[33] or Corin's friendly invitation to Rosalind and Celia.[34]

But much more common than these uses just discussed is the couplet which is used as some sort of conclusion to the speech. A climax, to be sure, is a form of conclusion; but here a climax is thought of as a distinct heightening of poetic effect, usually having to do with some kind of emotional outcry. A rhyme used in a conclusion, on the other hand, bears a predominant relationship to the thought rather than to the emotion of the speech. The emotion may be there, but it is not conspicuous. Also, though the couplet

---

29. IV. v. 219–20. 30. v. ii. 395–6.

31. *Tim.* IV. iii. 537–9. *Cf.* v. i. 55–6.

32. I. ii. 131–3. *Cf. Mac.* I. iv. 20–1; *Per.* II. i. 148–9.

33. *M. V.* III. ii. 315–16.

34. *A. Y. L.* II. iv. 86–7. *Cf. Hen. V* IV. i. 26–7.

rounds off the speech in a somewhat similar manner, it does not necessarily result in a heightening of the poetic tone. The word conclusion, accordingly, is used here in a broad sense to indicate a variety of relationships, all of which are alike in that they lend a sense of finish to the speech and that they achieve that sense of finish through their peculiar connection with the thought of the speech.

Of the several principal relationships the sententious observation supplies the largest number of rhymes. Gnomic utterances are very common in Shakespeare's plays—indeed, in Elizabethan drama in general—but as they are used at the ends of speeches they often enjoy a rhetorical as well as a moral value. Usually such rhymes present a wise reflection which grows out of the content, sometimes as a mere afterthought, but more often as a judgment, a summary, or a restatement of the specific thought in terms of the abstract, in terms, that is, of its moral implications. In *The Two Gentlemen of Verona*, for example, Julia concludes her reproaches to Proteus with an observation which passes judgment upon the subject under discussion:

> It is the lesser blot, modesty finds,
> Women to change their shapes than men their minds;[35]

and while this type of sententious utterance is frequently used in the comedies to give a tone of seriousness (or at least of mock seriousness),[36] it also appears in tragedies to create a tone of moral earnestness.[37] This gnomic couplet is also used to conclude unrhymed passages which are wholly sententious, thus giving the rhymed lines almost a climactic effect;[38] but at times the situation is somewhat altered, for the couplet may emphasize the application of the general gnomic remarks to the specific incident. Such a rhyme is the conclusion of Rosalind's advice to Phebe in *As You Like It*:

> Cry the man mercy; love him; take his offer.
> Foul is most foul, being foul to be a scoffer.[39]

There are several minor ways in which rhyme not containing sententious material effects a conclusion to a speech. It occasionally contains an explanation of the contents of the speech, as in

35. v. iv. 108–09
36. See *L. L. L.* I. i. 26–7; I. i. 31–2; *M. W.* II. ii. 215–16.
37. *R. J.* IV. v. 82–3; *Tim.* IV. iii. 492–3.
38. See *Rich. II* I. iii. 292–3; I. iii. 302–03; *Ham.* I. iii. 43–4; III. iii. 22–3.
39. III. v. 61–2. *Cf. 3 Hen. VI* III. iii. 19–20.

The Comedy of Errors when Antipholus of Syracuse, after order-
ing Dromio to prepare for immediate departure, explains,

> If everyone knows us and we know none,
> 'T is time, I think, to trudge, pack, and be gone.[40]

More often it accompanies a question, rhetorical or otherwise,
which sums up the whole idea of the speech. An excellent example of this is found in *Henry V.* The English king, having addressed a long appeal to the Governor and citizens of Harfleur,
concludes with these words:

> What say you? Will you yield, and this avoid,
> Or, guilty in defence, be thus destroy'd?[41]

The same effect is gained elsewhere without means of the formal
question. Thus, Marcus Andronicus finishes his speech to the
Romans with an implied question, a demand for a final decision:

> Speak, Romans, speak; and if you say we shall,
> Lo, hand in hand, Lucius and I will fall.[42]

In a less stately fashion, but with the same effect, Lucentio, in *The
Taming of the Shrew*, concludes his graceful argument for the vir-
tues of philosophy.[43]

Even these examples just noticed point to the one characteristic
which makes the couplet particularly well fitted to conclude a certain type of speech; namely, its ability to round off effectively a
speech of formal argument. C. V. Deane, speaking of the couplet
in its use later in the rhymed heroic play, makes this observation:

French spoken verse requires the enrichment of rhyme, for without it it
is not sufficiently distinguishable from prose; while in English dramatic
verse, which is not subject to this limitation, the employment of rhyme
seems to modify the whole expression and tone of thought. In both
languages, however, the couplet, with its capacity for antithesis and
sententiousness, tends to the production of long, formally built-up
arguments.[44]

In the plays of Shakespeare the speech-end couplet shows this
tendency, particularly in plays where the dialogue leans heavily
upon argumentation.

40. iii. ii. 157–8. *Cf. Ham.* iii. iv. 178–9.
41. iii. iii. 42–3. *Cf. T. C.* v. iv. 114–15.
42. *T. A.* v. iii. 135–6.   43. *T. S.* iii. i. 13–14.
44. *Dramatic Theory and the Rhymed Heroic Play* (London, 1931), p. 163.

In many speeches, accordingly, the real strength of the argument is reserved until the end, and there is given rhyme for double emphasis. Often this takes the form of a causal relationship. The situation is outlined, its implications are discussed, and then in the conclusion the actual cause of the situation is stated. Thus Northumberland, in *1 Henry IV*, concludes his plea for his son with these words,

> Either envy, therefore, or misprision
> Is guilty of this fault, and not my son.[45]

Again, syllogistic reasoning is used. Emilia, in *Othello*, after asserting that husbands, having strong desires, perform certain ills, declares that wives have the same desires; and then draws the logical conclusion:

> Then let them use us well; else let them know,
> The ills we do, their ills instruct us so.[46]

Sometimes the principle of climax is drawn upon: a series of arguments is presented, the most important reserved for the end and rhymed.[47] And, at other times, the order of the thought is from the general to the specific, from the general discussion to the specific point of the argument. In this way Adriana, in *The Comedy of Errors*, arrives at the real point of her shrewish berating of her supposed husband:

> Keep them fair league and truce with thy true bed;
> I live distain'd, thou undishonoured.[48]

These, then, are the major relationships between the rhyme which concludes a speech and the speech itself; for the most part there is little change to be noticed in the use of this type of couplet from the early plays to the late. The purpose is almost always one of emphasis and, although there is a decrease in number, examples of the principal types of relationship can be found in every period of Shakespeare's dramatic career. But Fleay was not altogether right in discarding this "tag-rhyme" as a means of estimating Shakespeare's development; for a comparative study shows some interesting variations.

In the early plays rhyme very often accompanies a speech of

45. I. iii. 27–8. *Cf. C. E.* v. i. 85–6.
46. IV. iii. 103–04. *Cf. T. A.* I. i. 7–8.
47. *Rich. II* I. i. 122–3; *T. C.* II. ii. 161–2.
48. II. ii. 147–8. *Cf. John* III. i. 170–1; *Rich. II* II. ii. 24–7; *M. V.* III. ii. 195–6.

verbal play, where the rhyme is merely a further stylistic embellishment in a speech already highly stylized and artificial. In *Romeo and Juliet* a passage of oxymoron, which otherwise might have continued indefinitely, is successfully rounded off with a couplet.[49] In the same play, Capulet's outcry at the death of his daughter, equalled in absurdity only by the earlier Ecphonisis[50] of the Nurse, uses the couplet merely as an additional ornament.[51] Or again, one might mention Juliet's play on the word "I," which is ultimately climaxed with a couplet.[52] All the early plays abound in the "love of verbal resemblances" which, as Bathurst rightly supposed, is "connected with this love of rhyme."[53]

Likewise, in the early plays rhyme which closes a speech is frequently dissociated from the main part of the speech; that is, though it may appear in one of the relationships just discussed, it is often not so closely coördinated with the body of the speech as it is in the later plays. This conclusion partially breaks down, of course, in such plays as *Pericles* and *Timon of Athens,* where there is reason to believe that at least some of the rhymes were added by another hand; but in general Shakespeare tends in the plays of his first period to conclude speeches with couplets which are either difficult to justify at all or which do not blend smoothly with the preceding lines.

With the gradual diminution of rhyme, however, there becomes evident in the speech-end rhymes a new coördinating facility which results in rhetorical and even grammatical unity. Whereas in the early plays the couplet was nearly always a syntactical unit, in the later it often grows directly out of the grammatical construction. But more important, the rhyme which in the early plays seems almost to be merely an embellishment tacked on to the speech becomes inseparably fused with the context in the later ones.

The most striking examples of Shakespeare's mature use of rhyme are to be found in *Troilus and Cressida,* a play whose dominant characteristic of argumentation and debate lends itself well to the natural tendency of the couplet to produce "long, formally built-up arguments."[54] An excellent example of this is the following speech of Aeneas:

49. I. i. 187–8.   50. Puttenham, p. 177.
51. IV. v. 63–4.   52. III. ii. 48–51.
53. Charles Bathurst, *Remarks on the Difference in Shakespeare's Versification in Different Periods of his Life and on the Like Points of Difference in Poetry Generally* (London, 1857), p. 8.
54. Above, p. 35.

In the extremity of great and little,
Valour and pride excel themselves in Hector;
The one almost as infinite as all,
The other blank as nothing. Weigh him well,
And that which looks like pride is courtesy.
This Ajax is half made of Hector's blood;
In love whereof, half Hector stays at home;
Half heart, half hand, half Hector comes to seek
This blended knight, half Troyan and half Greek.[55]

What Shakespeare is doing here—and it is characteristic of many of the speeches in this play—is roughly this: the speaker begins with a dual concept. Perhaps he is taking opposites or parallels or, as in this case, two aspects of the same proposition. First the one is discussed, then the other; then, as in a Baconian essay, the two ideas are either restated or expanded. Finally, the conclusion is reached, in which both ideas are shown in their true relationship;[56] and this conclusion is in rhyme. It cannot be separated from the body of the speech without destroying the basic thought-struc-ture. It might be said that the germ of such a speech is in the word-worrying of the earlier Shakespearian style; but here Shake-speare, somewhat like the metaphysical poets, is interested in the subtle relationship between ideas rather than sounds.

Thus, from this analysis of only the speech-end rhymes, certain suggestions can be found to explain partially the gradual diminu-tion of rhyme in Shakespeare's dramas. On the one hand, rhyme in the early plays seemed closely associated with the playwright's love for verbal similarities, which was expressed elsewhere in puns, stichomythia, oxymoron, anaphora, and the like. As he de-veloped a more dramatic medium, however, this proclivity be-came less marked, and rhyme at the end of highly stylistic speeches also diminished. On the other hand, as Shakespeare learned more successfully to coördinate rhyme with the rest of the speech, he tended more and more to reserve it for special effects, effects which had to do not so much with the sound as with the thought-structure of the entire speech; but in this use the couplet, as Shakespeare unquestionably realized, is most easily adapted to speeches of formal argument. Accordingly, one should expect to find fewer couplets being used in those plays, or in those parts of plays, where the dramatic scheme does not call for any form

55. iv. v. 78–86. Cf. ii. ii. 37–50; iv. i. 54–66.
56. Cf. M. B. Kennedy, "The Oration in Shakespeare," University of Virginia Abstracts of Dissertations (Charlottesville, Virginia, 1937), pp. 16–17.

of argument. Even in passages of argument, moreover, one would expect a diminution in the use of speech-end rhyme; for rhyme in blank-verse dramas is essentially an embellishment, an external method of producing an effect. As Shakespeare developed his facility with blank verse, he no longer needed effects outside his accepted medium; and thus rhyme is held more in reserve.

There is still a further observation which throws light on the diminution of the speech-end rhyme. The method in this chapter has been to examine Shakespeare's actual practice, to look at the rhyme in its context; and in every case, whether the rhymed line be in doggerel, heroic, or some other measure, it always constitutes a full close to the speech. Occasionally it is followed by another line, frequently a short one; but this line is rarely an organic part of the speech. In Shakespeare's early plays, moreover, nearly all the speeches end with a full line, whether the verse is rhymed or unrhymed; but as he developed in mastery of his medium the speeches tend more and more to end with a segment of a line. Statistics show an increase of these broken ends from none at all in the early *Henry VI* plays to as high as 391 in *Cymbeline*.[57] Although it can scarcely be maintained that the disappearance of rhyme brought about this gradual increase in broken speech endings, it can be maintained with some assurance that the converse is true. Since rhyme demands a full close to a speech, and since Shakespeare, in his development toward dramatic freedom, inclined toward a speech structure whose last line is divided with the first line of the next, rhyme had to give way.

Speech-Pause Rhyme

Closely associated with the speech-end rhyme is the rhyme which marks a pause within a blank-verse speech, a pause commonly indicated by a semi-colon, colon, or period. This classification is made here for the first time. Heuser, who alone attempted a complete listing of the couplets under their general uses, failed to notice it, possibly because none of the earlier critics had noticed it either. In a comment upon a couplet from *Richard III*, however, he gave a suggestion for this classification: "V, 3.171–172 schliesst nicht geradezu die Rede, sondern bezeichnet einen starken Schluss innerhalb derselben;"[1] but he dismissed the majority of such rhymes as accidental.

57. E. K. Chambers, II, 401. *Cf.* Frederick S. Pulling, "The Speech-Ending Test Applied to Twenty of Shakspere's Plays," *N. S. S. Trans.* v–vII (1877–79), 457–8.
1. p. 243.

Some of these couplets may be accidental, but that well over fifty of them, all marking more or less strongly a break in the movement of the speech, do so without the design of the playwright is not credible. Furthermore, an examination of the plays of Shakespeare's contemporaries and predecessors clearly shows that this use of the couplet was not uncommon. In such a play as *The Tragical Reign of Selimus* (1594), for example, there are more speech-pause than speech-end couplets, and in others the speech-pause are second in number only to the speech-end rhymes; nor was Shakespeare without precedent in this use of rhyme, for *The Spanish Tragedy* offers many excellent examples, and even *Tamburlaine*, despite Marlowe's opposition to rhyme in general, shows the speech-pause rhyme occasionally. Since Shakespeare availed himself of the other uses of rhyme found in his predecessors and early contemporaries, there is no reason to suppose he should not have done so with this.

As might be expected, the speech-pause rhyme, like the speech-end rhyme, is often separable from the structure of the entire speech. It may centre attention upon some important piece of information which, if the playwright were in a rhyming mood, would be rhymed regardless of its position in its context. A good example of this is the prophecy. Whether the lines containing the prophecy appear at the beginning, middle, or end of a speech, or even stand alone, one should not be surprised to find them rhymed. Thus Queen Margaret, in *Richard III*, pauses in one of her long diatribes against the king to predict his fast approaching doom:

> But at hand, at hand,
> Ensues his piteous and unpitied end.[2]

So, too, the titular lines of *Measure for Measure* are rhymed to call them to the particular attention of the audience and not to indicate any change in the movement of the speech;[3] and the two epitaphs which appear within blank-verse speeches in *Timon* are rhymed for the same reason.[4]

In some cases this couplet within the body of the speech gives the impression of being an interpolation either by the playwright or by some other hand. In the following passage from *Pericles*, for example, the couplet contributes nothing to the speech but its

2. IV. iv. 73–4.　　　　　　　　3. V. i. 415–16.
4. IV. iii. 380–1; V. iii. 3–4.

general wisdom and can be discarded without any real break in the sense:

> But I must tell you, now my thoughts revolt;
> For he's no man on whom perfections wait
> That, knowing sin within, will touch the gate.
> You are a fair viol, and your sense the strings;
> Who, finger'd to make man his lawful music. . . .[5]

Indeed, many of the gnomic utterances which appear in *Timon of Athens* and the first two acts of *Pericles* seem like interpolations.

Generally, however, speech-pause rhyme seems to perform a function organic to the speech in which it appears, a function varying according to the degree to which it alters the thought-progression of the speech. Frequently it merely indicates a light pause, with the rhyme and its accompanying punctuation merely a kind of stage-direction for the actor to come to a full stop, to raise or lower his voice, or to do whatever else the context may demand. Here and there the rhyme seems to lend a cadence to a long sentence within the speech, thus strengthening the normal mark of punctuation and the pause which it indicates.[6] Elsewhere it marks a change, however slight, in the tone of the speech or the tenor of thought. Thus, in *Timon,* a couplet which accentuates the period in a long sentence also introduces a change in the poetic medium from blank verse to rhyme;[7] and in *3 Henry VI* a rhyme heralds a distinct heightening of the emotional tone of one of the King's soliloquies:

> Would I were dead! if God's good will were so;
> For what is in this world but grief and woe?[8]

Prior to this couplet Henry has been thinking of the troubles of his reign, but with the rhyme he begins a passage of morbid self-deprecation. The following couplet from the same play climaxes a series of rhetorical questions which present one point of view:

> Was't you that revell'd in our parliament,
> And made a preachment of your high descent?[9]

and the speech continues with a somewhat different approach to the same idea. In *2 Henry VI* a couplet is used within the speech to focus certain general comments upon a specific situation, with

5. I. i. 78–82. *Cf.* II. iii. 62–3.
6. *Rich. II* II. i. 18–19; *Tim.* II. ii. 5–6.
7. IV. i. 35–6.   8. II. v. 19–20. *Cf. T. A.* I. i. 107–08.
9. I. iv. 71–2.

the ensuing lines stating an opposite point of view.[10] Indeed, this use of the couplet to mark the transition between two opposed attitudes is one of the most common functions of the speech-pause rhyme. Usually it is a grammatical, or at least a rhetorical, part of the first point of view, marking a strong pause before the beginning of the opposing view.

It is apparent from this discussion that the speech-pause rhyme bears a kinship with the speech-end rhyme, which performs many similar functions. Though the examples discussed so far mark only a kind of transition from one part of the speech to another growing immediately out of it, there are many rhymes in this division which emphasize a much stronger break in the speech, a break sufficiently complete to give the effect of two distinct speeches without the intervening words of another speaker. In *Richard III*, for example, a couplet forms the rhetorical conclusion to a lengthy passage of anaphora, and the speech continues in a lower stylistic level, almost as if some interruption had changed the mood and direction of the speech.[11] But even more marked is the deliberate change of subject initiated by the couplet in such a passage as the opening lines of *Twelfth Night*. Here Orsino, meditating on the beauties of music, puts a stop to his thoughts (and probably to the music) with these lines:

> Enough! no more!
> 'T is not so sweet now as it was before;[12]

and then undertakes to anatomize the fantasies of love. Similarly Hamlet winds up one thought, dismissing it from his mind with the words,

> O, 't is most sweet
> When in one line two crafts directly meet,[13]

and then turns his attention to other matters. The same effect is gained by a change of address within the speech, when, as in the passage noticed by Heuser,[14] the speaker turns from the person to whom he has been speaking and begins talking to another. Here the Ghosts of the Princes finish their words to Richmond with the couplet,

> Sleep, Richmond, sleep in peace, and wake in joy;
> Good angels guard thee from the boar's annoy![15]

---

10. III. i. 202–03. Cf. *T. A.* v. iii. 164–5.
11. IV. iv. 103–04.   12. I. i. 7–8.
13. *Ham.* III. iv. 209–10. Cf. *Cy.* IV. ii. 286–7; v. ii. 6–7.
14. See above, p. 39.
15. *Rich. III* v. iii. 155–6. Cf. *1 Hen. VI* IV. i. 16–17; *R. J.* v. iii. 175–6.

and then continue with their ominous words to Richard. The speech-pause couplet, accordingly, has the same effect of finality as the speech-end couplet and acquaints the audience clearly with the change in direction of the remarks.

The speech-pause rhymes do not constitute a large division, and are used rather sparingly by Shakespeare after the earliest of his plays. It is understandable that the early history plays, where the style tends to be heavy, with strong, well-marked periods, are most abounding in this type of rhyme. The early comedies, though full of rhyme, have scarcely any speech-pause rhymes; the tragedies and later history plays and comedies have somewhat more. With the disappearance of the speech-end rhyme came a more rapid disappearance of the speech-pause, probably because it was felt as more artificial. Since the end of the speech is logically the most emphatic part of it, and since rhyme, as Shakespeare uses it in his mature plays, is generally for emphasis, any rhyme which appears within the body of a blank-verse speech tends to destroy the effect of the whole and centre the attention on one of the parts. Both poetically and dramatically this is weak, and Shakespeare, who naturally thought in terms of the speech unit, the entire speech, early learned to reserve this pause rhyme for special effects.

This brings up the problem, however, of *Timon of Athens, Pericles,* and *Cymbeline,* all late plays and all containing a relatively high number of speech-pause rhymes. It is possible, of course, that these passages are un-Shakespearian, perhaps the work of Middleton, Tourneur, or Webster; but even so the technical reasons for the high number of speech-pause rhymes remain to be explained.

The explanation seems to lie in two facts. First, the majority of the speech-pause rhymes, particularly in *Pericles,* which has the highest number, are of a gnomic quality in keeping with the general tone of the plays. It is common for Shakespeare and his contemporaries to phrase their sententious utterances in such a way that the audience can set them down in their tables[16] and carry them away. These gnomic utterances, again particularly in *Pericles,* are rather poorly integrated with the rest of the speech and, though not out of keeping with the general tone of seriousness and social criticism, might well have been interpolated to meet some particular demand. Secondly, in *Pericles* and *Cymbeline* many of the speech-pause couplets, taken in conjunction with a following couplet and the blank-verse line which intervenes, form

16. *Ham.* I. v. 107.

a kind of stanza in which the first couplet is used not so much for itself as for the effect of the whole. When this appears, as it usually does, at the end of a speech or of a scene, it gives the effect of a delayed cadence, the first couplet suggesting the conclusion, the blank-verse line interrupting it, and the second couplet finally resolving it.[17] Thus, instead of actually having a speech-pause rhyme and then an end rhyme, there is in effect a double-tag with a single-line interruption. Although this use appears once in an earlier play,[18] it is only in these later plays that it becomes a marked characteristic.

Speech-Beginning, Speech-Link, and Single-Speech Rhymes

In Shakespeare's plays there are numerous isolated rhymes which are difficult both to classify and to explain. In many cases it is impossible to determine whether the sound similarity, resulting from words important to the sense of the lines, was not a mere accident. When this rhyme appears at a strong position in the context, such as at exits or speech-ends, unless the play is almost entirely devoid of rhyme, the probability is that the rhyme was intentional; but when, as is often the case, it appears in a place where neither Shakespeare nor his fellow playwrights seem particularly inclined to use it and where it does not produce any striking effect, then it must be held seriously in doubt.

The rhymes to be discussed in this section are a mixed group. Some of them, despite their not being used in the stronger positions,[1] are indisputably intentional and perform a function of genuine value to the dramatic structure; others, just as full-sounding rhymes, add nothing to their context and thus, particularly in the later plays, are questionable. The first, and least extensive, group consists of rhymes which occur at the beginning of speeches of three or more lines; the second, of rhymes which bind together either two long speeches or two speeches of a single line each; and the third, of couplets which themselves constitute the complete speech of a single speaker. All three, to be sure, show similarities in subject matter and poetic quality, but they are sufficiently different in their effect to merit separate discussion.

The use of rhyme at the beginning of speeches is not character-

---

17. See *Per.* I. i. 76–7; I. i. 132–3; *Cy.* IV. ii. 286–7; v. ii. 6–7.
18. *John* I. i. 142–3.
1. The strong positions for isolated rhymes are scene- and act-end, speech-end, cue and exit.

istic of Shakespeare nor, for that matter, of his contemporaries.[2] Though there are approximately thirty such rhymes in his plays, many in later plays are probably unintentional, and even some in the early plays do not seem to be used with a definite purpose. When there is a definite purpose, the couplet is often not so much an integral part of the speech as a separate unit intended solely to emphasize its own contents. Thus, the couplet which begins a speech near the end of *Macbeth* is used as an epitaph over young Siward and not as a striking opening to a long passage of lamentation:

> He's worth no more:
> They say he parted well, and paid his score:
> And so, God be with him![3]

The very brevity of this father's dismissal of his son's death, of course, gives it its power; but the rhyme helps to attract momentarily the attention of the audience without drawing it away from the more important business of the scene. Thus also, a riddle begins a speech in *Measure for Measure*,[4] where the rhyme is to be explained solely on the grounds that Shakespeare and his contemporaries were fond of rhyming riddles.

In two or three cases this rhyme at the beginning of speeches is used to mark the change from one medium to another, a function frequently performed by rhyme in other positions. For example, in *Julius Caesar*, a play with only a moderate amount of rhyme, a couplet introduces blank verse after a passage of prose,[5] and in *Measure for Measure* a rhyme begins a prose passage after some lines of verse.[6] Mechanical as this device is, it is not without effectiveness, particularly where the change of medium also marks a distinct change in the tone of the scene.[7]

When integrally a part of the speech, speech-beginning rhyme is quite similar to rhyme at the end of a speech. Where the latter serves normally to round off the passage with a strong cadence, the former tends to begin the passage with similar forcefulness. Several times, indeed, the rhyme seems merely a poetic link with what has gone before, a link which serves to continue the musical

---

2. M. Meiners (p. 31) says that such a use is not uncommon in Webster: "Auch im Anfang einer Rede und in der Mitte bei besonders dramatischen Stellen findet sich der Reim."

3. v. viii. 51–3.   4. v. i. 184–5.
5. I. i. 37–8.   6. IV. i. 14–15.

7. *Cf.* Gertrud Bordukat, *Die Abgrenzung zwischen vers und prosa in den dramen Shakespeares* (Königsberg, 1918).

quality of the verse. This is particularly noticeable when the speech-beginning follows immediately upon a speech-end or even a single-speech couplet. Accordingly, in *Romeo and Juliet,* a speech which follows an exit couplet begins with a couplet, thus maintaining the poetic mood which might naturally drop with the departure of one of the principal actors;[8] and in *2 Henry VI* Gloucester's answer to Margaret's accusing couplet begins with a couplet in order not to sound less emphatic.[9] Where the rhyme is not used for such a poetic link, it seems intended primarily to give the passage a forceful opening. An excellent example of this is the following rhyme from the great trial scene in *The Merchant of Venice,* a scene in which, with perfect mastery, Shakespeare manipulates his medium to fit the various emotional changes in the action:

> Tarry, Jew:
> The law hath yet another hold on you.[10]

Although this is the only couplet in the scene and although elsewhere such a rhyme might easily be considered accidental, its use here to call attention to the passage in which the tide is completely turned against Shylock is so dramatic as to make it almost certainly a deliberate rhyme.

In speeches of high passion this opening rhyme also appears to good effect. This is true, of course, only when the tone of the entire speech is consistently passionate; otherwise the emphasis gained by the opening rhyme throws the rest somewhat into the shadow and weakens the effect of the whole. A good example is to be seen in *Macbeth* when, with the reappearance of the ghost, the frenzied Macbeth tries to bolster up his courage with

> What man dare, I dare.
> Approach thou like the rugged Russian bear.[11]

The ensuing lines continue the heightened effect of the opening by a succession of vivid and terrible images. In a like manner a couplet occasionally begins speeches of intense anger, such as old York's bitter invective against the criminal foolishness of Richard II[12] and Gloucester's heated criticism of the church in *1 Henry VI.*[13]

8. v. iii. 161–2.

9. ii. i. 190–1.

10. iv. i. 346–7.

11. iii. iv. 99–100. *Cf.* iii. iv. 69–70.

12. *Rich. II* ii. i. 163–4.

13. i. i. 33–4.

The gradual disappearance of this sort of rhyme is easily understandable. In the first place, it seems never to have appealed strongly to Shakespeare, who, even in his early plays, used it sparingly and with no very marked effect. When it appears in the later plays, it must either be labeled unintentional or recognized as existing for an effect which only seldom is related to the entire speech. In the second place, it tends, along with much of the other rhyme in the early plays, to accompany some highly stylized pattern which Shakespeare rapidly abandoned in his dramatic growth.[14] And in the third place, it is not compatible with the normal tendency of the heroic couplet to develop toward formal argumentation; for, because of its shifting the emphasis to the beginning, it weakens the structure of the entire speech. Even in speeches of high emotion the emphatic opening rhyme places too much strain upon the following blank verse.

Because of its weaknesses, speech-beginning rhyme was restricted in use even in the very early plays where rhyme in general was used freely. Speech-link rhyme, on the other hand, because of its ability to produce certain highly desirable dramatic effects, is to be found in generous portions even in Shakespeare's more mature plays. As it is used here, the term "speech-link rhyme" refers actually to two slightly different uses of rhyme. The one is where the couplet binds together two speeches, one of which is more than a single line in length, the other, where it binds two single-line speeches. The latter is much more common and generally more effective, but even the former appears at times to good advantage.

It was seen that the speech-beginning rhyme often serves as a link with the concluding rhyme of the preceding speech, usually with the effect of maintaining the poetic level of the passage. The speech-link rhyme which connects two long speeches performs the same function but does it more neatly and efficiently. Where the former merely gives the impression of unity by continuing the verse pattern, the latter tightens the bond by fusing the connecting lines into a stylistic unit. It is this fact, indeed, which probably limits the use of this type of speech-link rhyme to a few cases, and those only in the early dramas; such close coupling lends itself well to only single-line speeches where the effect of rapid dialogue is needed. In a passage from *1 Henry VI*, this rhyme connecting

14. See *R. J.* I. i. 177–8; IV. v. 84–5.

longer speeches is very dramatic. The Bishop of Winchester, in a heated argument with the Duke of Gloucester, makes this threat,

> Gloucester, thou wilt answer this before the Pope,

and receives the taunting reply,

> Winchester goose, I cry, "A rope! a rope!"[15]

It must be noticed that Gloucester continues with another rhymed couplet; otherwise, just as with the speech-beginning rhyme, the level of passionate excitement might be lowered.

It is much more common to find a single line rhyming with the final line of a long speech. By means of this device, Shakespeare produced some very striking effects, humorous and serious alike. A well-known example is at the end of one of the Nurse's garrulous monologues in *Romeo and Juliet:*

> *Nurse.* "Wilt thou not, Jule?" It stinted and said, "Ay."
> *Jul.*   And stint thou too, I pray thee, nurse, say I.[16]

Here too the rhyme is used for emphasis. Though its primary theatrical result is probably a comic one, it gives a forceful, emphatic close which demands attention; and if anything could distract the Nurse from her own reflections, this might be expected to do it.

The ability of the linking rhyme to emphasize the content of the second line makes it well adapted to sharp, forceful answers. In the classifications discussed earlier, the couplet, for the most part, was a unit, the emphasis customarily being divided alike on both lines. Here, however, the couplet is in effect two distinct lines, with the dramatic strength of the second line being magnified by the rhyme with the first. Thus, in the following passage, also from *Romeo and Juliet,* a play which contains a high number of speech-link rhymes, the final line of old Capulet's speech is merely a kind of auxiliary to Tybalt's angry reply:

> *Cap.* Show a fair presence and put off these frowns,
>   An ill-beseeming semblance for a feast.
> *Tyb.* It fits, when such a villain is a guest.[17]

An interesting variation in this use of speech-link rhyme for a heated answer is in an earlier passage where Tybalt divides a quatrain with Benvolio, but here much of the sharpness is lost.

---

15. I. iii. 52–3. *Cf.* IV. iii. 30–3; *T. A.* V. i. 49–52.
16. I. iii. 57–8. *Cf. Cy.* IV. ii. 228–9.   17. I. v. 75–7.

The delayed rhyme scarcely conveys the tenseness of the situation.[18]

It is this same emphasis on the second line which enables the speech-link rhyme to produce a humorous, sometimes caustic, answer. In *The Comedy of Errors* this is done by means of a triplet, the answer in a single line rhyming with the couplet of the previous speaker;[19] and in *Antony and Cleopatra*, by means of two rhyming iambic lines of only three feet each, which speed up the reply and intensify its effect.[20] This rhyme even makes possible the dramatic outlining of a single-line aside in which the speaker makes some comment on the words of the previous speech. Thus Thaisa's emotional aside, in *Pericles*, is really a kind of answer to her father's weak praise of Pericles:

> *Sim.* He's but a country gentleman,
>   Has done no more than other knights have done,
>   Has broken a staff or so; so let it pass.
> *Thai.* [*Aside.*] To me he seems like diamond to glass.[21]

The rhyme, of course, helps indicate to the audience that the line is really an aside; but because it is surrounded by unrhymed asides, the rhyme here must be primarily to express the emotional intensity of Thaisa's reaction.

When the speeches are only a single line in length, however, this speech-link rhyme enjoys its greatest success. In the examples just examined, where the rhyme is divided between two speeches of unequal length, the sharpness of the second line is undoubtedly effective, particularly when it is an answer or reply to the speech which it follows; but if the speeches are both of only a single line, the resultant balance makes possible a grace and rapidity which is very well suited to produce certain special dramatic effects.

In serious plays this type of rhyme is commonly used at times of violent action where the desired effect is one of intense rapidity. The couplets frequently appear in multiples, depending upon the amount of action which has to be accomplished. For example, in *Titus Andronicus*, Titus' stabbing of his wronged daughter is accompanied by rhyme and then followed by two highly passionate speeches, rhymed, in which he explains the reason for his deed.[22] A generous sprinkling of such lines is to be found in the early history plays, where rhyme is frequently called on to accompany some startling action. The murdering of Prince Edward, in *3 Henry*

18. I. i. 75–8.   19. I. ii. 51–3. *Cf. 3 Hen. VI* IV. iv. 14–16.
20. II. vii. 99–100.   21. II. iii. 33–6.   22. V. iii. 46–9.

VI, is accomplished in two thrusts, each one prefaced with a single rhyming line:

> *Glou.* Sprawl'st thou? Take that, to end thy agony. [*Stabs him.*]
> *Clar.* And there's for twitting me with perjury. [*Stabs him.*][23]

Such lines may almost be said to take the place of the stage directions;[24] but the purpose is a stylistic one as well. The couplet, by linking these short speeches to one another, succeeds in giving to the dialogue a quick, energetic pace and to the action a strong finality. Although this finality is more marked in the single-speech rhyme, even in the present group it appears to advantage.

An angry, passionate exchange of words between two characters is not uncommonly couched in rhyme, because here again the tone is one of rapidity and excitement, and the single-line unit makes for compression and sharpness. Demetrius and Lysander, like two fighting cocks, prepare to come to blows with these words:

> *Dem.* I say I love thee more than he can do.
> *Lys.* If thou say so, withdraw, and prove it too.[25]

Of course, this is all midsummer madness; and the audience perhaps sees behind the lines and realizes that this strutting, serious as it is to the two bewitched youths, will result in nothing. It is a curious fact that Shakespeare rather frequently makes use of rhyme to indicate a certain artificiality or insincerity either in the situation as a whole or in the particular words of the speaker whose real intentions are being belied.[26] Demetrius and Lysander are in dead earnest, but the situation into which they have been thrust is fantastic; and this rhyme, after many lines of blank verse, might seem to indicate the absurdity of the fight. A similar use of the speech-link rhyme is to be seen in *Romeo and Juliet* where the word play in the lines points to a certain falseness in the emotions.[27]

A principal use of the speech-link rhyme is in passages whose tone is comic. The same rapidity which gives vigor to speeches of high passion or of dramatic activity, in speeches of a comic turn lends a sparkle and brilliance which is so effective that Shakespeare continues to employ this type of rhyme up to his very latest plays.

---

23. v. v. 39–40.   24. See *T. A.* v. i. 47–8.
25. *M. N. D.* iii. ii. 254–5.   26. See David, p. 35.
27. iii. iv. 7–8. One naturally thinks of the terrible bewailing over the supposed death of Juliet (iv. v.). Here various stylistic devices are used to create a sense of artificiality. *Cf.* iv. i. 18–21.

Although it was strengthened by the stichomythia which Elizabethan drama took from the plays of Seneca, such a use of rhyme
is indigenous to English comedy. In the early Tudor comedies,
with rhyme the accepted medium, there are many passages of
single-line dialogue whose rapidity of delivery determines the effectiveness of the wit. Much of this, as for example in *Gammer
Gurton's Needle*, is a coarse sort of humor most easily expressed
by the doggerel lines which appear even in the early plays of
Shakespeare.

Since Shakespeare's doggerel has received considerable attention,[28] it will be necessary to give only a brief notice of it here. In
general it is used only in single-line, divided rhymes, principally
for a comic effect; and, as Malone observed,[29] it appears mostly in
the early plays. While one immediately thinks of *The Taming of
the Shrew*, a relatively late play for its high number of doggerel
rhymes, there is reason to suspect here a revision or a reworking
of an earlier version.[30] Although an occasional speech-link rhyme
in doggerel is to be found as late as *As You Like It*,[31] Shakespeare
soon learned to prefer prose or a more legitimate verse to this
vulgar metre in passages of rapid comic dialogue.[32]

Doggerel is chiefly reserved for the speeches of comic figures,
usually those of the lower order. In *Love's Labour's Lost, The
Comedy of Errors*, and *The Two Gentlemen of Verona* it appears
mainly in the mouths of clowns,[33] but it is not limited to these
characters. Oliphant, speaking of *The Comedy of Errors*, said:

One might reasonably assert (as has often been asserted) that Shakspere
made the Dromios speak in doggrel because it suited their characters,

28. See particularly the following: G. König; G. Saintsbury, vol. II; Paul Reyher.
29. pp. 506–07.
30. See F. G. Fleay, "The Authorship of the Taming of the Shrew," *N. S. S.
Trans.* I, 87–8; Ellis, *N. S. S. Trans.* I, 119; E. H. C. Oliphant, "Shakspere's Plays:
An Examination," *Modern Language Review* IV (1909), 343.
31. III. iii. 96–8.
32. Reyer (p. 77) summarizes the disappearance of doggerel in Shakespeare's
time as follows: "Peu à peu, ce 'Doggerel' qui consiste en vers manqués par suite
de l'ignorance du poète, ou de propos délibéré en vue de produire un effet comique,
ce 'Doggerel' sans mesure, ou, si je puis dire, d'une mesure approximative, se fait
plus rare. La technique du vers s'améliore, grâce à une grande pratique et à l'étude
des questions de versification. D'autre part, la prose est le mode d'expression adopté
pour les rôles de gros comique. Mais le 'Doggerel' ne disparaît point pour cela; il
revêt de nouvelles formes, en reprend d'anciennes quelque peu modifiées, et, entre
les mains des rimailleurs d'une part, des satiriques et des humoristes de l'autre, il
est encore destiné à tenir dans la poésie anglaise une place intéressante."
33. König, pp. 118–19; Reyher, pp. 70–1.

but in III, i, Antipholus of Ephesus, Angelo, and Balthazar all speak the dialect of Dromio.[34]

A similar case of a high character speaking doggerel is in *The Merchant of Venice* when Portia closes a highly euphuistic prose scene with this couplet:

> Come, Nerissa. Sirrah, go before.
> Whiles we shut the gates upon one wooer, another knocks
>   at the door.[35]

The speech-link rhyme in regular metres is to be found scattered throughout the dramas when an effect of clever repartee is desired, except in the very latest works, where rhyme of any sort is used sparingly. While it occurs most frequently in certain of the comedies, it is by no means confined to them. In *1 Henry VI*, Margaret, who has let her mind wander from the subject, conceals the fact with a clever response:

> *Suf.* Lady, wherefore talk you so?
> *Mar.* I cry you mercy, 't is but *quid* for *quo*.[36]

Again, in *Romeo and Juliet*, a play whose tragic mood is frequently interrupted by effects belonging to comedy, the clever sallies of wit between various of the characters call on rhyme to heighten their comic tone.[37] In the comedies which avail themselves of the humor of rapid dialogue, however, this use of rhyme is most appropriate and most effective. At times the rhyme takes on the characteristics of stichomythia, as in this couplet from *The Taming of the Shrew:*

> *Bap.* The gain I seek is, quiet in the match.
> *Gre.* No doubt but he hath got a quiet catch;[38]

but elsewhere it produces the same effect without the repetition of any single word. An interesting use is in the following triplet from *Love's Labour's Lost:*

> *Prin.*   Some merry mocking lord, belike; is 't so?
> [*Mar.*] They say so most that most his humours know.
> *Prin.*   Such short-liv'd wits do wither as they grow.[39]

---

34. p. 350.

35. I. ii. 146–7.

36. v. iii. 108–09.

37. II. i. 32–3.

38. II. i. 332–3. *Cf. R. J.* IV. i. 18–21. Rhymed stichomythia is characteristic of the Senecan tragedies written by the Pembroke school, but appeared rarely in the professional tragedies (see A. M. Witherspoon, p. 91).

39. II. i. 52–4. *Cf.* II. i. 111–13; III. i. 60–2.

Here the rhyme is extended into a triplet[40] and the grace of the lyrical banter is increased. Then too, the striking alliteration adds to the general tone of gaiety.

The Taming of the Shrew is particularly rich in this use of rhyme, a fact which is explicable by the nature of the humor in this play. In such a play as 1 Henry IV the humor, though of several sorts, is mostly the result of the dominating personality of Falstaff. This is not to say that there is no lively exchange of wit in the comic scenes, for actually the Prince and Sir John join more than once in verbal conflict; but most of the humor is of a broad sort, often raucous and coarse. Or again, in A Midsummer Night's Dream the comedy—at least that of Bottom and his fellows—is crude and mechanical, depending for its effectiveness mostly upon the grotesque in character and situation. In both these plays, moreover, the comic scenes are in prose, a medium characteristically used by the low-comedy figures in Shakespeare. In The Taming of the Shrew, however, and in parts of The Comedy of Errors, Love's Labour's Lost, and even Romeo and Juliet, the method used to produce a comic effect is somewhat different. In the first place, the comic figures are not from the lower classes but generally belong to the level of society which has at least come into contact with education and refinement. In the second place, their humor grows not so much out of situation, though this naturally is involved, as out of the nimbleness of their wits. Falstaff's wit, to be sure, is nimble, but he is prone to fall back upon grossness. Petruchio, in The Taming of the Shrew, is not above coarseness, particularly when he designs to shock the shrewish Kate, but Petruchio is essentially a gentleman who, like Biron, engages with delight in the sophisticated banter of his class. Thus, even the doggerel rhymes which link two speeches in this play tend to reflect an intellectual, courtly grace, a clever repartee which, in Shakespeare's works, belongs principally to the high-comedy characters. It is the particular province of the speech-link rhyme, therefore, to accompany a rapid sally of wit which generally bears with it some flavor of sophistication.

This means, of course, that the speech-link rhyme is limited in use to those plays where such an effect is in harmony with the general nature of the piece. It would appear grossly inappropriate to have Falstaff and Hal arguing in graceful rhymed pentameters. It would seem equally inappropriate to convert the gracefully

---

40. See J. Schipper (A History of English Versification [Oxford, 1910], p. 217) for some comment on triplets in Elizabethan poetry.

lyrical rhymes of the Princess of France and Maria, or the sharply pointed repartee of Mercutio and Romeo, into robust prose. It is to be expected, then, that this type of rhyme will vary considerably from one play to another, depending on the general poetic atmosphere.

But that the speech-link rhyme seems to disappear altogether in the later comedy still requires an explanation. There are two possible explanations. First, the doggerel rhymes, which constitute a fairly large number, are used scarcely at all after *The Taming of the Shrew*. Doggerel was in bad taste at the time Shakespeare used it, and it has been pointed out that even Shakespeare's use is something of an anachronism.[41] That he should discontinue it, possibly out of deference to public taste, is not surprising. Secondly, the speech-link rhyme, whether doggerel or regular pentameter, suffered the same fate as stichomythia in Shakespeare's development.[42] The system had its day and then ceased to be; that is, stichomythia and speech-link rhyme, neither exclusive of the other, helped school Shakespeare in the composition of rapid dialogue, of quick exchanges of wit, or of words spoken in passion. But both were effects of stylization which tended to get in the way of free, natural conversation; and, consequently, as Shakespeare changed from a lyrical to a fundamentally dramatic medium, he discarded those earlier devices which he now no longer found necessary to produce his effects.

The third group of rhymes to be discussed here, the single-speech rhyme, has this in common with the other two: there is often difficulty in determining whether or not the rhyme has been used deliberately. When a strong justification for the speech-beginning rhyme is lacking, it is safe to assume that the rhyme is not deliberate; for neither Shakespeare nor his contemporaries made it a common practice. The speech-link rhyme, on the other hand, appears rather commonly for certain special effects, and thus it can usually be given the benefit of the doubt. The single-speech rhyme lies somewhere between the two. There are certain uses of this kind of rhyme which can be said to be characteristic of Shakespeare, uses which depend upon considerations other than the position in the context; yet there are many possible single-speech rhymes which do not fall into the more common categories and

---

41. Reyher, p. 69.
42. See Gustav Kramer, *Über Stichomythie und gleichklang in den dramen Shakespeares* (Duisburg, 1889).

thus make the problem of determining the intention of the poet a difficult one.

By the term "single-speech rhyme" is meant the couplet, usually a syntactical unit, which conveys the words of a single speaker. Included in this group are couplets the first line of which may be divided between two speakers, but whose rhyming words are contained in the syntactic unit; and included also are a few speeches containing a pair of couplets. These anomalous pairs are discussed here primarily because they do not fit easily into any of the other classifications and because they share one of the many functions of single-speech rhyme.

This single-speech rhyme seems particularly successful in conveying such things as farewells, prophecies, ominous forebodings, epitaphs, and the like.[43] Thus the Bishop of Carlisle, in *Richard II*, cries out,

> The woe's to come; the children yet unborn
> Shall feel this day as sharp to them as thorn.[44]

These words are not a rhetorical part of a long diatribe, but are set sharply against the surrounding speeches.

The epitaph and its dramatic variant, the elegiac lines spoken over the dead, seem naturally to fall into rhyme. In the case of Timon's epitaph, Shakespeare is merely drawing from his source,[45] and it is perfectly in keeping with tradition that such matter should be rhymed. From an epitaph to an elegiac speech spoken over the departed, moreover, is not a far step, and Shakespeare, along with some of his contemporaries, seemed often to think of this type of speech in terms of rhyme. For this reason Ajax, in *Troilus and Cressida*, pays homage to a fallen enemy in rhyme;[46] and the Duke of Suffolk, in *2 Henry VI*, adopts the same elegiac tone to mark the death of a powerful faction:

> Thus droops this lofty pine, and hangs his sprays;
> Thus Eleanor's pride dies in her youngest days.[47]

Death and rhyme in Shakespeare's plays have a more intimate connection than this, however, for, like the speech-link rhyme, single-speech rhyme frequently accompanies the physical action of stabbing and murdering. As a means of achieving a sense of fi-

43. For some farewell speeches, see *Rich. II* I. ii. 56–7; I. iii. 97–8.
44. IV. i. 322–3. *Cf. I Hen. VI* IV. vii. 92–3.·
45. V. iv. 70–3.   46. V. ix. 5–6.
47. II. iii. 45–6.

nality, a full-rounded close, this undivided couplet is more effective than the speech-link rhyme. The outstanding example is the
following couplet from *Othello:*

> I kist thee ere I kill'd thee: no way but this,
> Killing myself, to die upon a kiss.[48]

The rhyme might be said to punctuate the action, to sum up in
this one supreme moment of atonement an infinity of experience,
to focus in this act of self-determined justice the whole romantic
personality of the Moor and the fatal course of his ill-starred love.

Rhyme as an accompaniment of action seems inevitably to produce a kind of flourish. In *3 Henry VI*, when in a mood of angry
passion a challenge for combat is to be given, Sir John Mont-
gomery throws down his gauntlet with these words:

> And whosoe'er gainsays King Edward's right,
> By this I challenge him to single fight.[49]

Earlier in the play, in an entirely different mood, the action calls
for a rhyme to accompany the formal knighthood of Edward
Plantagenet.[50]

Though these uses of the single-speech rhyme are paralleled in
the other types already discussed, they seem here to gain an added
effectiveness by virtue of their standing alone and engaging the
full energy of the speaker. Frequently, however, this rhyme may
be justified only in a very general way by the lyrical or emotional
tone of a passage. The various isolated rhymes in *As You Like It*
can be explained only by the fact that they harmonize with the
general atmosphere of gaiety and lyricism pervading the play; and
it is the same with the following rhyme from *The Two Gentlemen
of Verona:*

> Ha! let me see; ay, give it me, it's mine.
> Sweet ornament that decks a thing divine![51]

for here the sole motive for rhyme seems to be a lady's glove!

There are two uses of single-speech rhyme which, though far
from being exclusive to it, may almost be considered characteristic: that is, in asides or in expressions of a gnomic order.

Abbott was the first to give any particular attention to the use
of rhyme in an aside, and in his statement he gave a probable rea-

48. v. ii. 358–9. *Cf.* v. ii. 124–5; *R. J.* v. iii. 119–20; *T. C.* v. viii. 9–10.
49. IV. vii. 74–5.   50. II. ii. 61–2.
51. II. i. 3–4. *Cf. Per.* I. ii. 113–14; *A. W.* v. iii. 69–70.

son for such a use: "Rhyme was also sometimes used in the same conventional way, to mark an *aside,* which otherwise the audience might have great difficulty in knowing to be an *aside.*"[52] How closely such an explanation conforms to Elizabethan stage practice is difficult to determine. Shakespeare certainly uses asides in many places without rhyme, in passages which might very easily be confused with dialogue. In *Cymbeline,* for example, there are two couplets in an aside, and yet a few lines later there appears another aside in blank verse.[53] Since there is no more reason for the audience to confuse the one than the other, Abbott's explanation, despite its having been widely received, is hardly acceptable. The aside could certainly be sufficiently marked by the position on the stage of the actor and by his manner of delivery of the lines. To a notion that the rhyme might have been used as a kind of stage direction to remind the actor how the lines were to be presented, the same objection offers itself. For why should an actor need a reminder for one aside and not for another in the same scene?

The most that can be said is that Shakespeare seemed, even in some of his latest plays, to be fond of rhymed asides, and that he was following a tradition which was well established when he began writing plays; for though Kyd did not include this type among the many rhymes in *The Spanish Tragedy,* Marlowe made rather generous use of it at least in *The Jew of Malta.*[54] It was not uncommon, either, in the works of Shakespeare's later contemporaries.

The rhymed aside in Shakespeare takes several forms. As was seen, it occasionally consists of a single line which rhymes with the final words of the previous speaker,[55] sometimes with a comic, sometimes with a serious, effect. More often it consists of two to six lines which, by means of the rhyme, are independent of the surrounding speeches, except, of course, in their relationship to the thought of the passage as a whole. In a few cases the rhymed lines are used in conjunction with blank-verse lines to constitute the entire aside, thus having the same effect as the speech-end or speech-pause rhyme.[56]

The *locus classicus* of the rhymed aside in Shakespeare is Act IV, Scene iv, of *Richard III.*[57] In this scene there are no rhyming

52. Sec. 515.   53. IV. ii. 26–9, 32–8.
54. See II. iii. 139–40, 235–6, 241–2.   55. See above, p. 47.
56. See *Cy.* IV. ii. 26–9. The necessary brevity of an aside, of course, makes it particularly susceptible to such a stylistic pattern as the couplet.
57. *Cf.* Abbott, sec. 515.

lines except the words which Queen Margaret utters while she is still unperceived by the rest of the actors on the stage. Her words have a little of the effect of the Greek chorus, for, as in the following couplet, they explain and pass judgment upon the principal action before the eyes of the audience:

> Plantagenet doth quit Plantagenet,
> Edward for Edward pays a dying debt.[58]

Though these asides, in addition to commenting on the action, also reveal the emotional state of Margaret, in other plays the rhymed aside is used more directly to indicate the inner workings of the speaker's heart. Saturninus, for example, in *Titus Andronicus*, reveals to the audience that Tamora's charm is beginning to take effect:

> A goodly lady, trust me; of the hue
> That I would choose, were I to choose anew;[59]

thus preparing for events to follow. In *Macbeth*, also, the fatalistic resignation of Macbeth to an approaching doom which he instinctively senses is expressed in an aphoristic rhyme.[60]

The rhymed aside is sometimes used, of course, merely to give information to the audience, information necessary to the course of the action but not to be overheard by others on the stage. Thus Pisanio, in *Cymbeline*, tells of his intention to deceive his master and save his wronged mistress.[61] But the numerous rhymed asides in the later plays seem mostly designed to convey moral observations upon the words or actions of the characters. Such an aside is spoken by Escalus in *Measure for Measure:*

> Well, Heaven forgive him! and forgive us all!
> Some rise by sin, and some by virtue fall.
> Some run from brakes of vice, and answer none;
> And some condemned for a fault alone.[62]

This tendency of the aside to offer a moral may explain the relatively high number of rhymes in such plays as *Measure for Measure, Pericles,* and *Cymbeline;* for the rhyme calls the wisdom of the lines to the special attention of the audience.[63]

---

58. IV. iv. 20–1. *Cf.* IV. iv. 15–16; IV. iv. 24–5.
59. I. i. 261–2.   60. I. iii. 146–7.
61. III. v. 104–05.   62. II. i. 37–40. *Cf.* IV. ii. 111–16.
63. Katherine Lever ("Proverbs and *Sententiae* in the Plays of Shakspere," *Shakespeare Association Bulletin* XIII [1938], 231) makes this observation: "*Sententiae,* characterized by brevity and concentration of meaning, make fine asides and are often used in this way."

Indeed, the other principal use of the single-speech rhyme is just that. It is a favorite medium for general sententiousness. It must be understood, however, that the rhyming of gnomic utterances is not limited to single-speech rhymes. Without exception, all the classifications of rhyme contain a high percentage of gnomic utterance.

It is unnecessary to find a single source for Shakespeare's use of rhymed *sententiae* and commonplaces, for he was merely following the practice of his fellow dramatists in meeting the demands of his audience. The sixteenth and seventeenth centuries produced a countless number of books of proverbs, adages, maxims, and *sententiae*. Such a collection as John Heywood's *Dialogue Conteynyng the Number of the Effectuall Prouerbes in the Englishe Tounge*, the earliest work of its kind in England,[64] was printed ten times between the years 1546 and 1598[65] and was imitated by many other collectors. The greatest single writer to satisfy this desire of the Elizabethan to add a cubit to his moral stature was Seneca, whose various writings afforded a wealth of gnomic material. His *Epistulae Morales* and his various dramas were widely quoted and misquoted by writers of Shakespeare's day, particularly by the dramatists.[66] It was common, moreover, to mark these *sententiae* by means of rhyme and thus render them more memorable. Such rhyme was not limited to the drama, for, as Paul Verrier demonstrated, it is natural for a proverb or maxim to have some sort of rhyme.[67] In the drama of the time this rhyme became almost an established custom. M. W. Croll said, "This principle of marking a 'sentence,' or maxim, by rhyme is more or less observed in all the Senecan plays;"[68] and the same might be said of the various other types of drama, private or public.

It is therefore quite natural to find Shakespeare, an Elizabethan writing for Elizabethans, scattering throughout his dramas wise sayings which could readily be caught and carried away in the minds of the listeners. On the whole, he managed them deftly and dramatically, using them only when the tone of the play and the demands of the particular action permitted. This couplet from

64. W. Carew Hazlitt, *English Proverbs and Proverbial Phrases* (London, 1907), p. xv.

65. Richard Jente, "The Proverbs of Shakespeare with Early and Contemporary Parallels," *Washington University Studies* XIII (1925–26), 393–4.

66. James H. Hewlett, "The Influence of Seneca's *Epistulae Morales* on Elizabethan Tragedy," *Abstracts of Theses. The University of Chicago Humanistic Series* IX (1930–32), 456.

67. *Essai sur les principes de la métrique anglaise* (Paris, 1909), I, 126–7.

68. p. 34.

King Lear, for example, seems very well fitted to the situation and the character:

> How far your eyes may pierce I cannot tell:
> Striving to better, oft we mar what's well.[69]

How appropriate it is that the weak-willed Albany, at a time when some definite action on his part might have averted the ultimate catastrophe, should take refuge in a bookish commonplace! In a lighter vein Proteus, in *The Two Gentlemen of Verona,* humorously anticipates the future course of the plot with a graceful aphorism:

> Indeed a sheep doth very often stray,
> An if the shepherd be a while away;[70]

and the Nurse in *Romeo and Juliet,* whose store of wisdom probably contained many homely adages, cautioned Romeo, "Two may keep counsel, putting one away," rhyming it with its prefatory line.[71] In such a play as *Pericles,* on the other hand, some of these gnomic rhymes have but faint justification in the action and suggest the presence of another hand.[72]

The variation in this type of rhyme results, of course, from the demands of the particular play. As was noticed before, certain plays are high in gnomic content because the general tone of the play is a moral one. In *Measure for Measure,* for example, all the single-speech rhymes are of a sententious nature, and the same is true of *Timon of Athens.* Both these plays are problem comedies, both deal with serious defects in the social order, and both contain a relatively high number of gnomic rhymes. In lighter plays, such as *A Midsummer Night's Dream* or *As You Like It,* despite the serious undertone in the latter, the atmosphere does not call for grave reflection, and consequently, though proverbial expressions are not totally absent, the number of gnomic rhymes is low.

Thus it is that the single-speech rhyme shows a fluctuation rather than a gradual diminution. The aside, combined with the sententious utterance, continued to employ rhyme in even the very latest plays. *Cymbeline* and *Pericles* show more single-speech rhymes than *The Comedy of Errors* and *The Two Gentlemen of Verona,* because the moral structure of the former makes neces-

---

69. i. iv. 368–9.   70. i. i. 74–5.
71. ii. iv. 208–09. *Cf. M. V.* ii. ix. 82–3.
72. See ii. ii. 34–5. This is more noticeable in the speech-end rhymes than in the single-speech rhymes, for it is much easier to tack a couplet on to a speech than to interrupt the dialogue.

sary the inclusion of *sententiae* both in asides and in the ordinary dialogue. The speech-beginning rhyme tended to disappear because it was a use which never was compatible with Shakespeare's general practice; the speech-link rhyme met the same fate because the playwright soon learned to produce its effects in a simpler, more natural way; but the single-speech rhyme, because it appeared to advantage in asides and sententious utterances, occurs as frequently in the latest as in the earliest of his plays.

Exit and Cue Rhyme

Among the most characteristic uses of rhyme in Elizabethan drama is that marking the exit or entrance of an actor or group of actors. Though Marlowe, except in the problematical *Doctor Faustus*, applied rhyme rather sparingly to exits, he did employ it frequently just before the entrance of an actor. His contemporaries, who followed his general revolt against the dominance of rhyme on the stage, clung tenaciously to its use at such places as entrances and exits, where there was a noticeable interruption in the dramatic action; and there was no marked alteration in this use throughout Shakespeare's career. It is not surprising, therefore, to find that this type of rhyme constitutes one of the most extensive classifications of Shakespeare's isolated rhymes.

Growing out of this use, moreover, just as with the speech-end rhyme, there are certain problems to which there is no satisfactory answer. Though the term cue rhyme is here offered to designate the rhyme which occurs immediately prior to the entrance of a character or which anticipates some off-stage sound-effect, it may not be a happy choice; for, if the couplet is actually a cue, if it is really designed to prompt some inexperienced Bottom who might miss a less conspicuous cue,[1] then why is there no greater uniformity in its use? One may search the pages of Shakespeare in vain to find him giving a cue repeatedly to a certain actor, or to certain minor rôles which might have been played by the less experienced members of the company, or even to several people in a massed entrance where a strong cue might be needed to avoid confusion. The same can also be said of the exit rhyme. If it was actually intended by Shakespeare to replace a stage cue, then one must explain why it was used in one place and not another, why an actor who knew enough to leave the stage in one scene needed a reminder in another, sometimes even in the same, scene.

1. *M. N. D.* III. i. 103–04.

The complete lack of any systematic practice in so far as the particular actor or group of actors is concerned forces the conclusion that, although rhyme at times seems to replace a stage cue, such matters were left in general to the individual actor or to the prompter, who followed the directions of the prompter's copy.[2] The rhyme, therefore, is used for a certain artistic effect, to give coloring to the words of the departing speaker or to prepare the scene for the entrance of the new characters; and it is this purpose alone which can be fruitfully analyzed.

There are some couplets which may be thought to give a cue for off-stage action. While an actor could be standing ready to come on stage the moment he heard his cue words, taking advantage of sight and sound in order to time his entrance perfectly, it is not likely that the men who produced the off-stage sound-effects could always be so advantageously situated. Perhaps the prompter gave them the signal, or perhaps they had to depend upon catching the cue words from the mouth of the speaker. Whatever may have been the situation, it can be seen that a stronger cue than could be given by the ordinary line might have been desired occasionally and that the dramatist may have been called on to write a rhymed tag in order that the sound-effect could be produced at the desired moment.

This, of course, is mere conjecture, as indeed is much of our present notion of Elizabethan stage conditions;[3] but there are a few rhymes in this class which seem certainly designed to give a cue. When the action calls for the sounding of an alarum in *Troilus and Cressida,* a couplet immediately precedes the written stage direction:

> Let Paris bleed; 't is but a scar to scorn;
> Paris is gored with Menelaus' horn.[4]

2. An excellent study of this subject is Dorothy Moody's *Shakespeare's Stage Directions: An Examination for Bibliographical and Literary Evidence* (unpublished dissertation, Yale University, 1938).

3. See George F. Reynolds, *Some Principles of Elizabethan Staging* (Chicago, 1905); Sir Edmund Chambers, *The Elizabethan Stage* (Oxford, 1923), 4 vols.; *A Series of Papers on Shakespeare and the Theatre, together with Papers on Edward Alleyn and Early Records Illustrating the Personal Life of Shakespeare, by Members of the Shakespeare Association* (London, 1927); M. C. Bradbrook, *Elizabethan Stage Conditions* (Cambridge, 1932); George F. Reynolds, *The Staging of Elizabethan Plays* (New York, 1940).

4. I. i. 114–15. It can be only coincidence that the most noticeable word in the couplet is "horn," with its suggestion of the possible instrument used in sounding the alarum.

The full-sounding rhyme, combined with the rhetorical structure of the lines, tends to throw the emphasis upon the final word and to mark the exact moment when the stage-effect is desired. (It should be noticed, however, that the couplet refers to one of the most popular Elizabethan subjects for humor, which might be a sufficient justification for the rhyme.) Again, in *Timon,* when the characters are supposed to rise from the table, a couplet gives them the cue, a couplet which has no other obvious reason for existing;[5] and in *Coriolanus* a couplet appears unexpectedly in a prose scene, seemingly to give the cue for off-stage sounds and for the entrance of actors.[6] There is even a possibility that this couplet was not from the pen of Shakespeare but was added for the specific purpose of giving a cue where it was needed.[7]

With the rhyme which appears before the entrance of a character, one must take a different approach. Though it cannot be said that the rhyme gives a cue to the actor to come on-stage, it can be said that it prepares the stage for his arrival. This preparation takes different forms, the most obvious of which is the direct comment upon the entrant before the audience has had an opportunity to see him. Such a rhyme is Queen Margaret's in *3 Henry VI:*

> O, but impatience waiteth on true sorrow.
> And see where comes the breeder of my sorrow![8]

While this might be considered a mere repetition rather than a rhyme, Shakespeare often accepted such identical rhymes in passages of consecutive rhyme and thus might be expected to do so elsewhere. Here it makes the entrance of Warwick doubly emphatic. A similar use of entrance rhyme is found in *Romeo and Juliet* when Benvolio's line, "Here comes the furious Tybalt back again," announcing the entrance of Tybalt, is answered by Romeo's "Alive, in triumph! and Mercutio slain!"[9] This second line, if the cue is correctly placed,[10] is really a comment on the actor after he has stepped into view of the audience, while the first heralds his approach. Thus the rhyme is obviously not a cue for his entrance, though it does make an effective accompaniment.

A less obvious but more common method of preparing the stage

5. I. ii. 149–50.   6. II. i. 177–8.
7. At least, the authenticity of the couplet has been doubted by various critics. See M. A. Bayfield, *A Study of Shakespeare's Versification* (Cambridge, 1920), p. 193.
8. III. iii. 42–3.   9. III. i. 126–7.
10. Concerning the position of this stage cue, see Heuser, p. 249.

for the new arrival is simply to create a dramatic pause by means
of the rhyme, a pause which enables the attention of the audience
to be shifted from one interest or focal point to another. In this
way the entrance is not so much an interruption of the action as a
fresh impetus. Where there is no rhyme, the entrance not infrequently breaks into the general movement of the dialogue, perhaps interrupting the train of thought by the introduction of a
new element or causing an unexpected turn in the action. When
rhyme is used immediately before the entrance, however, the dialogue is brought to a full close and the action neatly rounded off,
this by virtue of the fact that Shakespeare's isolated couplets are
for the most part end-stopped. They demand the completion of
the thought, the termination of whatever action or gesture they
may accompany. The result is a pause, varying in degree according to the particular situation; and it is in the pause that the
entrant makes his appearance.

Mechanical as this seems, it is not without effectiveness. Shakespeare seems very fond of using it at the end of long soliloquies,
where the couplet gives a distinct climax or conclusion to the
words of the speaker, before the advent of others can interrupt
his meditations and produce a sense of incompleteness. In this
manner Lord Clifford, in 3 *Henry VI*, dramatically finishes his
soliloquy and falls into a faint:

> Come, York and Richard, Warwick and the rest;
> I stabb'd your fathers' bosoms,—split my breast.[11]

His soliloquy having reached its highest emotional peak, marked
by a rhyme, there is a pause, or at least a break, in the action; and
the audience may now turn its attention to the characters who
enter.

But apart from soliloquies, this pause appears also in the normal
dialogue to accentuate an entrance. Occasionally it is within the
body of a speech, the speaker coming to a full close before the entrance and then continuing on a new subject inspired by the arrival of the new character. An example of this is Friar Laurence's
speech in *Romeo and Juliet* where he concludes his advice to
Romeo with this gnomic couplet:

> Therefore, love moderately; long love doth so;
> Too swift arrives as tardy as too slow.[12]

11. II. vi. 29–30.

12. II. vi. 14–15. This couplet is intensely ironical. If the Friar, in the final act of
the play, had moved more swiftly he might have anticipated Romeo and averted the
tragedy. *Cf.* II. v. 16–17.

Though the Friar undoubtedly had the ability to continue his platitudes almost indefinitely, there can be little question that this was intended for a final one by the speaker, as if he anticipated the exact moment when Juliet was to arrive. For with the couplet she enters; the Friar remarks, "Here comes the lady," and continues with a lyrical description of her.

This use of rhyme before an entrance—or before an exit—has frequently the effect of the scene- or act-end couplet, for it seems to indicate the completion of one part of the scene before the beginning of the next. Actually, many of the scene units accepted by modern editors may be divided into shorter scenes, marked by exits and entrances; and the couplet, in plays where rhyme fits into the general artistic scheme, is one of the common methods of marking such changes in the action. In *Richard II*, for example, the general discussion of the dispute between Bolingbroke and Mowbray is brought to a full-sounding end with the King's couplet,

> High-stomach'd are they both, and full of ire,
> In rage deaf as the sea, hasty as fire;[13]

then, with this necessary exposition conveyed, the entrance of the disputants follows and the important action of the scene is begun. Although there is here no real change in the subject matter of the scene, it is quite common for the entrance to introduce an action more or less unrelated to what has gone before. In such a case, of course, the rhyme tends to make questionable many of the accepted scene- and act-divisions. A good example occurs in *Titus Andronicus*. The Andronici have discovered the mutilated Lavinia, and make their passionate lament in nearly a hundred lines of blank verse, unbroken by rhyme. Finally Titus ends a speech, which in itself has a certain conclusive note, with a couplet; at this point Aaron enters with his supposed message from the Emperor, shifting the attention from Lavinia to the Emperor's inhuman demands.[14] Similarly the mood in *Twelfth Night* is changed from one of romantic lyricism to serious comedy by the couplet and the entrance which follows it;[15] and in *Julius Caesar* the couplet accompanies the suicide of Brutus, in a sense drawing the curtain upon one part of the action before the entrance of others introduces a new theme.[16]

An interesting use of the couplet occurs when it is related to an

13. I. i. 18–19.   14. III. i. 148–9.
15. V. i. 333–4.   16. V. v. 50–1. *Cf.* v. iii. 89–90.

exit as well as an entrance, that is, when it bridges the gap between the two. In 3 *Henry VI*, after the Father who has killed his
own son in the bloody civil strife has left the stage with the body,
the wretched king comments upon the departed in a single couplet:

> Sad-hearted men, much overgone with care,
> Here sits a king more woeful than you are.[17]

Immediately thereafter the battle makes itself felt upon the stage
and the king is told to flee for his life. The necessity of the transition is easily seen. An entry following directly upon the exit of the
Father would not only have cut short the emotional mood prema-
turely but it would have frustrated the purpose of the entire passage, which was not to show the sorrow of a son who killed his
father or of a father who killed his son but of a king whose weakness was wasting his entire realm. Another example deserves some
mention, because in it an even more obvious function is performed. In *Romeo and Juliet* the balcony scene calls, at one place,
for an exit and an almost immediate re-entry, leaving a slight gap
to be filled; and it is filled by a three-line speech from Romeo, the
first line rhyming with Juliet's exit line, the other two expressing
in couplet form a lyrical platitude.[18] Thus the couplet is a convenient device for filling what might otherwise be an awkward hiatus
in the dramatic action.

Yet more like the scene-end rhyme than the cue rhyme is the
exit rhyme, for the end of a scene is marked by the exit of the
characters from the stage. Both exit and scene-end rhymes include a great number of farewells, both suggest off-stage action,
and both anticipate later events in the play. But the exit rhyme
presents certain problems characteristic of it alone.

Although it is not difficult to see why a rhyme should be used
to mark the end of a scene on a stage where there may have been
no adequate mechanical means of indicating the division between
the actions, why the dramatist should have felt called on to accompany a simple exit with a rhyme may not be so apparent. One
theory is that the playwright was obliged by the actor to give him
a graceful or an emphatic couplet to make his exit the more dramatic and perhaps to offer a more memorable cue to his suc-
cessor.[19] Another is that the actors themselves added many of the
rhymes when they felt that the author had not sufficiently under-

17. ɪɪ. v. 123–4. *Cf. T. C.* v. iii. 95–6; *M. M.* ɪv. ii. 64–5.
18. ɪɪ. ii. 155–8.   19. D. L. Chambers, p. 18.

scored their departure from the stage. This view, however, has met with some objection. "If actors did add lines," argues Katharine Lever, "they would be likely to quote some old saying which they had heard rather than express a new opinion."[20] Even if some of Shakespeare's exit rhymes may not have come from his pen, the majority of them probably did; for, along with his fellow playwrights, he seemed to have no objection to punctuating a departure from the stage in this manner.

It is the dramatic effect which the couplet gives in such a situation which probably explains why it was used. Generally when rhyme accompanies the exit it calls particular attention to the one who is departing, either to the vital significance of his final words or to the important fact that he is leaving. For a moment it centers the entire attention of the audience upon him and makes his exit a matter of primary concern. He does not just leave the scene; he exits with a graceful flourish or with a forceful parting thrust.

Because the desired effect of the exit couplet is often this one of focusing the full attention of the audience upon the departure, the couplet itself is usually a particularly vigorous one, containing some words of striking grace or a message of vital significance to the progress of the play. The many exit rhymes in the *Henry VI* plays give ample proof of this. In these plays, where the tone is frequently intensified by the artificial stimulation of rhyme, exits are frequently punctuated with such an energetic couplet as the following:

> His fortunes I will weep, and, 'twixt each groan
> Say, "Who's a traitor? Gloucester he is none."[21]

Particularly effective in such a use are prophecies and curses or even premonitions of disaster to come, for all three tend to magnify the importance of the character who is leaving and to arouse suspense. Though there are many examples of these in the *Henry VI* plays, one must turn to some of the later works to find them used with the greatest dramatic skill. Cassandra's wild prophecies in *Troilus and Cressida* give her exits a terrifying importance as, pathetically aware of her ineffectuality, she leaves her words of doom in unheeding hearts.[22] In *Macbeth* the prophecies of the Apparitions punctuate several exits with magnificent dramatic irony. Macbeth leaves the stage with these words which are later to assume a fatal significance:

20. p. 232.   21. 2 *Hen. VI* III. i. 221–2.
22. II. ii. 111–12; v. iii. 89–90.

> I will not be afraid of death and bane,
> Till Birnam forest come to Dunsinane.[23]

And in *Othello* the parting words of old Brabantio,

> Look to her, Moor, if thou hast eyes to see:
> She has deceived her father, and may thee,[24]

though forgotten by the one to whom they were addressed, are later remembered by Iago to become an important tool for his villainy. In *Romeo and Juliet* nearly half the exit rhymes contain ominous forebodings of the tragedy to come.[25] These examples, and many others, serve really two purposes: they make the exit doubly emphatic and they give the fulfillment a particular poignancy. At the moment of exit, moreover, the benefits are reciprocal, for just as the couplet makes the exit more emphatic so the exit helps draw attention to the parting words.

Though the effect, as in these examples just discussed, is often of a very dramatic nature, there are many exits which take advantage of rhyme merely to gain a certain gracefulness. In comedies this tends to be true of couplets which are essentially humorous, like this one from *The Comedy of Errors:*

> As from a bear a man would run for life,
> So fly I from her that would be my wife.[26]

Under other circumstances the effect depends on the graceful turn which rhyme is capable of producing, on the decorous accompaniment which it gives the action. Thus the exit of the King in *Love's Labour's Lost* is accomplished by means of an elegant exchange of rhymed compliments between the King and Princess;[27] thus the farewell of the rejected suitor in *The Merchant of Venice* finds graceful expression in a well-turned couplet.[28]

A curious use of the exit rhyme is to be noted when the exit occurs before the rhyme has been completed, that is, when it comes between the two lines of the couplet. The effect is quite the opposite from that produced by the usual exit or entrance rhyme; for while they tend to interrupt the action, frequently to such an extent that the impression is as if a new scene were begun, the broken exit rhyme forms a strong link between the action before the exit and that which follows. It is customary, and natural, with

23. v. iii. 59–60. *Cf.* v. vii. 12–13.   24. I. iii. 293–4.
25. I. v. 91–4; III. v. 58–9; IV. v. 94–5.
26. III. ii. 159–60.   27. II. i. 178–9.
28. II. vii. 76–7. *Cf. T. N.* I. v. 306–07; *A. C.* v. ii. 188–90.

this type of rhyme that the second line should make some comment upon the character who has left the stage, as in the following couplet from *Romeo and Juliet,* a kind of answer to the final words of the departed:

> *Fri. L.* Come, go, good Juliet, I dare no longer stay.
> [*Exit Fri. Lau.*]
> *Jul.*   Go, get thee hence, for I will not away.[29]

Here the rhyme does not emphasize the exit so much as it does Juliet's determination to remain with the dead. The mood, which might otherwise have been interrupted by the departure, is to a certain extent maintained by means of the rhyme.

From the foregoing analysis one fact stands out. For the most part the rhymes discussed in this section, whether they be exit or cue rhymes, seem to demand a pause in the action. The entrance rhyme tends to bring the preceding action to a full stop in order to prepare for the new character; the exit rhyme frequently places so much emphasis upon the departure that when the action continues it seems often to be separated from what went before. This fact may be partially responsible for the gradual diminution in the use of this type of rhyme. Appropriate for certain plays and for certain scenes which demand sharply punctuated action, this use is out of place where the exit and entrance are of minor importance only or where the pause which the rhymed accompaniment seems naturally to give is not in keeping with the general movement of the scene. Always used for a specific effect, this type of rhyme grew less frequent because the effect was needed less.

As Shakespeare developed in his dramatic ability he found a more natural way of handling entrances and exits. A glance at the exits in the early history plays will show that even when rhyme is not used a somewhat similar effect is employed. The following example is chosen at random:

> An army have I muster'd in my thoughts,
> Wherewith already France is overrun.[30]

This rather vigorous pair of lines puts an end to a part of the scene and precedes an entrance, with a balance and emphasis equivalent to that produced by rhyme. The difference between these lines and the following, also chosen at random, from a later play is very striking:

29. v. iii. 159–60. *Cf. C. E.* iii. ii. 183–4; *L. L. L.* ii. i. 35–6.
30. *1 Hen. VI* i. i. 101–02.

> Turn out that eyeless villain; throw this slave
> Upon the dunghill. Regan, I bleed apace;
> Untimely comes this hurt. Give me your arm.[31]

The exit is just as effective, but less ostentatiously so. The full-stop, couplet effect so common in the earlier plays has been replaced by a freer, more smoothly flowing line, and the exit seems not so much a determined event as a natural occurrence. Hence, when the rhymed entrance or exit is used in the later plays, it is by contrast much more impressive.

Scene- and Act-End Rhyme

The scene- and act-end rhymes[1] constitute the largest class of isolated rhymes in Shakespeare's plays. Even in plays nearly devoid of rhyme there are to be found occasional scene-end rhymes. In *The Tempest*, for example, the one indisputable rhymed couplet appears at the end of a scene, fittingly spoken by Ariel, from whose lips come various rhymed songs.[2] In all Elizabethan and early Jacobean drama this use of rhyme to announce the close of the action was more or less consistently practiced, even by Fletcher, who showed a strong tendency to ignore rhyme altogether.[3] Despite the censure of scene-end rhyme by the editor of *A Mad World My Masters*,[4] this use of rhyme continued for many years to receive the approbation of critic and audience. Addison wrote in 1711: "I would not however debar the Poet from concluding his Tragedy, or, if he pleases, every Act of it, with two or three Couplets, which may have the same Effect as an Air in the *Italian* Opera after a long *Recitativo*, and give the Actor a graceful *Exit*."[5]

Hardin Craig, like Addison, interprets the scene-end rhyme as pertaining to the actor: "In order to mark strongly the cue for the first actor in the succeeding scene, so it is thought, the dramatist [Shakespeare] composed a couplet to mark the close of the scene."[6] But Abbott thought of the rhyme from the standpoint of the au-

---

31. *Lear* III. vii. 96–8.

1. For the sake of convenience this class will be referred to here by only the term "scene-end," since generally there is no important distinction between a scene-end and an act-end rhyme.

2. II. i. 326–7.

3. See Maurice Chelli, *Étude sur la collaboration de Massinger avec Fletcher et son groupe* (Paris, 1926), p. 43.

4. See above, p. 21.

5. *The Spectator* xxxix (April 14, 1711).

6. p. 43.

dience when he said, "When the scenery was not changed, or the arrangements were so defective that the change was not easily perceptible, it was, perhaps, additionally desirable to mark that a scene was finished."[7]

Both these suggestions rest upon the interpretation of Shakespeare's stage as "a stage where only the appearance of a group of actors was required for the shifting of the theatrical locality;"[8] a stage, that is, which neither possessed an outer curtain to indicate the change of the scene nor demanded that the playwright follow a formal division of his play into acts and scenes. Notwithstanding Richmond Noble's assertion that the close of certain actions in Shakespeare's plays necessitated the drawing of a curtain,[9] the present knowledge of Shakespeare's stage points to the fact that it was without a curtain, except to divide the inner from the outer stage. This means, of course, that the playwright was without our present mechanical facilities for indicating a change in the action. The great number of scenes in *Antony and Cleopatra*, for example, suggests that each action followed immediately upon the preceding one and that the audience readily accepted whatever shift in place and time the entrants might indicate. It is still a matter of dispute whether Shakespeare himself thought of his plays as being constructed according to act- and scene-divisions, at least so far as those divisions meant any intermission in the action. J. Dover Wilson makes this statement:

I do not assert that Shakespeare's plays were always acted at the Globe without interruption of any kind. I think it quite likely, for instance, that the company and the audience found a short break convenient in the middle of a long play like *Hamlet*. But such a break had no structural significance; might occur at any point in the play when the stage was left clear; and was a mere matter of theatrical convenience.[10]

If Wilson is correct, then the majority of Shakespeare's plays, at least those acted at the Globe, were acted without interruption, the new scene or act beginning as soon as the new actors entered.

The absence of a curtain and the immediate transition from one scene to the next might very naturally have obliged the play-

---

7. Sec. 515.

8. Allardyce Nicoll, *The English Theatre* (New York, 1936), p. 44.

9. Richmond Noble, "Shakespeare's 'Curtains,' " *London Times Literary Supplement* xxvii (May 3, 1928), 334.

10. "Act- and Scene-Division in the Plays of Shakespeare: A Rejoinder to Sir Mark Hunter," *Review of English Studies* iii (1927), 395. But see Sir Mark Hunter, "Act- and Scene-Division in the Plays of Shakespeare," *ibid.* ii (1926), 295–310; W. W. Greg, "Act-Divisions in Shakespeare," *ibid.* iv (1928), 152–8.

wright at times to indicate the change in the action by some stronger means than ordinary blank-verse or prose. The rhymed couplet, because of its ability to attract particular attention to itself, was one of the most natural means at hand, at least in the professional companies. The dramatist may have used it, as Craig suggests, only as a cue to the entering actors in order that there should exist no awkward break in the action; but, as indicated in the previous section, it is difficult to think of rhyme merely as a cue. On the other hand, he may have used it for just the opposite, that is, to indicate a pause, to distinguish clearly the new action from the old; of the two hypotheses this seems the more logical. Since the new scene usually meant a change of locale, a change in the action, and even a change in the poetic atmosphere, a rhymed couplet was often used to ring down an imaginary curtain so as to prepare the minds of the audience for a complete change in scene. In this way, the rhyme might often be considered a stage cue for the audience rather than for the actor, for it left no doubt that, with the entrance of the new group of characters on the stage, a complete change in the action was intended.

In using rhyme to indicate a change in scene, Shakespeare did not confine himself to the couplet but ran the gamut from the single line to the complex stanza of ten lines or more. To say he ended a scene with a single-line rhyme is not wholly a misstatement; in *Romeo and Juliet*, as modern editors have generally divided the scenes, there occurs a complete evacuation of the stage followed by a change of locale and an entrance, and yet the first line of the new scene rhymes with the final line of the preceding scene.[11]

The most common form of rhyme at the end of scenes is the single couplet, closely seconded by the double couplet or the double tag, as it is sometimes called; but various other forms occur with some frequency. A scene in *Love's Labour's Lost*, for example, ends with a couplet and a quatrain,[12] and another with a triplet.[13] Of the two, the quatrain and the triplet, the latter seems generally to be used more deliberately and with greater effect. Particularly in passages of consecutive rhyme or in scenes generously sprinkled with rhymed couplets, the triplet is employed to gain added emphasis. Its greatest success comes when it is divided be-

---

11. II. i. 42; II. ii. 1. For a further discussion of these lines, see Appendix B.

12. IV. iii. 381–6. For examples of other scenes ending in quatrains, see *T. G.* I. iii. 88–91; *John* I. i. 273–6; *M. V.* III. ii. 327–30.

13. IV. i. 160–2. Cf. *Rich. II* V. iii. 144–6; *Cy.* I. v. 85–7.

tween two or three speakers, as in this triplet from *The Merchant of Venice:*

> *Por.* Come, come, Nerissa, for I long to see
>   Quick Cupid's post that comes so mannerly.
> *Ner.* Bassanio, lord Love, if thy will it be![14]

for here the third, or answering line, conveys in a rapid and lively fashion a piece of news important to the action. In general, however, the longer forms of rhyme which are used to end scenes seem not to have any particular significance, but only to carry out the general lyrical tone of the scene.

A rather special form, already mentioned in connection with the speech-pause rhyme, is the *aabcc* pattern which is found in several of the later plays. The effect of this is only slightly different from that of the double tag, for it is simply the double couplet with a blank-verse line separation and produces what might be called a delayed cadence. The following passage from *Pericles* is a good illustration:

> I'll take thy word for faith, not ask thine oath;
> Who shuns not to break one will sure crack both;
> But in our orbs we'll live so round and safe,
> That time of both this truth shall ne'er convince,
> Thou show'dst a subject's shine, I a true prince.[15]

Instead of concluding his graceful farewell with a single gnomic couplet, Pericles emphasizes his trust in Helicanus with an additional couplet, separated from the first by a blank-verse line. The fact that this rather eccentric use of rhyme appears in no indisputably Shakespearian play suggests another hand.

Another peculiarity which deserves mention is the appearance of a shorter line after the rhymed couplet and before the close of the action. Never very frequently used, this extra line occurs somewhat more in the later than in the early plays. Steevens, in his edition of *Macbeth,* said:

It has been understood that local rhymes were introduced in plays to afford an actor the advantage of a more pointed exit, or to close a scene with additional force. Yet, whatever might be Shakspeare's motive for continuing such a practice, it may be observed that he often seems immediately to repent of it; and, in the tragedy before us, has repeatedly counteracted it by hemistichs which destroy the effect and consequently defeat the supposed purpose of the antecedent couplets.[16]

14. II. ix. 99–101.   15. I. ii. 120–4. Cf. *Cy.* v. i. 29–33.
16. *The Plays of William Shakspeare* (4th ed., London, 1793), VII, 566.

Since only four of the sixteen scene-end couplets in *Macbeth* show this extra short line, it is difficult to agree with Steevens' interpretation that Shakespeare was thereby repenting his having used the couplet at all; nor can one agree that the extra line destroys the effect of the couplet. Here is a double tag from Act V:

> The time approaches
> That will with due decision make us know
> What we shall say we have and what we owe.
> Thoughts speculative their unsure hopes relate,
> But certain issue strokes must arbitrate;
> Towards which advance the war.[17]

Shakespeare was too flexible an artist to limit himself to a fixed practice. It is true, as J. B. Mayor noticed, that in this play a short final phrase is often used "in the absence of the rhyming couplet as the natural close of the scene;"[18] when this short line is used in conjunction with the couplet it does not undo the effect of the couplet. All that can be said is that Shakespeare is merely varying his practice by calling upon an extra means of emphasis.

What, then, is the function of the scene-end couplet? As the term implies, the scene-end couplet is used primarily to indicate the completion of the action. The fact that the stage usually is cleared of actors indicates this visually; the use of the couplet indicates it phonetically. An examination of the scene-end couplets reveals three general methods by which the rhyme produces its effect.

The first of these may be seen where the rhyme is concerned merely with the preceding action. It has little to do with the general course of the play, and it does not look ahead to anything that may follow. It is concerned solely with the scene which it concludes, giving to the action a sense of finality sufficiently strong to leave no doubt in the minds of the audience of the change which is to follow. Sometimes the thought contained within the rhymed lines seems actually to have little to do with the context. Caldecott, inspired by such a rhyme from *Hamlet*,[19] made the following comment:

At the close of an act, or when the scene is shifted, and there is a pause in the action of the drama, it was the usage of our dramatists, down to the middle of the last century, not simply to divert attention from the

17. v. iv. 16–21.
18. *Chapters on English Metre* (London, 1886), p. 148.
19. II. i. 118–19.

main object, as here, by the introduction of a couplet or rhymes, but to make the subject of such couplet foreign altogether to the interests of the drama, an unconnected flourish, and that, not unfrequently, a labored and florid simile.[20]

There is, of course, a certain vagueness about this statement, particularly in the phrase "foreign altogether to the interests of the drama." The particular couplet from *Hamlet* which inspired the remark does sacrifice the sense somewhat for the rhyme, but since it comes from the lips of Polonius one might well interpret it as being deliberately nonsensical to fit the character of this sententious fool. It is true, however, that some of the rhymes in such plays as *Pericles* and *Timon of Athens* bear a very uncertain relationship to the context.

A common way of giving a concluding note to the scene is by presenting in the rhymed lines a chorus-like comment upon the action, thereby summing up and interpreting the main business of the scene. This may be in a series of rhymed couplets, such as Edgar's soliloquy at the end of the mad-symphony in the third act of *King Lear*.[21] In his six couplets Edgar reflects on how slight his own miseries are when he sees the King, his better, bearing greater ones. Thus he seems to be interpreting, like the Greek chorus, the moral lesson of the scene. His couplets serve still another purpose, in that they give an orderly, sane end to a terribly disturbed and uneven scene.

These chorus-like comments are more often in the form of single rhymed couplets, normally with a gnomic content. Nearly one quarter of the scene-end rhymes are sententious, and the majority of these are chorus-like observations on the preceding action. In *Measure for Measure* such a couplet issues from the heart of the pious hypocrite Angelo, who is beginning to feel the pangs of conscience. He remarks on his villainy with these lines:

> Alack, when once our grace we have forgot,
> Nothing goes right; we would, and we would not.[22]

Again, in *Timon of Athens* Alcibiades sums up his comments on the unpleasant scene in the senate-house with this couplet:

> 'T is honour with most lands to be at odds;
> Soldiers should brook as little wrongs as gods.[23]

20. Quoted in Furness, *The New Variorum Shakespeare: Hamlet* (Philadelphia, 1877), I, 129.
21. III. vi. 109–20.   22. IV. iv. 36–7.
23. III. v. 116–17.

A slight variation in this use of the couplet is the scene-end rhyme which gives a moral justification of the action. Thus Mistress Page excuses herself for her treachery to Falstaff,[24] and Cordelia explains to her audience the reason for her taking up arms against England;[25] in both cases, moreover, the rhyme has a strong gnomic undertone.

Such comments, to be sure, are not always gnomic. The following couplet from *As You Like It* has a different quality from the examples just given:

> Thus must I from the smoke into the smother,
> From tyrant duke unto a tyrant brother;[26]

but, of course, even this couplet carries with it the suggestion of a proverbial expression closely akin to the *sententiae*.

The second method by which the scene-end rhyme achieves its effect of giving an emphatic close to the action is by calling special attention to the stage of development reached by the plot. In this use the rhyme may be an aid in conveying certain important narrative details. In *The Merchant of Venice*, Gratiano indicates his course of action by means of a couplet:

> I am glad on 't. I desire no more delight
> Than to be under sail and gone to-night.[27]

Another interesting example is the couplet used to dismiss a character who is no longer to play a rôle of any importance in the play. The unmasking of Parolles and the end of his significance to the action is accomplished in scene-end rhyme;[28] and in *Henry V* Pistol is bowed out of the play with this couplet, which also ends the scene:

> And patches will I get unto these cudgell'd scars,
> And swear I got them in the Gallia wars.[29]

At times this special attention is called to a fact which has comparatively little relation to the narrative development. In *2 Henry IV*, for example, a scene ends with the Prince's general statement of policy, important to the patriotic tone of the play and as an anticipation of *Henry V*, but having little to do with the action of *2 Henry IV*. In the same way key lines are sometimes used to end

24. *M. W.* v. iii. 23–4.
26. i. ii. 299–300.
28. *A. W.* iv. iii. 371–5.

25. *Lear* iv. iv. 27–8.
27. ii. vi. 67–8.
29. v. i. 93–4.

scenes, lines in which either the title of the play is stated[30] or the moral of the entire action is given.[31] Likewise, a scene in *Othello* ends with a couplet designed solely to emphasize the beauty and innocence of Desdemona, thus heightening the tragic injustice which she suffers.[32]

More often the rhyme indicates certain important emotional developments in the action, developments which mark a significant stage in the plot. A paramount example is the lyrical stanza which ends a scene in *Much Ado About Nothing* by showing Beatrice's realization of her love for Benedick.[33] The rhyme, in addition, is used to vary what might otherwise be a monotonous repetition; for while Benedick confesses his love to himself in sprightly prose, Beatrice reveals hers in a graceful, lyrical stanza. Similarly the world-weariness of Macbeth is revealed in a scene-end rhyme.[34] In a way, this passage completes a cycle begun in the first act: in a scene-end rhyme Macbeth sells his soul to ambition and evil;[35] in a scene-end rhyme he screws his courage to the sticking point and leaves to murder the king;[36] in a scene-end rhyme he takes the second step in his downfall as he concludes the murder of Banquo,[37] and the third, as he determines upon a course of ruthless and bloody action;[38] and finally in a scene-end rhyme he comes to a realization that everything has been in vain and decides to throw himself on the mercy of fate.[34]

The third general method whereby the scene-end rhyme produces its effect is by anticipating later action, and in this use it achieves its greatest success. By pointing forward to something which is to happen in a subsequent scene, the rhyme excites the interest of the audience and creates a feeling of suspense.

The Senecan soliloquies in which a villain lays plans for his evil machinations are a favorite method of closing scenes even in the later plays, and with but few exceptions these soliloquies end in a vigorous couplet which presents the point of the whole speech. In *King Lear*, for example, three of Edmund's villainous soliloquies end in a rhyme, and each rhyme is designed to arouse the interest of the audience in the action which is soon to follow:

> Let me, if not by birth, have lands by wit:
> All with me's meet that I can fashion fit.[39]

30. *T. S.* IV. i. 213–14; *A. W.* IV. iv. 35–6.
31. *T. S.* V. ii. 184–9; *M. M.* I. iii. 53–4.
32. IV. iii. 105–06.   33. III. i. 107–16.
34. V. v. 47–52.   35. I. vii. 81–2.
36. II. i. 63–4.   37. III. i. 141–2.
38. III. ii. 54–5.   39. I. ii. 199–200. *Cf.* III. iii. 25–6; V. i. 68–9.

With this statement of his creed, Edmund is launched into his career of evil, a career which, before it is cut off, drags Lear and Cordelia to their deaths. Similar rhymes can be found in nearly every play, early or late, in which appears such a character as Edmund.

The determination of future action is not limited to rhymes in soliloquies, but frequently appears in dialogue. Ariel's couplet in *The Tempest* states a determined action in an aside,[40] while the following couplet from *1 Henry VI* is spoken in the hearing of all the characters:

> And now to Paris, in this conquering vein;
> All will be ours, now bloody Talbot's slain.[41]

Such a couplet is used also to suggest some further action after the close of the play.[42]

The prophecies, forebodings, and warnings which Shakespeare so frequently rhymes at exits are used also with great effectiveness at the ends of scenes. Somewhat akin to them is the couplet which, because of future events, produces an effect of dramatic irony. The English history plays seem particularly full of such scene-end couplets, though a good example is the following from *Troilus and Cressida:*

> The glory of our Troy doth this day lie
> On his fair worth and single chivalry.[43]

Aeneas' lines are a graceful compliment to the might of Hector, who, of course, is going to be killed in the battle which the lines announce. One cannot help mentioning here the dramatic irony in the words of King Claudius, in *Hamlet:*

> My words fly up, my thoughts remain below:
> Words without thoughts never to heaven go.[44]

Here is no anticipation of future events, nothing which depends for its effect upon subsequent developments, but an immediate realization of tremendous irony.

The most common method by which the scene-end rhyme prepares for coming events is by expressing a direct command. This command may be for an action which is of little importance to the

40. II. i. 326–7.   41. IV. vii. 95–6.
42. *T. A.* v. iii. 203–04; *Oth.* v. ii. 370–1.
43. IV. iv. 149–50. Cf. *1 Hen. IV* IV. i. 131–6; *2 Hen. IV* v. iii. 147–8; *Hen. V* III. v. 67–8.
44. III. iii. 97–8.

plot and which occurs off stage, as in this couplet from *As You Like It:*

> Support him by the arm.—Give me your hand,
> And let me all your fortunes understand.[45]

In *Hamlet* the same effect of continuity is gained by a couplet suggesting how the time is to be filled before the beginning of the next scene.[46]

On the other hand, this command may be for an action which is of great importance and which is later to constitute one of the important scenes of the play. Here also the history plays offer the most striking examples, for many of the scenes conclude with orders to prepare for battles that are to determine the course of the play.[47] But the other types of drama likewise show many examples of this use of the couplet. The following is a double tag from *As You Like It:*

> O, come, let us remove;
> The sight of lovers feedeth those in love.
> Bring us to this sight, and you shall say
> I'll prove a busy actor in their play.[48]

The promise is not belied when, in the next scene, Rosalind throws the love between Silvius and Phebe into a state of utter confusion.

The scene-end rhyme, though similar in its use to exit rhyme, differs from it—and from the other isolated rhymes—in one important respect. Whereas the exit rhymes show a marked tendency to decrease in number after the early plays, the scene-end rhymes show little decrease down to the very latest plays.[49] The simple explanation for this fact seems to be that the strong pause which the rhyme creates was felt by Shakespeare, after his early plays, to be inappropriate for the ordinary exit but helpful in indicating an important shift in the action.

---

45. II. vii. 199–200.   46. v. i. 321–2.
47. *1 Hen. VI* IV. ii. 55–6; *2 Hen. VI* v. ii. 88–9; *3 Hen. VI* II. ii. 173–4.
48. III. iv. 59–62.
49. The following list gives by plays the number of scenes or acts ending in rhyme, exclusive of those scenes whose final rhyme is part of an extended passage of rhyme. Indicated also is the total number of scenes in each play: *1 Hen. VI* 12/27; *2 Hen. VI* 8/24; *3 Hen. VI* 11/28; *Rich. III* 11/24; *T. A.* 3/14; *C. E.* 6/11; *T. G.* 7/20; *L. L. L.* 3/9; *R. J.* 11/24; *Rich. II* 10/19; *M. N. D.* 0/9; *John* 10/16; *M. V.* 11/20; *T. S.* 9/14; *1 Hen. IV* 8/19; *2 Hen. IV* 10/19; *M. A.* 2/17; *Hen. V* 13/23; *J. C.* 4/18; *A. Y. L.* 8/22; *T. N.* 10/18; *Ham.* 13/20; *M. W.* 3/23; *T. C.* 12/23; *A. W.* 10/23; *M. M.* 7/17; *Oth.* 7/15; *Mac.* 16/28; *Lear* 9/25; *A. C.* 7/42; *Cor.* 2/29; *Tim.* 13/17; *Per.* 11/22; *Cy.* 11/27; *W. T.* 0/15; *Tp.* 1/9; *Hen. VIII* 5/17.

Consecutive Rhyme

The extended passages of consecutive rhyme are of particular importance in this study for two reasons: they include a numerical majority of all the rhymes in Shakespeare's plays and they show the most considerable decline in the use of rhyme. While scenes or large parts of scenes are frequently rhymed in the early plays, they are rarely so in the late; when they do appear in the mature plays they are used with greater deliberation, and usually with a more carefully designed effect.

If it is an essential part of the dialogue, the consecutive rhyme is used normally to convey a mood of lyricism, of sprightly comedy, or of emotional intensity. Still other uses are in gnomic passages and in such external elements as rhymed letters, scrolls, and the like.

Concerning Shakespeare's use of rhyme A. W. Ward wrote:

The employment of rime was . . . already being narrowed when Shakspere began to write; but the strong lyrical element in his poetic individuality inspired him with a lingering affection towards it, especially in plays with a decidedly lyrical element in their conception.[1]

This lyrical element is partially responsible for the great number of isolated rhymes in the early plays; much more noticeably it is responsible for the numerous lines of extended rhyme which fill the pages of his youthful dramas, in such a play as *Love's Labour's Lost* outnumbering the blank verse almost two to one. It is a commonplace to say that Shakespeare's early medium was lyrical rather than dramatic, that he was more interested in composing passages rich in poetic flavor than in synthesizing his words with the dramatic movement. Concomitant with this is his love for verbal resemblances, for such devices as puns, stichomythia, oxymoron, devices which tended to call attention to the words themselves rather than to their dramatic significance. Rhyme must be considered as part of this strong lyrical element and this love for similarities in sound.

Although the earliest history plays have their share of rhymed passages, their subject matter on the whole gave Shakespeare little opportunity to exercise his lyrical inclinations. When, however, he broke away from the restrictions which these plays placed upon him, and when he emancipated himself from the Marlovian influence which found its strongest expression in *Richard III*, he

1. II, 288.

gave free rein to his lyrical disposition and indulged in the use of rhyme. This rhyme was not merely a matter of adoption with Shakespeare. He was not just experimenting with a medium foreign to him, attempting to beautify himself with borrowed feathers. Rhyme was as natural to him, to his manner of expression, as blank verse. That the latter finally took complete command resulted from a fundamental change in Shakespeare's mode of expression, that is, from the change to a more dramatic verse medium. While Shakespeare was writing plays whose atmosphere was essentially lyrical, it was natural for him to use rhyme. As Hiram Corson said of A Midsummer Night's Dream,

the reader must feel that it [rhyme] is *essential* to the poetic pitch of the play. The poet, with a more dramatic purpose, might have previously written a number of plays on a lower poetic key, and have used, in consequence, fewer rhymes. It is quite certain that he did previously write such plays. That he could not have written a more dramatic play at the time he composed A Midsummer Night's Dream, is not for a moment to be supposed.[2]

On the other hand, that he would have written such a play as A Midsummer Night's Dream at a later period in his dramatic development is also not to be supposed, for the excessive lyricism, found likewise in such plays as Love's Labour's Lost, Romeo and Juliet, and Richard II, was supplanted by other interests.

In some of the early lyrical plays the use of rhyme seems almost indiscriminate. David, speaking of the shifts from blank verse to prose, to rhyme, to sonnets, and to rhyme-royal stanzas in The Comedy of Errors, says, "Admirable as the invention is, it is hard to find any poetic method in such a hotch-potch."[3] In such a play as A Midsummer Night's Dream, however, Shakespeare is to be seen using extended rhymed passages with careful deliberation.

The rhyme in this play is fundamental to the general structure, and, of course, to the pervading atmosphere of lyricism and romance. The four groups of characters, all centered in Theseus, are differentiated not just by their separate positions in the action but by the very language they speak. Theseus and Hippolyta and their immediate coterie speak for the most part in a dignified blank verse. The "rude mechanicals," except in their play, use prose, language fitting men of their low station. The young lovers express themselves principally in rhyme, as do the fairies.

2. An Introduction to the Study of Shakespeare (Boston, 1889), pp. 69–70.
3. p. 18.

Throughout the play these distinctions in medium are carefully kept.

The lovers speak in a graceful pentameter, mostly in couplets though here and there in other stanzaic forms. In a rather interesting fashion they switch occasionally to blank verse. In the first scene of Act I they are not introduced speaking rhyme, for when they are hailed before Theseus they are part of the courtly group and speak in blank verse. Nor do they begin using rhyme immediately upon their being left alone on the stage. It is not until Lysander and Hermia have been speaking of their love for nearly fifty lines that Shakespeare, as if by a sudden inspiration, has them begin talking in the metre which is to characterize their conversation through most of their subsequent scenes.[4] In the central scene of their plot the lovers, thrown into a state of angry confusion by the mistakes of Puck, begin a quarrel, still using their characteristic rhyme. When the quarrel reaches a state bordering on violence, however, rhyme is forgotten.[5] The ultimate awakening of the lovers is in blank verse[6] and their scattered comments in the final act are either in this medium or in prose, but by this time they seem again to be part of the courtly group and thus use its medium.

The use of rhyme for the plot of the lovers has been variously explained. One critic considers it "particularly appropriate, since it prevents us from taking the lovers' scenes too seriously,"[7] while another asserts that it "gives the formal effect of an old English square dance, as the four lovers, all much of one pattern, change partners."[8] Perhaps more essential is the fact that the rhyme, with its musical richness, helps convey the dream-like quality, the mood of lyricism and romance, which is the prevailing atmosphere of the play.

The fairies, who also speak in rhyme, are differentiated from the lovers by the fact that their metre is brighter and more lyrical. Although Oberon, by his royal prerogative, speaks occasionally in blank verse and in rhymed pentameter—as in the beautiful lyrical passage beginning, "I know a bank where the wild thyme blows"[9]— the fairies generally use the shorter line, the trochaic tetrameter, which Shakespeare characteristically gives to his supernatural

---

4. The rhyme begins with line 171 and continues to the end of the scene.
5. III. ii. 195 is the turning point from rhyme to blank verse, and except for an occasional rhyme the remainder of the dispute between the lovers is in blank verse.
6. IV. i. 191–203.   7. Hardin Craig, p. 99.
8. Oliver Elton, p. 16.   9. II. i. 249–68.

figures.[10] Guest says of this metre, "Under Shakespeare's sanction, it has become classical, and must now be considered as the *fairy dialect* of English literature."[11] The metre as used here, and also in the speeches of the three weird sisters in *Macbeth*, produces a lyricism which is in marked contrast to the other metres, even to the rhymed lines of the lovers. Wherever it is used, it seems to convey a sense of unreality; and thus, after weaving its mysterious charms through the action of the play, it fittingly closes the dream with a fairy blessing.[12]

In some respects this lyric use of rhyme in *A Midsummer Night's Dream* is characteristic of many of the early plays. In *The Comedy of Errors*, though much of the rhyme is comic, there are some passages of pure lyricism. This is more true in *Love's Labour's Lost*, where the various love poems composed by the King and his companions are all couched in rhyme. In *Romeo and Juliet* also, despite the fact that the play is a tragedy, the predominant atmosphere of romance and lyricism includes many passages whose sole justification is their lyrical quality. Thus Capulet's description of Juliet and of the "old accustomed feast" is presented in rhyme,[13] and Romeo's exquisite description of Juliet, whom he sees for the first time, is given in five highly imaginative couplets.[14]

To digress for a moment, *A Midsummer Night's Dream* suggests a still further use of rhyme. In this play rhyme differentiates certain groups of characters. Elsewhere it seems to differentiate one particular character from the rest in the play. In *King John*, for example, the Bastard is much more inclined to use rhyme than are any of the other characters. Though usually in a single couplet, his humorous, caustic comments sometimes take longer forms, most often the rhyme-royal stanza.[15] Similarly in *Richard III* the speeches of the women, primarily in their expressions of grief and sorrow, exhibit rhyme along with other stylistic embellishments; and in *Richard II* the words of the King and of Gaunt are very often couched in rhyme, "as if for the purpose of marking them off from other characters."[16] This must not be overemphasized, however, for it is never particularly obvious. In no play does Shakespeare limit his rhyme to one character, and though occasionally there is, as in Richard II, a strong lyricism of

10. See Appendix B, p. 129.
11. *A History of English Rhythms* (ed. W. W. Skeat: London, 1882), p. 179.
12. v. i. 378–445.   13. i. ii. 16–37.
14. i. v. 46–55.   15. i. i. 170–5; ii. i. 504–09.
16. Hardin Craig, p. 313.

character, the use of rhyme to distinguish character is not a common practice with Shakespeare.[17]

After the early plays, rhyme as the medium for passages of lyricism is used with much reserve, just as such passages themselves are used with reserve. In *As You Like It*, a play whose atmosphere is not unlike that of *A Midsummer Night's Dream*, there are a few couplet passages of pure lyricism, though for the most part the lyricism appears in songs, poems, and rhymed letters. Pandarus quotes a lyrical rhyme on love in *Troilus and Cressida*,[18] and the unwinding of the plot in *All's Well* is accomplished in a series of rhymed couplets.[19] The witches' scenes in *Macbeth*, possibly un-Shakespearian,[20] are perhaps the last passages of lyricism for its own sake to be found in the dialogue of the plays. When Shakespeare finally returned, in *The Tempest*, to a quiet pastoral mood, he was no longer interested in the purely lyrical. The love between Ferdinand and Miranda, which in an early play might have inspired at least some rhymed lyricism, is thrust into the background. The verse of the entire play, often free and graceful, is dramatic and meditative rather than lyrical; and in this type of verse rhyme seems to have little place.

A considerable portion of the extended rhyme in the early plays is used in passages of comic dialogue where an effect of clever, rapid repartee is desired. As with the speech-link rhyme, this comic effect is produced not only by the five-foot iambic but often by some other metrical line. In any of the three early comedies can be found examples of various types of lines used for rhymed comic dialogue. In *The Comedy of Errors* the first passage of extended rhyme, a clever dialogue on the subject of marriage, is in iambic pentameter couplets, combining speech-link and single-speech rhymes.[21] In the next act, when a coarser type of humor is called for, the metre changes to doggerel, to the direct descendant of the old alliterative line.[22] The effect, as Antipholus of Ephesus and his servant try in vain to gain entrance to their own house,[23] though decidedly humorous, is very similar to the raucous street fights, in doggerel, which occur in such a play as *Ralph Roister Doister*. Though none the less appreciative, the discriminating Elizabethan play-goer must have felt the crudity of such a scene.

---

17. Such a practice, however, was not uncommon in the Tudor interlude. See Bernard, p. 200.

18. iv. iv. 17–18, 20–1.   19. v. iii. 314–19, 325–34.
20. See D. L. Chambers, p. 14.   21. ii. i. 10–43.
22. Schipper, *A History of English Versification*, p. 118.
23. iii. i. 32–83.

Similar passages are to be found in *The Two Gentlemen of Verona* and *Love's Labour's Lost;* even as late as *The Taming of the Shrew* doggerel is used to accompany a low sort of horse-play, as Petruchio and his man Grumio dispute over which shall knock at the gate.[24] Though these examples have all been of the longer doggerel line, in *Love's Labour's Lost* Shakespeare makes use of a short iambic line of three accents to produce a comic rapidity in the dialogue.[25]

Despite its appearance in *The Taming of the Shrew* and occasionally in other plays,[26] the doggerel line in comic rhymed passages does not hold a position of any importance after the early plays. The heroic line, however, continues to be used in comic rhymed passages in some of the later plays, usually with a studied effect. A good example is the rhyme which accompanies Cressida's reception in the Greek camp.[27] As Dowden has observed, "there is a flippancy in the speeches which they would lose if turned from rhyme into blank verse."[28] Here the rhymes are interrupted by blank-verse lines and are not divided in the manner of stichomythia—one line to each speaker. In the doggerel passage from *The Comedy of Errors* which was just mentioned, the single-line speech of the characters outside the house is answered by a rhyming line from within. In this passage from *Troilus and Cressida* the line unit is broken, the single line at times being divided between two speakers, and the rhyme itself ceases to be the major factor in the movement of the dialogue. The function of the rhyme seems to be, as Dowden said, to heighten the flippancy of the lines and perhaps to anticipate the later events of the play by underlining the suggestion of wantonness in Cressida's behavior, the wantonness which Ulysses openly condemns at the end of this passage.[29]

Another example of this use of rhyme in a later play is not from a comedy but from a tragedy. In *Othello,* Iago, trying to amuse the nervous Desdemona until her husband arrives, voices his witty, cynical remarks mostly in couplets, eleven in all, though with several interruptions.[30] The occasion seems to call for rhyme. Othello's ship is overdue. Desdemona is naturally concerned, and honest Iago, who does everything efficiently, undertakes to divert

24. I. ii. 11–17. *Cf.* I. ii. 225–36.
25. II. i. 123–8, 186–93, 202–03, 209–12.
26. See *A. Y. L.* III. iii. 98–107 (probably sung) and *M. W.* II. i. 15–19.
27. *T. C.* IV. v. 28–31, 33–8, 40–1, 43–6, 49–52.
28. p. 45.   29. IV. v. 54–63.
30. II. i. 115–16, 130–1, 133–4, 137–8, 142–3, 149–61.

his mistress. To do this he assumes a tone of cynical bantering, the wit and artificiality of which are heightened by the use of rhyme.

Like speech-link rhyme, these passages of comic consecutive rhyme in the early plays generally sharpen the repartee and speed up the dialogue. Often the couplet is divided between two speakers; that is, it is a speech-link rhyme. That Shakespeare felt this to be artificial and mechanical seems evident from the fact that he uses consecutive rhyme for a comic effect in the later plays only when the general tone is one of artificiality. Then too, the doggerel which is so common in the early plays rapidly passes out of favor. When, in the later plays, the playwright wishes to produce the effect of the early doggerel he seems to prefer prose.

Consecutive rhyme for the expression of pure lyricism disappeared as Shakespeare's medium changed from the lyrical to the dramatic; and for the expression of a comic mood consecutive rhyme lost ground because its effect seemed more naturally gained by prose and because the playwright seemingly came to think of it as artificial. Consecutive rhyme for the communication of deep emotional feeling, however, continued to be used with some frequency except in Shakespeare's very latest plays.

The early plays, with their high number of rhymes, are particularly full of rhymed passages used to express deep feeling. In *Richard III*, a play with somewhat less rhyme than the other plays of Shakespeare's first period, there is a good example of this use of rhyme when the Duchess of York passionately answers her taunting son:

> No, by the holy rood, thou know'st it well,
> Thou cam'st on earth to make the earth my hell.
> A grievous burden was thy birth to me;
> Tetchy and wayward was thy infancy;
> Thy school-days frightful, desperate, wild, and furious,
> Thy prime of manhood daring, bold, and venturous;[31]

and then continues in blank verse. In *Romeo and Juliet* the final parting of the lovers is in rhyme as, with hearts full of foreboding, they express their sorrowful farewell.[32] And in *Richard II* one of the most pathetic passages in the play, the parting between Richard and the Queen, is conducted in rhyme, rhyme that gives lyrical expression to their grief.[33]

As Shakespeare developed he continued to use rhyme for the

31. IV. iv. 165–70.   32. III. v. 23–6, 33–6.
33. v. i. 79–102.

expression of emotional excitement, but to use it in a somewhat equivocal manner. In *The Merchant of Venice*, one of the first plays to show complete synthesis of action and language, one hears Bassanio addressing his newly-won bride in a passage of five couplets full of restrained emotion[34] in conscious contrast with the unrestraint of Portia's blank verse; and yet David's contention that the scene is fundamentally unrealistic may be justifiable.[35] The rhyme may have been used to emphasize the artificiality of the scene. The same might be said of Helena's emotional soliloquy in *All's Well that Ends Well*,[36] and certainly may be said of the long passage of rhyme in Act II where Helena pleads with the King to accept her as his healer.[37] In her reasoning with the King, as in her later dismissal of the suitors,[38] there is, to be sure, no strong emotion, though there is an emotional undertone. There is, however, a fundamental artificiality about the entire situation. In *The Merchant of Venice* the unreality lies in the selection of a husband on the basis of his choice of a casket; here it is the selection of a husband by virtue of the strange knowledge of therapeutics which Helena, alone of all the world, possesses. It might almost seem, then, that Shakespeare was deliberately using rhyme in these passages to point out the absurdity of the situations which they present.

On the other hand, there can be little question that Macbeth's passionate speech at the disappearance of the Third Apparition is deliberately rhymed to heighten the tone of excitement which the lines contain.[39] The words of the Apparition, of course, are rhymed, and it may therefore be that Macbeth's speech is merely made to harmonize; but his determination earlier in the play to revisit the witches, a resolve made out of the greatest distress of mind and soul, is also rhymed, seemingly to accentuate emotional intensity.[40] Similarly might be mentioned Cordelia's attempt to console her grief-stricken father[41] and Coriolanus' passionate soliloquy in which he expresses his utter disgust with having to beg favors from the populace.[42]

There seems to be, accordingly, a somewhat ambiguous usage in the later plays. Although at times the rhyme suggests a certain artificiality either in the emotions or in the situation which inspires them, elsewhere it cannot be so interpreted, but must be

34. III. ii. 140–9.
36. I. i. 231–44.
38. II. iii. 78–83, 86–91, 95–8, 102–03, 109–10.
39. *Mac.* IV. i. 94–101.
41. *Lear* v. iii. 3–6.

35. p. 35.
37. II. i. 133–44, 146–213.
40. *Mac.* III. iv. 135–40.
42. *Cor.* II. iii. 120–31.

accepted as a method of heightening the emotional tenor of the passage. As a sincere means of conveying emotions, however, rhyme lost its favor with Shakespeare as soon as he had realized the full mastery of blank verse, for rhyme was too inflexible to convey the subtle shades of emotion which are drawn in his mature plays. That Macbeth continues to use it can be explained only by the fact that he is the most poetic of all Shakespeare's great tragic heroes. Like Richard II and Romeo, he thinks in terms of the imaginative, the poetic, the lyrical; and thus, perhaps out of fidelity to the basic concept of the character, Shakespeare has him occasionally express himself through the lyrical medium of rhyme.

The persistence of consecutive rhyme in Shakespeare's mature plays is partially to be explained by the continued use of certain intrusive passages which, strictly speaking, are not part of the dialogue though they are part of the play. The lyrical love poems, for example, which are so conspicuous in *Love's Labour's Lost* find their lineal descendants in Orlando's ridiculous love poems in *As You Like It*,[43] poems which are made the butt of ridicule for their paucity of rhyme and absurdity of sentiment. The rhymed love letter in *The Two Gentlemen of Verona*[44] has many parallels in the later plays. Phebe's "challenge" to Rosalind,[45] Malvolio's supposed love note from Olivia,[46] Helena's letter in sonnet-form in *All's Well that Ends Well*[47] are just a few examples. The rhymed scroll which appears for the first time in *The Merchant of Venice*[48] is used in *Much Ado About Nothing*[49] and again in *Pericles*.[50] For the most part these intrusions are lyrical in nature, often being written in a short metre and usually presenting an eccentric rhyme scheme. Their separation from the context is thus rendered the more complete, and probably they should not be included in a study of Shakespeare's use of rhyme, except that they do show his continued willingness to use rhyme for special embellishment.

There remains to point out another characteristic of the passages of consecutive rhyme, a characteristic which has a significant relationship to the gradual disuse of this type of rhyme. Fleay observed that "there is not only a gradual lessening, as we advance in time, of rhyme lines in general: but also a gradual dying-out of

43. III. ii. 93–100, 133–62. *Cf.* III. ii. 107–18.
44. III. i. 140–9.
45. *A. Y. L.* IV. iii. 40–1, 44–5, 47–8, 50–63.
46. *T. N.* II. v. 107–10, 115–18. *Cf. Ham.* II. ii. 116–19.
47. III. iv. 4–17.
48. II. vii. 65–73; II. ix. 63–72; III. ii. 132–9.
49. v. iii. 3–8. *Cf. Tim.* v. iv. 70–3.   50. III. ii. 68–75.

different arrangements of rhyme lines."[51] The early works display
a considerable amount of rhyme which is not in couplet form but
which adopts some other stanzaic pattern. The most common of
these patterns is the quatrain, reserved usually for the passages of
greatest lyricism. In *The Comedy of Errors,* many of the comic
passages are in couplets; but when Antipholus of Syracuse declares his love for Luciana he does so principally in quatrains.[52]
The same is true in *Love's Labour's Lost.* The lyrical first scene,
for example, shows a haphazard mixture of couplets, triplets, and
quatrains, with as many quatrains as couplets.[53] But other stanzaic
patterns are also common, particularly the rhyme-royal stanza and
the sonnet. Both of these have been used to give approximate
dates to the plays in which they appear, for Shakespeare seemed
particularly in the mood for them while he was composing *Venus
and Adonis* and the *Sonnets.* The rhyme-royal stanza is used for a
great variety of purposes, ranging from the cynical observations
of the Bastard[54] to the tender lyricism of Paris[55] and the passionate
outcry of Richard II;[56] the sonnet, less flexible in the dramatic
medium, usually stands apart as a distinct unit, though it is used
in *Romeo and Juliet* to lend a courtly grace to the first meeting of
the lovers.[57] And in his last use of the sonnet within a drama,
Shakespeare has it tell of the melancholy mood of the frustrated
Helena.[58]

But in general Shakespeare discarded such alternate rhymes
from his plays almost immediately after the composition of *Richard II, A Midsummer Night's Dream,* and *King John.* This fact, of
course, may be interpreted in two ways. His general tendency
away from passages of consecutive rhyme may have resulted in
the abandonment of all such stanzaic patterns; but it seems more
likely that it was the unnaturalness of such special patterns in the
dialogue which induced the poet to discard them. They are, of
course, essentially lyrical and constitute a higher degree of stylization than the heroic couplet. As lyrical embellishments they are
desirable in plays whose atmosphere permits such embellishments. Where a less obtrusive style is desired in the dialogue, they
are out of place.

The disappearance of consecutive rhymed passages, therefore,

---

51. "On Metrical Tests," in Ingleby, p. 52.
52. III. ii. 1–52.
53. I. i. 47–103, 105–18, 126–9, 134–81.
54. *John* II. i. 504–09. 55. *R. J.* v. iii. 12–17.
56. *Rich. II* III. ii. 76–81. 57. I. v. 95–108.
58. *A. W.* III. iv. 4–17.

results from a combination of causes. A distaste for rhyme in more complicated stanzaic forms is partially responsible. The development of Shakespeare's medium from lyrical to dramatic, the shift from doggerel to prose for lively comic dialogue, and the mastery of a flexible blank verse to convey deep feeling account for the rest.

External Rhyme

The rhymes considered in this class are not part of the dialogue of the plays which they accompany. If Shakespeare actually thought of them as separate, as a kind of writing which might be far different in stylistic requirements from ordinary dramatic dialogue, then it is obvious that the changing use of rhyme within the organic parts of his plays neither influenced, nor was influenced by, the rhyme in these external passages. Many of the rhymes included here, moreover, have had their authenticity doubted, some with justification. Thus the external rhyme should be excluded from the discussion of Shakespeare's development.[1]

Included in this class are really two distinct types of rhyme: the rhyme appearing within the body of the play, such as masques and plays within the play, and that which is strictly external, such as choruses, prologues, and epilogues. The use of rhyme in such passages was by no means limited to Shakespeare. David Klein, speaking of the one respect in which Marlowe's campaign against rhyme was unsuccessful, said: "His successors refused to follow his example of casting the prolog and epilog into blank verse, showing that they did not feel these to be an intrinsic portion of the play."[2] It was the common practice to rhyme such things as prologues and epilogues, just as it was the common practice to employ rhyme in masques and interpolated plays.

Shakespeare's prologues are not all in rhyme. The prologues to the various acts of *Henry V* (they might well be considered choruses) are mostly in blank verse, though they all end with a single or double rhyme-pair; and the same is true of the prologue to *Troilus and Cressida*. On the other hand, the prologues to the first two acts of *Romeo and Juliet* and to *Henry VIII* are totally in rhyme, the first being in the form of sonnets. Shakespeare's epilogues, if they are rhymed at all,[3] are totally in rhyme. It may be

1. Cf. Anna Kerrl, p. 117.
2. *Literary Criticism from the Elizabethan Dramatists* (New York, 1910), p. 235.
3. *As You Like It* ends with a prose epilogue.

that while in the prologues he uses the rhyme in much the same way as the speech-end rhyme to give a sense of finality to the passage, in the epilogue such an effect is not needed, since the epilogue cannot escape a sense of finality. Then too, the epilogues are generally shorter than the prologues. The epilogue to *Henry V*, rather surprisingly, is a sonnet,[4] while the epilogue to *Henry VIII* consists of seven rhymed couplets. The other two rhymed epilogues which are specifically called epilogues are quite different, the one concluding *All Well's that Ends Well* having only six pentameter lines, the one concluding *The Tempest* having twenty lines of trochaic tetrameter.[5]

In this connection must be mentioned the closing rhymes of *A Midsummer Night's Dream* and *Troilus and Cressida*. In both instances, though the lines have the effect of an epilogue, they are not indicated as such. In the former, Puck, left alone on the stage at the end of the fairy masque, steps forth and begs the indulgence of the audience;[6] in the latter, Pandarus ends his meditative soliloquy with five couplets directly addressed to the "traders in the flesh" who might be in the audience.[7] These two passages have caused the chronologists considerable difficulty since Furnivall first pointed them out,[8] for if the epilogues and prologues are not to be counted in the ratios of rhymed to unrhymed verse, what is to be done with these passages which are obviously epilogues and which are yet inseparable from the context? The choice must be an arbitrary one. Here they have not been included with the external rhyme because they grow directly out of the dialogue and therefore may be considered as part of it.

Really indistinguishable from prologues and epilogues are the choruses which Shakespeare uses, in some of his plays, primarily to indicate the passage of time and to bridge the gap in the narrative. The prologues in *Romeo and Juliet* and *Henry V* are, in fact, spoken by a chorus. In *The Winter's Tale* there is a more formal use of the chorus, for Time bridges, in thirty-two rhymed lines, the gap of sixteen years which occurs between the third and fourth acts. The chorus in this play is used only this once. In *Pericles*, however, the Gower speeches, actually choruses, are used throughout the play to connect the rather loosely knit scenes and to lend continuity to the narrative. In some respects these speeches

---

4. See F. G. Fleay, in Ingleby, p. 53. 5. See Appendix B, pp. 153–4.
6. v. i. 430–45. 7. v. x. 48–57.
8. *N. S. S. Trans.* I, 34.

seem un-Shakespearian.[9] The metre, though mostly in iambic tetrameter, is highly irregular. The chorus at the beginning of Act V consists of six rhymed quatrains in iambic pentameter, a stanzaic form which Shakespeare had discarded early in his dramatic career. Also, the rhymes are peculiar, showing a much greater license with sounds than Shakespeare exhibits elsewhere. Even if not by Shakespeare, however, the Gower speeches cannot be separated from the play but are an essential part of its basic structure. Then too, Gower himself confesses a certain antiquity in his lines,[10] an antiquity which these stylistic eccentricities may have been deliberately chosen to produce. The final Gower speech, the epilogue, is perfectly regular in metre and rhyme, but this is no longer part of the play. The atmosphere has been broken with the completion of the action, and this epilogue is like any of the other rhymed epilogues.

The other external rhymes which must be mentioned are to be found in the plays within a play and the masque. In a sense these are not external, for at least in A Midsummer Night's Dream, Hamlet, and Merry Wives they are fundamental to the entire structure; yet strictly speaking they are not part of the dialogue and should not, therefore, be considered in the development of Shakespeare's style. In A Midsummer Night's Dream, and also in Hamlet, it is perfectly obvious that the poet was deliberately striving for a different style, possibly just to differentiate the language and tone from that of the rest of the play, though in both there seems to be a more important reason for the style. In the "Pyramus and Thisbe" play produced by Bottom and his companions, Shakespeare was being satiric. Probably written by Peter Quince, the play was intended to represent the absurdities of amateur productions, particularly those of the small country town; for though the scene is ostensibly Athens, the fact that the players represent many trades is alone sufficient indication of the society which Shakespeare had in mind. By the garbled prologue, by the immature treatment of the story, by the stilted, mechanical metres, by the rodomontade of the language, and by the uncouth rhymes, Shakespeare has created here one of the most delightful burlesques in the language.[11]

The Mouse-trap in Hamlet is not a burlesque, though its style

9. "It is widely accepted that the author mainly responsible for Acts I and II and the Choruses was . . . George Wilkins" (W. A. Neilson, The Complete Dramatic and Poetic Works of William Shakespeare, p. 355).

10. I Gower 11–12.   11. See G. D. Willcock, p. 5.

also is distinguished from that of the rest of the play. While this is done partially by the use of consecutive rhyme, it is also done by a deliberate stiffness in the lines, a stiffness that is in sharp contrast to the freedom of Shakespeare's mature style. Though there are a few run-on lines in Hamlet's play, the majority of them are end-stopped, most of the couplets coming to a full close. In addition to that, the caesura, which Shakespeare developed to give variety in his rhymed lines as well as in his blank verse, is here almost totally lacking, with the result that the lines have a mechanical, wooden movement. A possible explanation for this is that here, as in the Gower passages, Shakespeare was attempting to give the flavor of age to his lines, was trying to create the impression that here was a play produced a long time ago. This explanation, of course, assumes that Shakespeare concerned himself with making his dramas conform to the demands of time and place—which in general is certainly not true.

The masque in *The Merry Wives of Windsor* is similar to the two plays just discussed in that it also is an inseparable part of the action, essential to its development. It contains the final unmasking of Falstaff and makes possible the winding-up of the plot. Though the rhymes show few irregularities, there is a peculiarity in the metre which deserves mention. The speakers in the masque are all dressed as fairies and thus might be expected to use the trochaic tetrameter, or fairy metre, which Shakespeare customarily gives to his supernatural beings. Actually he begins in this metre[12] and then changes to iambic pentameter, with some uneven lines. Heuser's explanation for this change seems reasonable: "Dies lässt vermuthen, dass Shakespeare anfangs beabsichtigte, die Reden der verkleideten Personen, ganz als wären es Reden übersinnlicher Wesen, in vorwiegend trochäischem Metrum zu verfassen, dass er nachher aber seinen Entschluss änderte und, da es sich nur um verkleidete Personen handelte, den regelrechten 5-Füssler auch für die Verkleidungsscene wählte."[13]

The masques in *Cymbeline* and *The Tempest* are not so definitely an integral part of the plays in which they appear. Posthumus' vision in *Cymbeline*[14] adds nothing to the plot and could be removed without necessitating many alterations in the text. The metre is iambic tetrameter, changing to pentameter, and the rhyme-scheme is irregular, varying from the old ballad pattern (*abcb*) to a more or less regular alternate rhyme in pentame-

12. V. V. 41.   13. p. 190.
14. V. iv. 30–122.

ter. The masque in *The Tempest*[15] could likewise be removed without detriment to the plot, since its inclusion is only for the amusement of the lovers. There is an irregularity of metre to be observed here, too, for while the major portion of the masque is in iambic-pentameter couplets, there is a song of trochaic tetrameter. That the latter was not chosen as the metre for the entire masque is difficult to explain, except that in his latest plays Shakespeare showed little inclination to depart from the pentameter as the metrical standard. The authorship of these two masques has been argued for many years,[16] but any view must be mere conjecture. Shakespeare, of course, showed little fondness for passages of extended rhyme in his later dramas, but if he were called on to include a masque in order to meet public tastes, there is no reason to suppose he could not have done it.

15. IV. i. 60–117, 128–38.   16. See Appendix B, pp. 152–4.

V

Shakespeare's Couplet Rhetoric

THE decrease of rhyme in Shakespeare's dramas resulted from the fact that he came less and less to desire its particular effects. At the same time, the increase of feminine and weak endings, of run-on lines, and of the flexible use of caesuras was a manifestation of growth toward freedom in blank verse. As Lanier said, the decrease of rhyme is related to this tendency in the blank verse:

We found that he tended more and more, from the early plays to the late ones, to disuse rime; and since the rime recurring at the end of each line is a very striking method of marking off a *regular* line-group for the ear, of impressing a regular pattern of fives upon the ear, the *disuse* of rime is clearly an advance towards *freedom,* towards the *relief from monotony,* towards the greater display of *individuality* in verse.[1]

As Shakespeare advanced toward greater freedom in his blank verse, he naturally—perhaps unconsciously—felt less and less the urge to use the rhymed heroic line along with his blank verse, since it represented restraint and order. When he did use it, moreover, he did so because it represented restraint and order, and thus was capable of producing certain needed effects.

The analysis in the preceding chapter showed how to a great extent this was true, but in order further to test it I propose here to examine a representative group of rhymed couplets to see whether the couplet itself reflects the development evident in Shakespeare's blank verse or whether the couplet rhetoric in his later dramas retains the rigid character it possesses in the earlier ones. If the late couplet shows a much greater freedom than the early, then the degree in which it can be considered a thing of restraint, a sharp contrast to the blank-verse medium, is considerably lessened.

Since the passages of consecutive rhyme fall off rather sharply after the first period and since the rhymed couplets in weak positions are of secondary importance, not infrequently questionable or irregular, I have chosen for study only the rhymed couplets in

1. *Shakspere*, II, 245.

the strong positions: the speech-end, exit and cue, and the scene-
and act-end rhymes. In such isolated positions, with the couplet
usually a self-enclosed unit, its true nature can most easily be
ascertained; as Ruth Wallerstein has said,

> If we examine further into the aesthetics of established pattern and
> variation in verse, we find in large stanzas, in blank verse, or in run-on
> couplets that, where a number of lines form the unit of perception and
> give the design, there is room for ample and subtle variation from pat-
> tern in the individual line; whereas if the unit of perception be limited
> to two lines, the pattern, to be firmly kept, must be more sharply and
> formally perceptible in the two individual lines on which the sense of
> design depends.[2]

The term "couplet rhetoric," as here employed, does not conform to Bright's definition: "By the rhetoric of verse, or the rhetoric of poetry, is meant the emphasis elicited by verse-stress, when
it is at variance with the usual (prose) emphasis."[3] An attempt to
examine Shakespeare's couplets from the standpoint of such vari-
ants in the verse stress proved so inconclusive that it was discarded. The term "couplet rhetoric," therefore, is used here in a
broad sense to indicate the position of the caesura, the quality of
the ending of the line, the rhythmical relation of the lines to each
other and to the context, the metrical character of the individual
lines, the nature of the rhyming words, and the thought-pattern
of the lines.

Shakespeare's heroic couplet is generally very regular. Indeed,
F. E. Schelling has remarked, "It is a mistake to consider that the
Elizabethans often practised the couplet with the freedom, not to
say licence, that characterizes its nineteenth century use in the
hands of such poets as Keats."[4] Because of Shakespeare's tendency
toward freedom from restriction and rule in matters of verse, it
might be expected that his practice in the couplet would likewise become freer. Schipper asserted dogmatically that such is
actually the case: "Gleichwohl ist eine ähnlich freie Behandlung
des *heroic verse* in den späteren Dramen Shaksperes, wie dieje-
nige seines späteren. *blankverse,* unverkennbar."[5] If Schipper's
conclusion is correct, then to a certain extent the couplet must
cease to represent regularity and order, and Shakespeare's use of

2. "The Development of the Rhetoric and Metre of the Heroic Couplet, Especially in 1625–1645," *PMLA* L (1935), 171.
3. "The Rhetoric of Verse in Chaucer," *PMLA* XVI (1901), 42.
4. "Ben Jonson and the Classical School," p. 239.
5. *Englische Metrik,* II, 204.

it in his mature dramas must seem somewhat less for deliberate contrast with the movement of the surrounding verse. But Schipper drew this conclusion mainly from looking at the rhymed prologue and epilogue to *Henry VIII*. The isolated rhymes used in the strong positions within the text reveal no such marked analogy to the blank verse. Though there is some development in the thought-structure, and though in a few of its characteristics the couplet shows a slight tendency toward freedom, for the most part the pattern established at the beginning of Shakespeare's career is retained to the end.[6]

Puttenham, in *The Arte of English Poesie* (1589), wrote, "The meeter of ten sillables is very stately and Heroicall, and must haue his *Cesure* fall vpon the fourth sillable, and leaue sixe behinde him."[7] Of well over two thousand lines examined for their structural characteristics nearly three-fourths follow Puttenham's stricture in spirit, though not in letter. That is, a great majority of Shakespeare's couplets show a medial caesura, but not always at the end of the fourth syllable. The caesura is considered to be medial when it appears after the fourth, fifth, or sixth syllables; when elsewhere, it is variant. It can be asserted, of course, that every five-foot line must have a pause somewhere within it, but here such a pause is recognized as a caesura only "when there is grammatical or rhetorical pause so considerable as—in most cases—to require marks of punctuation."[8]

Next in number are the lines which contain no caesura at all, the type of line which Sir George Young considers characteristic of the standard verse of Shakespeare's day.[9] Schelling's tables of the non-dramatic verse of Spenser, Marlowe, Drayton, Chapman, and Sandys show that this continuous line was somewhat more common than the line with a medial caesura.[10] In Shakespeare's couplets the line is more flexible; but it is not so flexible as to contain, even in the later plays, many lines with a variant caesura, the type of caesura which could be expected to increase rather rapidly if Shakespeare's heroic line actually grew more flexible along with his blank-verse.

A glance at the chart in Appendix C shows that in the matter of caesura there was no appreciable change in Shakespeare's couplet. The predominance of medial caesurae indicates that Shakespeare,

6. The conclusions in this chapter are based upon the table given in Appendix C.
7. p. 60.
8. Raymond M. Alden, *English Verse* (New York, 1903), p. 438.
9. p. 89.   10. p. 237.

even in his earliest dramas, recognized the value of following generally such a rule as Puttenham's.[11] The line with no caesura is
just as evident in the late as in the early plays. *Timon of Athens*
and *Pericles* have a relatively high number of such lines, as do
Troilus and Cressida, *Macbeth*, and *Cymbeline*. The variant caesura, though there is scarcely any fluctuation, seems, if anything,
more frequent in the early plays. Thus, in the matter of the caesura Shakespeare's heroic couplet, as an isolated unit in the blank-
verse passage, shows Schipper's statement to be false.

Another manifestation of freedom in the poetic line is an increase in the use of weak endings. Shakespeare's early blank verse,
possibly influenced by the traditional patterns of rhyme,[12] tended
to end the line on a strong, full-sounding word. As he advanced
toward a more flexible verse this rigidity was relaxed and the lines
came more and more to end in monosyllabic prepositions and con-
junctions, and thus the emphasis was drawn away from the end of
the line;[13] but in the heroic couplet no such change is evident. In
all the couplets considered here, there are only nine lines which
have other than a strong ending, and these are scattered throughout the plays. Shakespeare's rhyme continued to throw the emphasis upon the end of the line, and consequently in the later
plays stood at variance with the endings of the blank verse.

In blank verse Shakespeare showed an ever increasing predilec-
tion for enjambed or run-on lines. In his couplets, as might be expected, there is a much smaller percentage of enjambed lines; as
the table in Appendix C indicates, the number increases slightly
in the later plays.[14] There are comparatively few run-on couplets
indicated in the table, but that is natural since the couplets under
consideration are all couplets which conclude a speech or a part
of a scene. Occasionally, when a line follows the rhyme-pair, the
sense is run on into this third line. This happens in none of the
earliest plays and only once in the latest, though it occurs several

---

11. Rushton (*Shakespeare and 'The Arte of English Poesie'* [Liverpool, 1909])
shows that certain of the figures described by Puttenham occur in Shakespeare's
work, and thus maintains·that the playwright had studied *The Arte of English
Poesie*.

12. See Sir George Young, pp. 106, 149.

13. The definition of light and weak endings which I have used in this study is
the one given by the Tests Committee of the St. Petersburg Shakspere Circle, p.
482. *Cf.* John K. Ingram, pp. 442–64.

14. In general the line is considered to be run-on or enjambed only when a mark
of punctuation concludes it. Occasionally, however, there is such a clear phrase-
pause as to justify its being considered end-stopped despite the absence of punctuation. *Cf.* George Saintsbury, II, 6; R. M. Alden, p. 438.

times in plays of the middle periods. This increase might be interpreted as indicating that Shakespeare's heroic couplet was, as Schipper asserted, growing freer along with the blank verse. If there were no run-on couplets in the early plays and a great many of them in the late, then one might assume a development toward a more flexible couplet. Since neither of these conditions is met, however, Saintsbury's comment on the Elizabethan couplet in general seems to apply to Shakespeare: "In the uncertainty of the Elizabethan grasp of the couplet—in the veering and yawing between the stopped and enjambed forms which is the evident result, not of a designed combination of the two, but of an irresolute and unclear grasp of either—there is evidence that the prosodic mind was not made up about it."[15]

In the problem comedies and later tragedies it is somewhat more common than in the early plays to find some words of the first line of the couplet a syntactic part of the preceding lines. Such a couplet is Hamlet's

> The play's the thing
> Wherein I'll catch the conscience of the King.[16]

This division of the first line, of course, disrupts the regular two-line pattern of the heroic couplet and is therefore a tendency toward freedom; but the effect is really not one of freedom. As Granville-Barker has observed, every section of the soliloquy which this couplet concludes ends in mid-line, thus minimizing the pause and keeping the speech whole. This couplet represents really the first definite full stop, and thus is "a musical full close."[17]

The metrically irregular lines indicated on the chart have little significance, for the majority of them, as Heuser demonstrates in "Der Coupletreim in Shakespeare's dramen," result from some mutilation of the text. It occasionally happens that Shakespeare will give his couplet a short first line, as in this exit rhyme from *The Merchant of Venice:*

> Fast bind, fast find;
> A proverb never stale in thrifty mind.[18]

15. ɪɪ, 203. It must be noted, however, that certain passages of consecutive iambic pentameter couplets in the late plays display a high number of run-on couplets. Time's speech in *The Winter's Tale* (ɪᴠ. i. 1–32) contains twelve out of sixteen; and the prologue and epilogue to *Henry VIII*, seven out of twenty-three. The consecutive heroic couplets in *Macbeth* contain six out of twelve. But these are all suspect passages. In *Lear* there is only one in twenty-two.

16. *Ham.* ɪɪ. ii. 633–4.

17. *Prefaces to Shakespeare* (London, 1927), ɪɪɪ, 233.

18. ɪɪ. v. 54–5.

More rarely he uses a short second line.[19] Any other metrical eccentricity in the heroic line may be interpreted more safely as a flaw in the text than as licence on the part of the playwright.

The rhyme in Shakespeare's rhymed heroic couplets follows generally a rather rigid pattern, for just as most of the lines end on a strong word, so most of the rhymes are masculine, concluding the line on the stressed syllable. Charles Bathurst thought Shakespeare particularly fond of double rhymes, what he calls the Italian as opposed to the French mode of rhyming;[20] but Shakespeare was not fond of this rhyme, especially not in his heroic couplets. Occasionally the couplet contains a single rhyme upon the hypermetrical, weak termination, a method of rhyming with which Wyatt experimented but which has never gained any popularity among English poets.[21] Shakespeare seems not to use it for any particular effect. The same can be said for the rather rare cases where a hypermetrical syllable makes an approximate rhyme with an accented or masculine ending, a characteristic device of both Peele and Dekker.[22]

For the most part Shakespeare's rhymes are single and on the stressed final syllable, with a preponderance of monosyllabic rhymed words. As Young says, "The exigency of rime, in the scarcity of words accented on other than the last syllable but one, led to the prevalence of a monosyllabic ending."[23] Double rhymes, not infrequent in passages of doggerel, appear occasionally in isolated heroic couplets, usually for a comic effect. It is very unusual to find such a rhyme used in a serious play for a serious effect, though the Duke's advice to Brabantio in *Othello*[24] "is rendered more emphatic by being a double rhyme."[25]

If Shakespeare had used many feminine endings in his heroic couplets, it could be said that his couplets were leaning toward a more flexible form; for the feminine ending leads naturally to the run-on line. But the heroic couplets examined here show very few such rhymes. It might be added that the increase in feminine endings in the blank verse was held by Fleay to be in direct ratio to the decrease in rhyme; but, as Hermann Isaac pointed out, this is not true.[26]

19. *Hen. VIII* I. ii. 213–14.   20. pp. 159–60.
21. See Young, p. 110.
22. Examples of such irregular rhymes are noted in Appendix B.
23. p. 149.   24. I. iii. 202–03.
25. Hiram Corson, p. 90. *Cf.* J. M. Robertson, *Did Shakespeare Write "Titus Andronicus"?* (London, 1905), pp. 191–2.
26. "Die Hamlet-periode in Shakesperes leben," *Archiv für das studium der neueren sprachen und literaturen* LXXIII (1885), 176.

Some of the foregoing remarks may seem to indicate that Shakespeare's heroic couplet, in its failure to follow the blank verse toward freedom of form, was moving in the other direction, that is, toward the neo-classical couplet. The marked medial caesura and the ascendancy of the strong ending with masculine rhyme are characteristics of the Popean couplet, but they are also characteristics of the English closed couplet from the time it originated as "a naturalization of the Latin elegiac distich."[27] The couplet becomes neo-classical in nature when it shows along with such metrical characteristics a style which is predominantly epigrammatic,[28] that is, when the arrangement of the words and development of the thought consistently fall into such rhetorical pattern as parallelism and balance, inversion, and antithesis and contrast. The neo-classical couplet contains these rhetorical devices in great abundance. The Elizabethan heroic couplet in general contains them, just as its classical model contains them. In Shakespeare's couplets these devices are an occasional embellishment, not the common pattern.

Numerically, the lines containing balance or parallelism are the most striking. F. G. Hubbard, speaking of Elizabethan dramatic verse in general, said, "The nearer the play is to Seneca the more repetition and parallelism it has."[29] In Shakespeare's heroic couplets, however, the parallelism as well as the repetition seems not to follow this generalization, for some of the most Senecan plays show comparatively few lines of parallelism or repetition. Then too, the early plays contain as much as the later ones, and there is comparatively little change in the nature of these rhetorical devices from the time of Shakespeare's apprenticeship to his full mastery of his craft. For example, the following couplet from *1 Henry VI*,

> God and Saint George, Talbot and England's right,
> Prosper our colours in this dangerous fight![30]

has the same balance in the first line and between the first and second lines as this couplet from *1 Henry IV*:

> Harry to Harry shall, hot horse to horse,
> Meet and ne'er part till one drop down a corse.[31]

27. Ruth Wallerstein, p. 166.
28. George Williamson, "The Rhetorical Pattern of Neo-Classical Wit," *Modern Philology* XXXIII (1935–36), 61.
29. "Repetition and Parallelism in the Earlier Elizabethan Drama," *PMLA* XX (1905), 369.
30. IV. ii. 55–6.   31. IV. i. 122–3.

And in *Timon of Athens* the following couplet, though it is some-what more flexible than most of the couplets around it, shows a similar balance:

> Make war breed peace, make peace stint war, make each
> Prescribe to other as each other's leech.[32]

This last example uses the balance as a reinforcement of the antithesis between "war" and "peace," and is in many respects characteristic of Shakespeare's antithetical couplets; for antithesis implies balance. The couplets which have any marked stylistic structure show a rather high percentage of antithesis, and many of the antithetical couplets are almost indistinguishable from the pure neo-classical couplet. Often the antithesis is limited to one line—as in the following, to the second line:

> To end a tale of length,
> Troy in our weakness stands, not in her strength.[33]

Occasionally there is antithesis in the first line:

> Let me, if not by birth, have lands by wit:
> All with me's meet that I can fashion fit.[34]

It is characteristic also to have a gnomic or semi-gnomic comment for the second line when there is antithesis in the first.[35] And fi-nally there is antithesis between the two lines of the couplet, as in the following couplet from *Henry V*:

> What say you? will you yield, and this avoid,
> Or, guilty in defence, be thus destroy'd?[36]

Quite frequently the antithesis in a couplet is enforced by some other stylistic device. Common among such devices is inversion, which was later to become one of the prime characteristics of the neo-classical couplet. In such a couplet as this from *King Lear* the inversion seems to sharpen the contrast within the line and even to point a certain opposition in the rhyme words:

> Time shall unfold what plighted cunning hides;
> Who covers faults, at last shame them derides.[37]

Inversion is used, of course, even when there is no antithetical relationship in the thought-structure of the couplet, sometimes

---

32. v. iv. 83–4.
33. *T. C.* i. iii. 136–7. *Cf. T. C.* v. iv. 108–09.
34. *Lear* i. ii. 199–200.
35. *Rich. II* ii. iv. 23–4.
36. iii. iii. 42–3. *Cf. Per.* i. ii. 99–100.
37. i. i. 283–4. *Cf. A. W.* ii. i. 126–7; *A. C.* i. iii. 64–5.

with the purpose of placing a particular word in a position of emphasis. Thus one might say that the inversion in this couplet from *Timon of Athens* is used to place the verb in the strongest position in the line:

> And with their faint reply this answer join;
> Who bates mine honour shall not know my coin.[38]

And similarly in Romeo's dying speech inversion is used to throw the major emphasis upon the word "die."[39] Elsewhere, however, there seems to be no justification for the inversion other than the necessity of completing the rhyme.

Another device used often by Shakespeare to sharpen the antithesis in the couplet is alliteration, and this not merely in the early dramas, where he was particularly prone to indulge in word play. A good example from an early play is the following couplet from *2 Henry VI:*

> Sword, hold thy temper; heart, be wrathful still.
> Priests pray for enemies, but princes kill.[40]

A close parallel from a late play are these words of the Third Senator in *Timon of Athens:*

> In, and prepare;
> Ours is the fall, I fear; our foes' the snare.[41]

Though in general repetition and word play purely for their own sake left Shakespeare's verse as his early poetic exuberance gave way to a more mature dramatic instinct, the heroic couplet retains many of these stylistic elaborations. In *Timon of Athens* he makes use of the device which Puttenham calls Traductio, or the tranlacer:[42]

> I will say of it,
> It tutors nature. Artificial strife
> Lives in these touches, livelier than life.[43]

Here the implied contrast is rendered more effective, though more artificial, by the play on the word "life." Internal rhyme, such as in this couplet from *Romeo and Juliet,* is not uncommon:

> But that a joy past joy calls out on me,
> It were a grief, so brief to part with thee;[44]

38. iii. iii. 25–6. *Cf. Oth.* v. ii. 370–1. 39. v. iii. 119–20.
40. v. ii. 70–1.   41. v. ii. 16–17.
42. p. 170.   43. i. i. 37–8.
44. iii. iii. 173–4. *Cf.* Guest, p. 127.

and akin to this are the several examples of Puttenham's Re-
bounde: "A young man married is a man that's marr'd."[45] Repetition appears in various forms in the couplets. Sometimes it is the
immediate repetition of the word in the line (Epizeuxis);[46] sometimes the repetition has a word between (Ploche). When this second type appears in the middle of the line it creates a nice balance: "We scorn her most when most she offers blows."[47] In this
couplet from *Troilus and Cressida* there is fourfold repetition:

> Half heart, half hand, half Hector comes to seek
> This blended knight, half Troyan and half Greek.[48]

Another stylistic device not uncommon in Shakespeare's heroic
couplets is the device which Puttenham called Brachiologa, or the
cutted comma.[49] A good example is this couplet from *Love's Labour's Lost:*

> Well, I will love, write, sigh, pray, sue, groan:
> Some men must love my lady, and some Joan.[50]

It is by no means limited to the early plays.

Shakespeare's couplets, accordingly, have the rhetorical features which are later to assume significant proportions in the neo-
classical couplet. These features are particularly noticeable in the
couplets whose contents are sententious, a fact which substan-
tiates Williamson's statement that the neo-classical couplet "is
foreshadowed in the sententious development of the couplet in
the Elizabethan sonnet and play, or in the Jacobean epigram."[51]
Balance, parallelism, antithesis, inversion, and repetition are to be
found in Shakespeare's heroic couplets, early or late, and along
with them still other stylistic devices; but as the table in Appendix
C indicates, these devices cannot be considered major characteristics. They are still, with Shakespeare, embellishments rather
than principal stylistic patterns.

They do, however, suggest formalization and even restraint. In
general antithesis and balance were used in the early plays with
somewhat more regard to sound than to sense, but there is no
marked difference between the late and the early couplets. Shakespeare's heroic couplets cannot be said to share in the movement
toward freedom which the blank verse enjoyed. Although in the

45. *A. W.* II. iii. 315.   46. *Rich. II* III. ii. 71; *R. J.* IV. i. 67.
47. *A. C.* III. xi. 74.   48. IV. v. 85–6.
49. p. 178.
50. III. i. 206–07. Cf. *1 Hen. VI* IV. iii. 52–3; *Tim.* I. ii. 131–3.
51. p. 64.

early plays he was somewhat more prodigal of his effects, using the couplet with less discrimination, the basic structure of the couplet underwent little or no change. With the blank verse becoming more free and with the couplet remaining static, the contrast between the two mediums of expression became sharper; consequently the couplet tended to be reserved for places where the contrast was needed to produce some special effect.

VI

Conclusion

THERE have been many attempts to explain Shakespeare's gradual disuse of rhyme. Malone's suggestion that the playwright, as his taste matured, came to feel the inherent impropriety of rhyme in drama, or, as Malone rephrased it, that Shakespeare felt rhyme to be a form of bondage and thus grew weary of it,[1] received many followers.[2] Hertzberg maintained that this bondage was made doubly grievous because when rhyme was used the blank verse had to move in a more precise and fixed measure in order not to contrast too sharply.[3] Other critics have attempted a more mathematical interpretation of the tendency away from restriction and toward freedom by declaring that rhyme decreased in direct proportion to the increase of double or feminine endings and run-on lines,[4] which is virtually the same as saying rhyme disappeared with the increased mastery of blank verse.[5] It has also been suggested that a strong public distaste for rhyme and a marked abandonment of rhyme by Shakespeare's fellow playwrights influenced his use,[6] and even that the new king's dislike of rhyme led to Shakespeare's disuse of it.[7]

Similarly varied are the explanations for its continued use. Certain critics, thinking that Shakespeare could not possibly have continued using rhyme, suggest that other hands are responsible for much of it in the later plays.[8] Some of the rhyme is said to be the remains of source material,[9] or again of early versions of the playwright's own work which he revised for a new production.[10]

1. See above, p. 1.
2. *Cf.* Richard Grant White, *Studies in Shakespeare* (New York, 1886), p. 17; *N. S. S. Trans.* I, 31; Sidney Lanier, *Shakspere*, II, 245; Anna Kerrl, p. 122.
3. pp. 251–2.
4. R. Boyle, "Blank Verse and Metrical Tests," pp. 442–3; but see W. Wilke, p. 514.
5. T. M. Parrot, *William Shakespeare: A Handbook* (New York, 1934), p. 242; Hiram Corson, p. 68.
6. See above, p. 21. 7. J. W. Draper, p. 39.
8. D. L. Chambers, pp. 20–1. 9. E. H. C. Oliphant, pp. 190–9.
10. W. A. Neilson and A. H. Thorndike, *The Facts about Shakespeare* (New York, 1933), p. 73.

Or it is said to be used only for the taste of the pit.[11] More sympathetic views state that it is used because the lyrical character of the play demands it,[12] that it does not linger merely because it is a stage tradition but because it serves certain very special purposes.[13]

It has been the chief purpose of this study to reject some of these explanations, to refine upon others, and to show that no single one is adequate. The conclusions reached may be summarized as follows:

Little can be gained from a study of the contemporary attitude toward rhyme in general or from the comments on rhyme in Shakespeare's plays, for though rhyme seemed somewhat in disfavor among many of Shakespeare's contemporaries, there is nothing to indicate that it was not acceptable as an occasional embellishment for certain dramatic effects. Moreover, a study of contemporary plays, chosen to represent major and minor writers, the different dramatic companies, and the several types of drama popular on the public stage, does not reveal any marked diminution in the use of rhyme during Shakespeare's dramatic career.

The explanation for the change in Shakespeare's use of rhyme lies within and depends upon the effect which rhyme produces in the different positions in which it is commonly used.

At the end of speeches the rhyme in the early plays served often as an additional embellishment to a highly stylized passage. As Shakespeare lost some of his youthful exuberance for the mere sound of words, he learned to reserve this speech-end rhyme for special effects and to coördinate it better with the rest of the speech. The most common of these effects was derived from the natural tendency of the heroic couplet to become a medium for formal argumentation. Since formal argumentation was appropriate to only certain plays, this use of rhyme was limited. Then too, the increase of broken speech-ends in Shakespeare's blank verse tended to eliminate rhyme.

The speech-pause and speech-beginning rhymes disappear for somewhat the same reason. In several of the early plays, and even in a few of the later, when a sharply punctuated style is needed, Shakespeare occasionally uses a rhyme to mark a strong pause within a speech. This destroys the unity of the speech, however,

11. A. W. Pollard, Introduction to Peter Alexander, *Shakespeare's Henry VI and Richard III* (Cambridge, 1929), p. 27.
12. Jakob Schipper, *A History of English Versification*, p. 225.
13. J. W. Hales, *N. S. S. Trans.* I, 25.

by breaking it in the middle and weakening the emphasis of the end. As Shakespeare came to think of the speech more in terms of the entire unit, such interruptions are less frequent. The rhyme at the beginning of a speech likewise seems to draw the emphasis away from the end, the most important part of the speech, and thus is not compatible with the proclivity of the heroic couplet to lend itself to formal argument. Never very popular with Shakespeare, when such a use of rhyme appears in the later plays it seems to have little relation with the speech as a whole but is used to emphasize its own content.

The speech-link rhyme is limited mostly to plays where the effect of clever repartee is desired, and often uses stichomythia or appears in a doggerel measure. Like stichomythia, this speech-link rhyme seems to have been considered artificial by Shakespeare and is held in reserve after the early plays. The doggerel measure appears in some of the mature pieces, but possibly only as a hangover of an early version of the play. Doggerel enjoyed general ill repute, and was used very seldom by Shakespeare's fellow playwrights or by Shakespeare himself after his early works.

In the single-speech rhyme there is a fluctuation rather than a diminution. Because of its characteristic uses in asides and particularly for gnomic utterances, it occurs as often in late plays as in early, varying according to the tone of the play.

Exit and cue rhymes, by throwing particular attention upon the characters concerned in the action, result usually in a pause in the action. Where such a pause is out of keeping with the general movement of the scene or where the exit and entrance are relatively unimportant, such a rhyme is inappropriate. A glance at his unrhymed exit speeches shows that Shakespeare learned to use exits more gracefully as he advanced in dramatic power, to make them not so much a special event as the natural outgrowth of the action. Since rhyme emphasizes the exit or entrance, it accordingly came to be reserved for only special occasions.

The scene- and act-end rhyme varies in the different plays but does not diminish until the very latest plays. By rounding off the action of the scene, by indicating the stage of development of the plot, or by creating suspense through anticipating later events in the play, the rhyme here seemed to compensate for the probable lack of a curtain and to indicate the important shift in the action. The rhyme, therefore, is not so much a cue to the actor as to the audience, and Shakespeare was inclined to continue this practice because of the exigencies of the Elizabethan stage.

Passages of consecutive rhyme vary in the early plays according to the atmosphere of the play. A general tone of lyricism seems usually to inspire frequent use of long rhymed passages. The disappearance of such passages resulted probably from these conditions: a distaste for rhyme in more complicated stanzaic forms, the development from a lyrical to a dramatic medium, the shift from doggerel to prose for lively comic dialogue, and the mastery of a flexible blank verse to convey complex emotional states.

It is wrong to say that the disappearance of rhyme was regular, that it followed a fixed rate of decline. As the foregoing summary indicates, Shakespeare came to reserve rhyme for particular effects. Where the play seemed to require these effects, there the rhyme was used, whether the play was written in 1600 or in 1610. The particular effects were heightened, moreover, by the fact that, while Shakespeare's blank verse advanced rapidly toward freedom of form, his heroic couplet remained static and unchanging.

It is wrong to say further that in his practice of rhyme Shakespeare adopted and followed a consistent plan. Like a skilful craftsman he availed himself of all the tools of his trade. When he had mastered a better tool for a certain task he seldom reached for the old; yet where the old could well perform the task he did not hesitate to use it. Dramatist and poet, he was sensitive to both the advantages and disadvantages of rhyme, and consequently in its use exercised a freedom licensed by understanding.

APPENDICES

Appendix A. List of Supplementary Plays

THE following is the list of plays by Shakespeare's immediate predecessors and contemporaries which have been examined for their use of rhyme. Since no attempt has been made in this investigation to get more than approximate figures and thus to discover general tendencies, no statistical information is given here. The general results of the investigation are summarized in Chapter III.

For the sake of consistency the following dates of plays are, whenever possible, those given in Henry W. Wells, *A Chronological List of Extant Plays Produced in or about London 1581–1642* (New York, 1940); they are the dates of production, not of publication, for only the former can be of particular value to this study. Questionable dates are indicated by an asterisk.

The Arraignment of Paris, G. Peele, 1584.*
The Famous Victories of Henry the Fifth, anon., 1586.*
Tamburlaine, C. Marlowe, 1587.*
Endymion, J. Lyly, 1588.
Doctor Faustus, C. Marlowe, 1588.*
Friar Bacon and Friar Bungay, R. Greene, 1589.*
The Spanish Tragedy, T. Kyd, 1589.*
The Jew of Malta, C. Marlowe, 1589.*
The Battle of Alcazar, G. Peele, 1589.*
The Taming of a Shrew, anon., 1589.*
The Troublesome Reign of King John, anon., 1590.*
The True Tragedy of Richard the Third, anon., 1590.*
James the Fourth, R. Greene, 1591.*
Edward the First, G. Peele, 1591.*
The Four Prentices of London, T. Heywood, 1592.*
Edward the Second, C. Marlowe, 1592.*
George a Greene, the Pinner of Wakefield, anon., 1592.*
The Cobbler's Prophecy, R. Wilson, 1592.*
Leire, anon., 1592.*
Selimus, anon., 1592.*
The Woman in the Moon, J. Lyly, 1593.*
Dido Queen of Carthage, C. Marlowe and T. Nashe, 1593.*
David and Bethsabe, G. Peele, 1593.*
The Old Wives Tale, G. Peele, 1593.*

A Knack to Know an Honest Man, anon., 1594.
The Blind Beggar of Alexandria, G. Chapman, 1596.
Two Lamentable Tragedies, R. Yarington, 1597.*
Englishmen for My Money, W. Haughton, 1598.
Every Man in His Humour, B. Jonson, 1598.
The Shoemaker's Holiday, T. Dekker, 1599.
Every Man Out of His Humour, B. Jonson, 1599.
Antonio and Mellida, J. Marston, 1599.
Look About You, anon., 1599.
Cynthia's Revels, B. Jonson, 1600.
The Poetaster, B. Jonson, 1601.
The Pilgrimage to and Return from Parnassus, anon., 1601.
The Royal King and the Loyal Subject, T. Heywood, 1602.
A Woman Killed with Kindness, T. Heywood, 1603.
Sejanus, B. Jonson, 1603.
Bussy D'Ambois, G. Chapman, 1604.
Philotas, S. Daniel, 1604.
The Wise Woman of Hogsdon, T. Heywood, 1604.
The Malcontent, J. Marston and J. Webster, 1604.
Eastward Ho! G. Chapman, B. Jonson, and J. Marston, 1605.
If You Know Not Me, You Know Nobody, T. Heywood, Part I, 1605;
    Part II, 1606.
The Woman Hater, F. Beaumont and J. Fletcher, 1606.
Volpone, B. Jonson, 1606.
The Tragedy of Julius Caesar's Revenge, anon., 1606.
The Tragedy of Tiberius, anon, 1607.
Cupid's Revenge, F. Beaumont and J. Fletcher, 1608.
Appius and Virginia, J. Webster, 1608.*
Philaster, F. Beaumont and J. Fletcher, 1609.
The Faithful Shepherdess, J. Fletcher, 1609.
The Coxcomb, F. Beaumont, J. Fletcher, and P. Massinger, 1609.
The Knight of the Burning Pestle, F. Beaumont, 1610.
The White Devil, J. Webster, 1610.*
The Insatiate Countess, J. Marston and W. Barksteed, 1610.*
The Captain, F. Beaumont and J. Fletcher, 1611.
A King and No King, F. Beaumont and J. Fletcher, 1611.
The Maid's Tragedy, F. Beaumont and J. Fletcher, 1611.
The Second Maiden's Tragedy, anon., 1611.
The Honest Man's Fortune, J. Fletcher, 1613.
The Duchess of Malfi, J. Webster, 1613.

Appendix B. Classified List of Shakespeare's Rhymes

IN the following pages are listed by act, scene, and line the rhymes in Shakespeare's plays, exclusive of the rhyme in songs. No attempt has been made to differentiate the rhymes on the basis of the metrical line; in general, unless otherwise indicated, the metre is iambic pentameter. Nor has any attempt been made to distinguish between the couplet or other patterns of rhyme. Metrical peculiarities are noted and references given to Julius Heuser's "Der Coupletreim in Shakespeare's dramen," a work which deals primarily with abnormalities in the rhymed lines; or, in cases where Heuser's work necessitates some supplement, to other critical works.

Where a rhyme is not an exact one according to modern pronunciation it has been verified by reference to Alexander J. Ellis, *On Early English Pronunciation with Especial Reference to Shakspere and Chaucer* (London, 1871), vol. III;[1] Wilhelm Viëtor, *A Shakespeare Phonology, with a Rime-Index to the Poems as a Pronouncing Vocabulary* (London, 1906); Henry Cecil Wyld, *Studies in English Rhymes from Surrey to Pope* (London, 1923); or whatever other phonological work the particular case demands. This treatment has been given all rhymes not in consecutive passages or listed as unintentional. An asterisk after the line number indicates that a line follows in the same speech.

The following division of the rhymes has been observed:[2]
Speech-end rhyme. When a rhyme at the end of a speech accompanies an exit or entrance, or occurs at the end of a scene or act, it is not listed here.
Speech-pause rhyme. Since this classification is here proposed for the first time, the rhymes have been very carefully weighed before being accepted as intentional. Doubtful cases are so indicated.
Speech-beginning rhyme. The couplets in this classification are difficult at times to justify. Though many of them may be unintentional, if the rhyme is a strong one, if there are other rhymes in the scene, and if the couplet seems to emphasize its content, it is counted here.
Speech-link rhyme.
Single-speech rhyme. Here are included mainly those rhymes which

1. Hereafter, except when otherwise indicated, all references to Ellis will be to this book.
2. For a further description of these divisions, see pp. 25–6.

stand in an isolated position among blank-verse or prose lines and which contain the total words of a single speaker.

Scene- and act-end rhymes. These are grouped together, for they perform an identical function.

Exit and cue rhymes. Exit rhymes are, of course, often similar to scene- or act-end rhymes and must have been so considered by Shakespeare. Cue rhymes either herald the entrance of an actor or group of actors or are a cue for some action on or off the stage. In the latter case the couplet has usually been listed elsewhere.

Consecutive rhyme. Since in a passage of consecutive rhyme peculiarities in the sound likeness between two words cannot cast doubt upon the intention of the rhyme, little cognizance is taken of the matter of pronunciation which in the isolated rhymes is often necessary to establish the validity of the couplet. There are, to be sure, some questionable rhymes in these consecutive passages, but it is not the purpose of this study to examine Shakespeare's pronunciation any more than is necessary to test the authenticity of certain dubious rhymes.

This classification includes many exit rhymes, scene- and act-end rhymes, and the like, for in a passage of consecutive rhyme these can have little individual weight.

External rhyme. This group consists of such rhymed passages as do not belong to the dialogue. Prologues, epilogues, choruses, and inductions are listed here, as are masques and plays within plays. It might be argued that rhymed letters, scrolls, epitaphs, and the like, should be included here also; but it seems better to consider them an integral part of the dramatic dialogue.

Accidental rhyme. All the rhymes listed here show a sound likeness which is above question, but because they fail to meet other requirements they are discarded from the classifications of intentional rhymes. Because it is impracticable to discuss all such rhymes individually, this general basis of selection is offered: a rhyme outside of a consecutively rhymed passage or otherwise heavily rhymed scene is considered accidental (1) if it does not appear in one of the strong positions of rhyme, such as speech-end, exit- or cue-lines, scene- or act-end; (2) if it is what might be called a weak rhyme, that is, the rhyme in such words as *majesty-embassy, me-thee,* sounds which are of frequent recurrence;[3] (3) if the lines do not follow the normal rhetorical pattern of the Shakespearian couplet. Exceptions are discussed individually.

1 HENRY VI

28 lines of speech-end rhyme: I. i. 143–4, 155–6; I. ii. 91–2; II. iv. 17–18, 57–8, 126–7; II. v. 15–16*; IV. iii. 28–9, 37–8; IV. iv. 8–9, 38–9; IV. vii. 89–90; V. ii. 19–20*; V. v. 77–8.

3. Because of their frequency and because it would be vain to attempt a selection, such weak rhymes are not even listed here.

II. iv. 126–7. This couplet gains a double justification by the prophecy which it states. Similarly IV. iv. 38–9.

IV. vii. 89–90. For a discussion of the rhyme see Heuser, pp. 235–6.

v. ii. 19–20 might plausibly be considered a scene-end couplet, since the single line following brings the action to a close.

8 lines of speech-pause rhyme: II. v. 8–9, 118–19; IV. i. 16–17; v. iii. 58–9.

II. v. 118–19. This might possibly be an aside, though it is not so marked. Richard, after having spoken a kind of epitaph over the dead Mortimer, addresses this couplet to his own soul before turning to the Gaolers with the rest of the speech.

6 lines of rhyme at speech-beginnings: I. i. 33–4; I. ii. 13–14; II. i. 72–3.

24 lines of speech-link rhyme: I. iii. 43–6, 52–5; II. iii. 59–60; II. iv. 68–9; IV. iii. 30–3; IV. v. 11–12; v. iii. 85–6, 108–09, 115–16.

I. iii. 45–6 do not actually link speeches, but merely continue the rhyme. Similarly I. iii. 54–5 and IV. iii. 32–3.

IV. v. 11–12: *gone-son.* Cf. *V. A. gone-one,* 227, 520, 1071.

v. iii. 108–09. See Heuser, pp. 237–8, for a discussion of the irregularities of these lines.

8 lines of single-speech rhyme: II. ii. 57–8; III. i. 184–5; IV. vii. 92–3; v. ii. 16–17.

III. i. 184–5. An exit follows the next speech.

IV. vii. 92–3. See Heuser, p. 237, for a discussion of the irregularities in these lines. The couplet contains a prophecy.

v. ii. 16–17: *there-fear.* See Ellis, p. 965.

26 lines of scene- or act-end rhyme: I. i. 176–7; I. iii. 90–1; I. vi. 30–1; II. iv. 133–4; II. v. 128–9; III. ii. 136–7; IV. i. 193–4; IV. ii. 55–6; IV. iii. 52–3; IV. iv. 45–6; IV. vii. 95–6; v. i. 59–62.

I. iii. 90–1: *bear-year.* Cf. *T. A.* III. v. 38–9 and see Ellis, p. 964.

II. iv. 133–4 contains a prophecy. Cf. IV. vii. 92–3.

II. v. 128–9: *blood-good.* See Ellis, p. 961.

III. ii. 136–7: *die-misery.* Cf. *C. E.* IV. ii. 2–4.

v. i. 59–62 consists of four lines, all ending with the same vowel sound.

6 lines of exit and cue rhyme: I. i. 87–8; I. ii. 20–1; IV. ii. 37–8; (v. iii. 58–9).

I. i. 87–8: *eyes-miseries.* Cf. *eyes-infamies, R. L.* 637–8.

I. ii. 20–1. For a detailed discussion of this couplet see Heuser, pp. 238–9. Though the first and second lines are separated by considerable stage action, it seems to be used as an exit rhyme.

IV. ii. 37–8 also contains a prophecy.

(v. iii. 58–9). Although there is no exit here, this couplet, listed above under speech-pause rhyme, probably originally replaced the stage cue: *She is going. Cf.* Heuser, p. 235.

156 lines of consecutive rhyme: I. ii. 113–16; IV. iii. 39–46; IV. v. 16–55; IV. vi. 2–57; IV. vii. 1–32, 35–50.

IV. v. 16–55 consists of the rather melodramatic debate between Old Talbot and his son. The emotional tone is meant to be powerful and intense, and the sudden shift from blank verse to rhyme in line 16 may indicate a deepening of feeling as the argument gets under way. Actually this entire scene has little value to the plot and could easily be omitted. *Cf.* IV. vi. 2–57; IV. vii. 1–32, 35–50. Since these Talbot scenes are so full of rhyme, it might well be supposed that they were written by the same hand.

2 lines of accidental rhyme: I. ii. 130–1.

Total lines of rhyme: 264.

2 HENRY VI

20 lines of speech-end rhyme: II. i. 75–6, 196–9; II. iii. 30–1, 43–4; III. i. 264–5, 300–01, 325–6; IV. ii. 152–3*; IV. x. 24–5.

III. i. 264–5. The rhyme here is identical, but the position of the couplet, as well as the gnomic content, justify its being considered as rhyme.

III. i. 325–6. See Heuser, p. 240, for a scansion designed to rid 326 of its seeming Alexandrine.

4 lines of speech-pause rhyme: III. i. 202–03; IV. x. 20–1.

4 lines of speech-beginning rhyme: II. i. 190–1; IV. ii. 192–3.

II. i. 190–1. The rhyme here follows a couplet in the previous speech and emphasizes Gloucester's defence.

8 lines of speech-link rhyme: II. i. 161–2; III. i. 243–4; IV. iv. 24–5; v. ii. 72–3.

4 lines of single-speech rhyme: II. i. 188–9; II. iii. 45–6.

II. iii. 45–6 contains a striking simile. *Cf. 1 Hen. VI* II. v. 8–9.

18 lines of scene- or act-end rhyme: I. i. 258–9; I. ii. 106–07; II. i. 204–05; III. i. 382–3; III. ii. 411–12; v. i. 213–16; v. ii. 88–9*; v. iii. 32–3.

II. i. 204–05 is possibly also the cue for an off-stage flourish.

26 lines of exit and cue rhyme: I. i. 145–6, 170–1, 212–13; II. i. 163–4; II. iii. 33–8; III. i. 193–4, 221–2; III. ii. 298–9; IV. iv. 47–8; v. ii. 29–30, 70–1.

I. i. 145–6: *gone-long*. Though this is not an exact rhyme, both the position and the content force one to agree with Walker (*A Critical Examination of the Text of Shakespeare* [London, 1860], I, 137) that "the place seems to require rhyme."
I. i. 170–1: *delay-presently*. Cf. Ellis, p. 954.
III. i. 193–4: *were-fear*. Cf. *were-appear*, *R. L.* 631.
III. i. 221–2: *groan-none*. Cf. Viëtor, p. 233.

4 lines of unintentional rhyme: IV. i. 77–8; IV. vii. 105–06.

Total lines of rhyme: 88.

3 HENRY VI

28 couplets to mark speech-ends: I. iv. 107–08; II. i. 187–8; II. ii. 173–4; II. iii. 46–7; III. iii. 19–20, 36–7, 127–8; IV. iii. 5–6; IV. iv. 14–15, 23–4; IV. vi. 30–1, 43–4, 97–8; IV. viii. 60–1.

IV. iv. 14–15. Queen Elizabeth's reply begins with a line which rhymes with this couplet. While this may be unintentional, a similar linking of speeches by means of rhyme is not unusual in the early plays. Cf. *C. E.* I. ii. 51–3.

14 lines of speech-pause couplets: I. iv. 71–2, 97–8; II. i. 123–4; II. v. 10–11, 19–20; IV. vi. 14–17.

2 lines beginning a speech: III. iii. 163–4.

11 lines of speech-link rhyme: I. iii. 47–8; III. ii. 74–5, 107–10; IV. iv. 16; v. v. 39–40.

I. iii. 47–8 and v. v. 39–40 accompany stabbings and deaths. Cf. *J. C.* v. iii. 89–90; *T. C.* v. viii. 9–10; *Oth.* v. ii. 358–9.
IV. iv. 16. This line forms a triplet with a speech-end couplet. Cf. *C. E.* I. ii. 53.

8 lines of single-speech rhyme: II. ii. 61–2; IV. i. 104–05, 110–11; IV. vii. 74–5.

II. ii. 61–2 accompanies the formal ceremony of knighthood. *Cf. John*
I. i. 161–2.

IV. i. 104–05, 110–11 might both be considered speech-end couplets.
They have such a distinctly separate identity, however, that they have
been included here. The second couplet is a literal repetition of Warwick's words in III. iii. 231–2.

IV. vii. 74–5. *Cf. T. C.* I. iii. 287–90.

26 lines of scene- or act-end rhyme: II. ii. 176–7; III. ii. 194–5; III.
iii. 264–5; IV. i. 148–9; IV. iv. 34–5; IV. v. 28–9; IV. vi. 99–102; IV.
vii. 87–8; v. i. 112–13; v. vi. 90–3; v. vii. 45–6.

II. ii. 176–7 also contains a prophecy.
v. i. 112–13: *way-victory. Cf. key-may, M. V.* II. vii. 59–60.

26 lines of exit and cue rhyme: II. v. 121–2, 123–4; II. vi. 29–30;
III. iii. 42–3, 231–2,* 254–5; IV. iii. 58–9; IV. vi. 75–6, 87–8; IV.
vii. 38–9; v. ii. 3–4, 27–8; v. v. 81–2.

II. v. 123–4: *care-are. Cf.* Ellis, p. 964.
III. iii. 42–3 is identical rhyme.
v. v. 81–2: *hence-prince. Cf.* Ellis, p. 958.

10 lines of unintentional rhyme: I. i. 223–4; I. ii. 70–1; II. i. 117–18;
IV. i. 133–4; IV. viii. 29–30.

Total lines of rhyme: 125.

RICHARD III

24 lines of speech-end couplets: I. i. 39–40,* 99–100, 136–7; II. iv.
14–15; IV. i. 51–2, 96–7; IV. iv. 114–15, 122–3, 130–1, 209–10,
395–6, 416–17.

I. i. 39–40 might rightly be considered a cue rhyme, for the next line
speaks of the entrance of Clarence. It is such an organic part of the
long Senecan soliloquy which it concludes, however, that it is listed
here.

I. i. 136–7. This is one of the relatively few cases of a feminine ending rhyming with a masculine. *Cf.* G. C. Moore Smith, "The Use of
An Unstressed Extra-Metrical Syllable to Carry the Rime," *Modern
Language Review* xv (1920), 300–01 and R. E. Neil Dodge, "An Obsolete Elizabethan Mode of Rhyming," *University of Wisconsin Shakespeare Studies* (Madison, Wisconsin, 1916), p. 177.

II. iv. 14–15. *Fast-haste* was a natural rhyme for Shakespeare. *Cf.
V. A.* 55; *R. L.* 891.

IV. iv. 416–17. For the rhyming of *-n* with *-m* see Ellis, p. 955.

20 lines of speech-pause couplets: I. i. 56–9, 64–5; III. vii. 188–9; IV. iv. 73–4, 103–04; IV. v. 4–5; V. iii. 155–6, 182–3, 198–9 (?).

III. vii. 188–9. The comparative lack of couplets in this scene, the weakness of the rhyme, and the enjambement plus the absence of any caesura make this appear accidental. On the other hand, it emphasizes an important idea in the speech and marks a strong pause.

IV. iv. 73–4 contains a prophecy.

IV. v. 4–5: *head-aid. Cf. said-maid, M. N. D.* II. ii. 72–3; *said-read, L. L. L.* IV. iii. 193–4.

V. iii. 198–9 is doubtful. It appears in a soliloquy where there is a great amount of repetition of words at the end of the lines; *guilty* could rhyme with several lines both before and after.

4 lines of rhyme at the beginning of speeches: III. vii. 204–05; V. iii. 304–05.

III. vii. 204–05 tends to call attention to the hypocrisy in Richard's words.

V. iii. 304–05. This jingle is a note found pinned upon a tent, and thus is not actually part of the speech.

6 lines of speech-link rhyme: I. iv. 171–2; II. iv. 8–9; IV. iv. 24–5.

I. iv. 171–2 consists of two iambic lines of three accents. *Cf. R. J.* I. i. 190–1 and *A. C.* II. vii. 99–100.

IV. iv. 24–5 is also an aside.

8 lines of single-speech rhyme: III. vii. 221–2; IV. iv. 15–16, 20–1, 162–3.

III. vii. 221–2: *suit-rue it.* Heuser's classification of this rhyme as one of mounting passion is absurd. Actually the couplet shows Richard's hypocrisy, and the odd rhyme, which is more fitting a comic than a serious mood, accentuates this falsity.

IV. iv. 15–16, 20–1 are both asides. *Cf.* IV. iv. 24–5. See also Abbott, sec. 515.

30 lines of scene- or act-end rhyme: I. i. 161–2; I. ii. 261–4; I. iv. 289–90; III. iv. 108–09; III. vi. 13–14; IV. i. 103–04; IV. ii. 123–6; IV. iii. 54–7; V. i. 28–9; V. ii. 23–4; V. v. 38–41.

I. ii. 261–2: *grave-love* is without parallel in Shakespeare, though short *o* sometimes rhymed with short *a. Cf.* Ellis, p. 954.

IV. iii. 54–7. Quartos 3–8 have *wings,* but this still would not cancel the rhyme or explain why Heuser did not include the couplet.

22 lines of exit and cue rhyme: (I. i. 39–40); I. iv. 82–3; III. i. 91–4;

IV. ii. 64–5; IV. iv. 122–5, 194–5; V. iii. 17–18, 149–50, 165–6, 269–70.

(I. i. 39–40) is listed under the speech-end rhymes.
III. i. 94 is spoken in aside.
V. iii. 17–18 has the effect of a scene-end couplet, for the scene actually shifts from one camp to another.

16 lines of consecutive rhyme: IV. iv. 165–70; V. iii. 171–6, 310–13.

V. iii. 171–6 puts an end to the visitations of the Ghosts and thus might be considered an exit rhyme.

10 lines of unintentional rhyme: I. ii. 240–1; I. iii. 9–10; II. ii. 142–3; IV. i. 6–7; IV. iv. 68–9.

Total lines of rhyme: 140.

TITUS ANDRONICUS

22 lines of speech-end rhyme: I. i. 7–8, 60–1,* 94–5, 167–8, 366–7; II. i. 35–6, 130–1; V. i. 47–8, 57–8; V. iii. 135–6, 139–40.

I. i. 60–1. A line follows, but it is not an organic part of the speech.
I. i. 167–8. Though some editions have an entrance immediately following these lines, the couplet is listed here because in others the entrance is somewhat earlier. The sense of the passage demands that the entrance follow line 156.

6 lines of speech-pause rhyme: I. i. 107–08; V. iii. 164–5, 168–9.

4 lines of rhyme at the beginning of a speech: II. i. 97–8; V. iii. 147–8.

12 lines of speech-link rhyme: V. i. 49–52; V. iii. 46–9, 53–6.

V. i. 51–2 is actually not speech-link but continues the rhyme to give an order for gruesome action.
V. iii. 46–9 accompanies stabbing and death. *Cf. 3 Hen. VI* I. iii. 47–8.

8 lines of single-speech rhyme: I. i. 261–2, 271–2, 341–2; II. iii. 179–80.

I. i. 261–2 is spoken in aside. This might also be considered a speech-beginning rhyme.
I. i. 271–2 may be accidental, but the high number of rhymes in the scene, as well as the graceful ring of the lines, makes it seem intentional.

8 lines of scene- or act-end rhyme: II. ii. 23–6; II. iv. 56–7; v. iii. 203–04.

II. ii. 23–4. For the rhyming of *m* with *n* see Ellis, p. 955.

14 lines of exit and cue rhyme: I. i. 285–6; II. iii. 8–9, 190–1; III. i. 148–9, 205–06, 287–8; v. ii. 146–7.

II. iii. 190–1: *Moor-deflower.* Cf. Ellis, pp. 954 and 960.
III. i. 205–06 is spoken in aside.

2 lines of unintentional rhyme: v. iii. 17–18.

Total lines of rhyme: 76.

THE COMEDY OF ERRORS

22 lines of speech-end rhyme: I. i. 95–6, 155–6; I. ii. 51–2; II. ii. 147–8, 152–3; III. i. 105–6; III. ii. 150–1, 157–8; v. i. 83–6, 405–06.

I. i. 155–6: *die-custody* was probably an exact rhyme for Shakespeare. *Cf. S.* 94.10, *R. L.* 1052 and 1139.
I. ii. 51–2. The first line of the next speech rhymes with this couplet. *Cf. 3 Hen. VI* IV. iv. 14–15.
III. i. 105–06. Though this is an uneven couplet, Heuser, p. 194, rightly accepts it in its traditional form. *Cf. A. W.* II. iii. 312–13.
III. ii. 150–1. A doggerel couplet here ends a prose speech.
v. i. 83–4. *Rest-beast. Cf. M. W.* v. v. 47–8.

5 lines of speech-link rhyme: I. ii. 53; v. i. 67–8, 335–6.

I. ii. 53 forms a triplet with a speech-end rhyme. *Cf. 3 Hen. VI* IV. iv. 16.

8 lines of single-speech rhyme: I. i. 1–2, 27–8; II. ii. 48–9; v. i. 87–8.

II. ii. 48–9 is doggerel.
v. i. 87–8. The different forms of the adverbs in line 88 suggest that *wild* may have been changed to *wildly* by some copier for the sake of rhyme. On the other hand, rhyme is in keeping with the general spirit of the passage.

12 lines of scene- or act-end rhyme: I. i. 158–9; III. i. 120–3; IV. i. 112–13; IV. iii. 96–7; v. i. 424–5.

11 lines of exit and cue rhyme: II. i. 84–5; III. ii. 159–60, 168–9, 183–4; IV. iii. 79–81.

II. i. 84–5: *hither-leather.* See Ellis, p. 958.

317 lines of consecutive rhyme: ii. i. 10–43, 86–116; ii. ii. 173–204, 211–21; iii. i. 11–85; iii. ii. 1–70, 185–90; iv. ii. 1–40, 44–5, 50–1, 53–66.

iii. i. 54 is an unrhymed line, difficult to justify in a passage of rhyme. See Heuser, pp. 197–8. For a discussion of the metre of this entire passage see Schipper, *A History of English Versification*, p. 118.
The excessive amount of rhyme is used in scenes of comic banter and general lyricism. In the former considerable doggerel is used. *Cf.* A. Gaw, "Evolution of 'The Comedy of Errors,' " *PMLA* v (1926), 632.

2 lines of unintentional rhyme: iv. i. 1–2.

Total lines of rhyme: 377.

THE TWO GENTLEMEN OF VERONA

22 lines of speech-end rhyme: i. i. 9–10; i. ii. 39–40; v. iv. 43–4, 51–2,* 71–2, 80–3, 108–09, 112–15, 117–18.

i. ii. 39–40. Alexandrines are rare in Shakespeare. *Cf. M. W.* ii. ii. 215–16; *T. S.* i. ii. 227; and the sonnet of Alexandrines in *L. L. L.* iv. ii. 109–22.
v. iv. 80–3. See Sir George Young, pp. 167–8.

6 lines of rhyme at speech-beginnings: iii. ii. 42–3; v. iv. 124–7.

iii. ii. 42–3: *advantage him-endamage him.*
v. iv. 126–7: *death-wrath.* Though similar in sound, this word pair has no parallel in Shakespeare.

12 lines of speech-link rhyme: i. i. 80–1; ii. i. 1–2, 166–7; ii. ii. 6–7; ii. iv. 165–8.

i. i. 80–1; ii. i. 166–7 are doggerel.
ii. i. 1–2: *on-one.* See Wyld, p. 121.
ii. iv. 165–6: identical rhyme.

6 lines of single-speech rhyme: i. i. 74–5, 115–16; ii. i. 3–4.

i. i. 115–16: *over-lover.* The doggerel metre makes such an unusual rhyme acceptable, particularly if, as C. and M. C. Clarke (*The Shakespeare Key* [London, 1879], p. 673) say, "Considerable licence was taken in forming rhymes from words that merely sounded somewhat alike."

16 lines of scene- and act-end rhyme: i. iii. 88–91; ii. ii. 20–1; ii. iv. 213–14; ii. vi. 42–3; v. i. 11–12; v. ii. 55–6; v. iii. 14–15.

II. ii. 20–1 contains a short first line, a use not uncommon in Shake-speare.

v. i. 11–12: *off-enough* is without parallels in Shakespeare's rhymes.

v. ii. 55–6: repetition used as rhyme appears frequently.

8 lines of exit and cue rhyme: I. i. 68–9; I. ii. 48–9; I. iii. 84–7.

54 lines of consecutive rhyme: I. ii. 10–21, 27–32; II. i. 141–6, 171–4; III. i. 90–105, 140–9.

I. ii. 29–32. See Sir George Young, p. 165.

II. i. 141–2: *invisible-steeple*. Ellis, p. 955, says the rhyme was inten-tionally quaint and absurd. Speed's rhymes are generally eccentric, just as his metre tends to be doggerel. *Cf.* II. i. 171–4.

III. i. 140–9 is a love letter consisting of two quatrains and a final couplet.

6 lines of unintentional rhyme: I. i. 37–8; II. i. 127–8; III. i. 251–2.

Total lines of rhyme: 130.

LOVE'S LABOUR'S LOST

12 lines of speech-end rhyme: I. i. 22–3, 26–7, 31–2, 47–8; IV. iii. 379–80; v. ii. 821–2.

4 lines of speech-pause rhyme: IV. iii. 297–8; v. ii. 783–4.

9 lines of speech-link rhyme: II. i. 52–4; II. i. 111–13; III. i. 60–2. All three are triplets, in clever speech sallies.

5 lines of scene- and act-end rhyme: III. i. 206–07; v. i. 160–2.

v. i. 160–2 are doggerel lines. *Cf.* Walker, I, 7.

12 lines of exit and cue rhyme: I. i. 308–11; II. i. 35–6, 178–9; III. i. 65–6, 135–6.

III. i. 65–6 is doggerel.

The many other exit and cue rhymes in this play are listed be-low, for they are actually only part of the general lyricism of the rhymed scenes.

1076 lines of consecutive rhyme: I. i. 49–118, 128–9, 134–81; I. ii. 104–11; II. i. 120–1, 123–8, 186–95, 197–200, 202–08, 209–14, 215–29, 234–53, 255–8; III. i. 67–9, 71–2, 82–3, 85–6, 90–3, 96–

100, 101–07, 116–17; IV. i. 11–40, 49–50, 53–9, 90–120, 127–30, 131–47, 149–50; IV. ii. 24–5, 29–36, 40–1, 58–63, 99–100, 109–22; IV. iii. 26–41, 42–58, 60–73, 74–82, 85–100, 101–20, 121–94, 200–89, 381–6; V. ii. 30–1, 43–135, 139–56, 203–14, 216–309, 313–84, 387–8, 393–444, 446–83, 485–90, 513–14, 516–21, 541–2, 547–58, 565–72, 592–7, 627–8, 632–3, 657–60, 823–6, 833–5, 837–46, 880–1, 883–8.

I. ii. 104–11. Moth's "dangerous rhyme" may have been sung, but stage directions are lacking.

II. i. Many of the lines in this scene are either short iambic or doggerel lines. Although 205 has no line rhyming with it, it has been included in the tabulation, since it interrupts two rhymed lines.

The rhymed passages of this play have many different forms in addition to the couplet. There is a high number of triplets, quatrains, and other stanzaic patterns, including the rhyme-royal and the sonnet. A similar freedom is found in the length of the lines, which varies from two or three feet to the old fourteener. The rhyme shows considerably more freedom than is evident in Shakespeare's rhyme in general, and there are even several examples of sectional rhyme (cf. Edwin Guest, p. 127).

4 lines of unintentional rhyme: II. i. 167–8; V. ii. 30–1.

Total lines of rhyme: 1122.

ROMEO AND JULIET

42 lines of speech-end rhyme: I. i. 121–2, 147–8, 187–8*; I. ii. 10–11, 91–2; I. iv. 38–9; I. v. 60–1; II. i. 19–20*; II. ii. 21–4,* 123–4; III. i. 179–80; III. ii. 48–51, 59–60, 125–6*; IV. i. 66–7; IV. v. 63–4, 82–3; V. iii. 66–7, 301–02.

I. i. 121–2 is repetition rather than rhyme, but the general nature of the couplet necessitates its being considered a rhyme. Similarly II. ii. 23–4 and III. ii. 48–9.

IV. i. 66–7. Cf. C. E. I. i. 155–6; R. J. v. iii. 303–04.

10 lines of speech-pause rhyme: I. i. 182–3; II. i. 37–8; III. iii. 133–4; IV. v. 77–8; V. iii. 175–6.

II. i. 37–8: were-pear. Cf. were-bear, S. 13.6; were-swear, P. P. 241–2.

6 lines of rhyme beginning speeches: I. i. 177–8; IV. v. 84–5; V. iii. 161–2.

V. iii. 161–2 is assonance rather than rhyme.

42 lines of speech-link rhyme: I. i. 75–8, 166–7; I. ii. 12–13; I. iii. 57–8; I. v. 62–5, 76–7, 119–22; II. i. 32–3; III. i. 126–7, 156–7; III. ii. 127–8; III. iii. 73–4; III. iv. 7–8; III. v. 11–12, 40–3; IV. i. 18–21.

 I. i. 75–8. Alternate rhymes are used here for a swashbuckling effect.
 I. i. 166–7: *young-long.* Cf. Ellis, p. 962.
 I. ii. 12–13. W. L. Rushton, p. 17, lists this as an example of Puttenham's Rebound.
 I. v. 76–7: *feast-guest.* Cf. Ellis, p. 957.
 III. i. 126–7. This is possibly an entrance cue, though many editions have the entrance of Tybalt after line 125. The earlier entrance seems better because line 126 indicates that Tybalt is already visible to the speaker.
 III. ii. 127–8 is assonance rather than rhyme.
 III. iv. 7–8: *ago-woo.* See Ellis, p. 961.
 IV. i. 18–19 is identical rhyme, but obviously intentional.

8 lines of single-speech rhyme: I. i. 123–4; I. v. 136–7; II. iv. 208–09; III. v. 49–50.

 I. v. 136–7: *marrièd-bed.*

29 lines of scene- or act-end rhyme: I. i. 243–4; I. iii. 105–06; I. v. 145–6; II. i. 42–(3); II. ii. 187–90; II. v. 77–80; II. vi. 36–7; III. ii. 140–3; III. iii. 173–4*; III. v. 241–2*; IV. i. 124–5*; v. i. 85–6.

 I. v. 145–6: *anon-gone.* Cf. Ellis, p. 239.
 II. i. 42–3 in most modern texts is divided between two scenes. This awkwardness was unnoticed on the Elizabethan stage where there was no scene change at this place.
 II. vi. 36–7: *alone-one.* Cf. Ellis, p. 239.
 III. ii. 140–3 is a quatrain divided between Juliet and the Nurse.
 III. v. 241–2: *remedy-die.* Cf. *1 Hen. VI* III. ii. 136–7.

46 lines of exit and cue rhyme: I. i. 86–7, 108–09,* 160–1; I. iii. 96–9; I. v. 91–4; II. ii. 136–7,* 155–8, 185–6; II. v. 16–17; II. vi. 14–15; III. i. 124–5,* 140–1, 143–6; III. v. 58–9; IV. v. 94–5; v. iii. 19–20,* 43–4, 119–20, 159–60.

 I. i. 86–7. For a discussion of the seeming Alexandrine in 86 see Heuser, p. 249.
 I. v. 93–4: *shall-gall.* See Ellis, p. 956.
 III. i. 124–5. See the discussion of III. i. 126–7.
 v. iii. 43–4 is spoken in aside.
 v. iii. 119–20. See Walker, I, 116–17, for other examples of the masculine rhyming with feminine endings.

281 lines of consecutive rhyme: I. i. 162–5, 190–7, 199–204, 208–09, 213–17, 221–30; I. ii. 16–37, 46–51, 93–106; I. iii. 83–94; I. iv.

44–53; I. v. 46–55, 95–108, 140–43; II. iii. 1–94; III. i. 147–54, 181–202; III. ii. 130–37; III. v. 23–6, 33–6; v. iii. 12–17, 303–10.

I. i. 190–1. For a discussion of these lines see Heuser, p. 252.

I. i. 198. A line has probably been lost here. *Cf.* I. ii. 14–15.

I. v. 95–108 is the sonnet which Romeo and Juliet divide between them.

v. iii. 303–10. The play ends with a couplet and a sixain.

28 lines of external rhyme: prologues to Acts I and II, both in sonnet-form. *Cf.* I. v. 95–108.

6 lines of unintentional rhyme: III. iii. 66–7, 85–6, 105–06.

Total lines of rhyme: 498.

RICHARD II

90 lines of speech-end rhyme: I. i. 41–6, 67–8, 82–3, 106–07, 122–3, 150–1; I. ii. 54–5; I. iii. 93–6, 172–3, 211–12, 214–15, 221–4, 292–3, 302–03; II. i. 27–30, 86–7, 143–4, 297–8; II. ii. 24–7, 31–2; III. ii. 71–4, 102–03, 119–20, 139–40, 184–5; III. iii. 70–1, 175–6, 194–5; III. iv. 65–6, 90–1; IV. i. 148–9, 174–5,* 188–9; v. i. 24–5; v. iii. 34–5, 70–3; v. vi. 22–3.

I. i. 41–6. Although six lines are possibly too many to deserve this classification, their use here is decidedly to heighten the climax of a passionate speech.

I. i. 106–07. With the addition of line 105 this might well be considered a triplet. The only reason it has not been so listed here is that lines 106 and 107 form a grammatical unit.

II. ii. 25. For a discussion of this line see Heuser, p. 230.

6 lines of speech-pause rhyme: I. i. 133–4; II. i. 22–3, 130–1.

I. i. 133–4. Heuser, p. 228, denies this rhyme, declaring it does not have the syntactic unity that all the other rhymes in the play possess. His meaning, however, is not clear; the rhyme seems perfectly justifiable.

II. i. 130–1: *good-blood. Cf.* Wyld, p. 81.

8 lines of rhyme at speech-beginnings: II. i. 163–4; IV. i. 201–02; v. ii. 50–1; v. v. 67–8.

v. v. 67–8. For a discussion of the metrical peculiarity of line 67 see Heuser, p. 229.

2 lines of speech-link rhyme: II. i. 90–1.

24 lines of single-speech rhyme: I. ii. 56–7; I. iii. 97–8, 249–52, 304–05; II. i. 139–40, 209–10; II. ii. 142–3; III. iii. 131–2; IV. i. 322–3, 324–5; v. iii. 49–50.

II. i. 139–40: *have-grave.* See Ellis, p. 955.
II. ii. 142–3 contains a prophecy and a farewell. *Cf.* IV. i. 322–3.

47 lines of scene- and act-end rhyme: I. i. 200–05; I. ii. 69–74; I. iii. 308–09; II. i. 297–300; II. ii. 146–9; II. iii. 168–71; II. iv. 21–4; III. i. 42–(4); III. iv. 102–07; IV. i. 333–4; v. iii. 142–6; v. iv. 10–11.

II. i. 299–300: *fear-there. Cf.* Ellis, p. 954.
II. iii. 170. For the scansion of this line see Heuser, p. 226.
III. i. 42–(4). Elze's transposition of these lines seems plausible. See Heuser, p. 231.

41 lines of exit and cue rhyme: I. i. 18–19; I. iii. 206–07, 247–8; II. i. 135–8, 145–6, 211–14, 222–3; II. ii. 39–40, 121–2; II. iv. 16–17; III. ii. 61–2; III. iii. 180–3; III. iv. 27–8; IV. i. 317–18; v. ii. 37–40; v. v. 95–7.

II. i. 137–8: *grave-have. Cf.* II. i. 139–40.
II. i. 222–3: *part-short.* See Ellis, p. 954.
II. ii. 121–2: *uneven-seven.* For a summary of opinions on these vowel sounds see Heuser, p. 226.
v. v. 95–7 is a triplet divided between three speakers.

298 lines of consecutive rhyme: I. i. 154–95; I. ii. 60–1, 63–4, 66–7; I. iii. 55–62, 65–8, 144–7, 174–7, 225–32, 235–46, 249–52; II. i. 7–16, 149–54; III. ii. 76–81, 186–97, 209–18; III. iii. 168–71, 202–09; III. iv. 96–101; IV. i. 190–9, 214–21; v. i. 79–102; v. iii. 75–136; v. v. 110–19; v. vi. 7–10, 24–9, 31–52.

II. i. 7–16. Hardin Craig, p. 485, says, "The rhyming measure here and elsewhere characterizes Gaunt's exalted manner of speech."
III. iii. 202–03: *eye-remedy. Cf. 1 Hen. VI* III. ii. 136–7.
v. i. 91–2: *short-heart.* See Gavin Bone, "The Clue of Pronunciation," *London Times Literary Supplement* (March 21, 1929), p. 241.
v. vi. 24. For a discussion of the metrical peculiarities of this line see Heuser, p. 229.

8 lines of unintentional rhyme: II. i. 18–19, 262–3; v. ii. 54–5; v. v. 98–9.

Total lines of rhyme: 514.

The great number of rhymes in this play has occasioned much comment. Though Pope found them despicable and un-Shakespearian, Thomas Edwards, pp. 26–7, thought them very desirable. The rhymes are sometimes used to place the date of this play earlier than *Richard III*, but Dowden, p. 45, makes this comment: "We should consider whether a special reason for the great predominance of blank verse did not exist in the case of *Richard III*. It was written in continuation of *Henry VI.*, and more than any other play of Shakspere under the influence of the great master of blank verse, Marlowe. In *Richard II*. Shakspere is far more independent of external influence, and he may have been pleased to return to his early manner of rhymed dialogue after a grand experiment in the severer manner of his contemporary." It should be added that the rhyme is in keeping with the general poetic mood of the play.

A MIDSUMMER-NIGHT'S DREAM

4 speech-end rhymes: III. i. 143–4; v. i. 21–2.

v. i. 21–2: *fear-bear. Cf.* II. i. 27–34.

This low number of speech-end rhymes in a play so fertile of rhyme is explained by the fact that rhyme, used here mostly to distinguish the different groups in the play, appears generally in long consecutive passages.

4 lines of speech-link rhyme: II. i. 138–9; III. ii. 254–5. There is no strong justification for these rhymes. In a play as full of rhyme as this one they might easily have slipped in without the deliberate intention of the playwright.

24 lines of exit or cue rhyme: II. i. 144–5; II. ii. 25–6; III. i. 90, 109–14; III. ii. 2–3, 340–4; IV. i. 188–9*; v. i. 104–05, 376–7.

II. ii. 25–6 follows a song and was probably also sung. Furness lists it as part of the song.

III. i. 90 is Puck's rhymed answer to Bottom's lines from the play, the so-called "capping verse." See K. Elze, "Nachträgliche bemerkungen zu 'Mucedorus' und 'Fair Em,'" *Jahrbuch* xv (1880), 344.

III. i. 109–14 is a rhyme-royal stanza. The second line has only four accents, while the rest have five.

III. ii. 342–4 is a triplet, the third in this scene. All three are used with a definite purpose of emphasis, here to put an end to the quarrel between the lovers. The third line, as in the previous triplet, is an answer to the first two. The line is omitted in the Folio, but seems rightly included in the modern editions.

v. i. 376–7 is actually a scene-end couplet, for the remainder of the play is concerned with the masque of the fairies.

745 lines of consecutive rhyme: I. i. 171–8, 180–251; I. ii. 33–40; II. i. 2–59, 241–6, 249–68; II. ii. 27–34, 35–65, 66–83, 84–156; III. i. 109–14, 155–64, 168–77, 202–06; III. ii. 5–48, 50–101, 102–21, 122–35, 137–94, 350–95, 396–9, 401–36, 437–41, 442–7, 448–63; IV. i. 1–4, 74–7, 78–81, 83–4, 86–96, 97–106; v. i. 378–445.

These rhymes are mostly spoken by the fairies and the lovers. The play within a play is not included here.

I. ii. 33–40 is a doggerel poem recited by Bottom.

II. i. 2 ff. The fairy metre is mostly trochaic tetrameter, a metre normally reserved by Shakespeare for the speech of supernatural figures. *Cf.* Abbott, sec. 504; Collier, *English Dramatic Poetry*, pp. 185–6; Guest, pp. 179, 186.

II. ii. 27–34 is Oberon's charm, in trochaic tetrameter. *Bear, hair, appear, dear,* and *near* were probably pronounced alike. *Cf.* v. i. 21–2.

II. ii. 77 is an uneven line. *Cf.* Heuser, pp. 211–12.

III. i. 168–77. All the lines end in the same sound. *Cf.* III. ii. 396–9.

III. ii. 49. There is no explanation for this short line which interrupts a passage of rhyme. It marks a strong pause and perhaps accompanied some dramatic action. *Cf.* III. ii. 136.

III. ii. 122–7, 128–33, 431–6, 442–7 are rhyme-royal stanzas fitting for "materis of love" (*cf.* Guest, p. 360). Shakespeare uses this stanza frequently in his early plays and in *Venus and Adonis*.

159 lines of external rhyme: III. i. 84–9, 95–9, 105–06; v. i. 108–17, 128–52, 156–65, 171–82, 190–208, 222–9, 244, 248–9, 267, 276–92, 296–311, 331–54.

These lines constitute the masque of the mechanicals, both as it appears in the interrupted rehearsal and as it is finally presented before the court. Included are lines which actually do not rhyme but which, barring interruptions, probably would have rhymed.

v. i. 108–17, 128–52. This prologue is in imitation of the famous letter to Dame Constance in *Ralph Roister Doister* (III. ii.). See Saintsbury, II, 23. It has also been suggested, however, that Shakespeare is here parodying Gascoigne's prologue to *The Glasse of Governement* (John W. Cunliffe, "Gascoigne and Shakspere," *Modern Language Review* IV [1909], 233).

v. i. 140 is curiously without rhyme. Wm. N. Lettsom (Walker, *A Critical Examination of the Text of Shakespeare*, III, 76) wrote: "The triplet which is given by many modern editions in Midsummer Night's Dream, v. i, was produced by a transposition of Theobald's. Theobald, however, thought that a verse might have 'slipt out;' this seems to me certain, though Capell dissents." C. C. Clarke, p. 674, maintained that the line was deliberately unrhymed to show the slipshod style of the doggerel interlude.

6 lines of unintentional rhyme: IV. i. 114–15, 117–18; V. i. 86–7.

Total lines of rhyme: 783.

KING JOHN

23 lines of speech-end rhyme: I. i. 82–3, 145–7, 161–2, 257–8; II. i. 145–6, 406–07; III. i. 63–4,* 170–1; IV. i. 83–4; IV. ii. 151–2; V. vii. 68–9.

    I. i. 145–7. Triplets are not usual at the end of speeches unless the speeches have been totally in rhyme. The triplet here, however, is justified by the general tone of levity and mockery in the Bastard's words.

    I. i. 161–2. Anna Kerrl, p. 119, makes the following comment on this rhyme: "Der obige Reim der Vokale bietet keine Schwierigkeit, es findet sich auch *great: get* Lucr. 878 usw."

    III. i. 63–4. Although this couplet may be accidental—Heuser and Kerrl disagree—it has been included here as intentional. The case is similar in IV. i. 83–4.

    IV. ii. 151–2. The couplet contains a prophecy. The rhyme is not exact in modern English, but was probably acceptable in Shakespeare's time. See Heuser, p. 224.

4 lines of speech-pause rhyme: I. i. 142–3, 203–04.

    I. i. 142–3. This couplet is separated from the triplet which ends the speech by only one blank-verse line. This suggests the *aabcc* structure which appears frequently in some of the later plays. *Cf. Cy.* v. iv. 125–6.

2 lines of rhyme at the beginning of a speech: IV. ii. 90–1. This might well be accidental, though the couplet emphasizes the King's passionate answer.

23 lines of speech-link rhyme: I. i. 150–3, 168–9; II. i. 293–4, 415–16; III. i. 219–20, 320–2, 325–6, 337–8; III. iii. 28–9; V. iv. 21–2.

8 lines of single-speech rhyme: I. i. 158–9, 163–6; II. i. 413–14.

    I. i. 158–9. See Heuser, p. 224, for discussion of the irregularities in these lines.

    II. i. 413–14 is spoken in aside.

28 lines of scene- and act-end rhyme: I. i. 271–6; II. i. 595–8; III. i. 346–7; III. iv. 182–3; IV. i. 133–4; IV. ii. 268–9; IV. iii. 158–9; v. i. 78–9; v. ii. 179–80; v. iv. 60–1; v. vii. 117–18.

I. i. 271–6 consists of a couplet and a quatrain. *Cf. L. L. L.* IV. iii. 381–6.

II. i. 595–8. These lines all have the same rhyme.

III. i. 346–7: *jeopardy-hie. Cf. 1 Hen. VI* III. ii. 136–7.

IV. ii. 268–9: *haste-fast.* See Ellis, p. 955.

16 lines of exit and cue rhyme: I. i. 42–3, 180–1; II. i. 48–9; III. i. 73–4; IV. ii. 99–102; IV. iii. 7–8, 9–10.

I. i. 42–3 is spoken in aside.

II. i. 48–9: *blood-shed.* This rhyme is without parallels in Shakespeare, but the passage seems to demand a rhyme.

IV. iii. 7–8 accompanies the Prince's leap to death, and thus is a kind of exit.

16 lines of continuous rhyme: I. i. 170–9; II. i. 504–09. Both of these are rhyme-royal stanzas, the second of which is spoken aside. *Cf. M. N. D.* III. ii. 122–7.

4 lines of unintentional rhyme: IV. i. 54–5; IV. ii. 53–4.

Total lines of rhyme: 124.

THE MERCHANT OF VENICE

18 lines of speech-end rhyme: II. vii. 59–60; III. ii. 61–2, 106–07, 195–6, 231–2,* 313–16*; v. i. 144–5, 231–2.*

II. vii. 59–60: *key-may.* Ellis, p. 957, said, "It is not quite certain whether this last is meant for a rhyme. The only word in the authorities is *may*, which Gill writes (mai);" but Viëtor lists *key-survey*.

III. ii. 231–2 might well be accidental. Since Shakespeare seems to be in a rhyming mood in this scene, however, it has been included.

4 lines of speech-beginning rhyme: IV. i. 346–7; v. i. 151–2. Both of these may be accidental, but particularly IV. i. 346–7 calls special attention to the information given in the speech.

8 lines of single-speech rhyme: I. iii. 155–6; II. ix. 80–1, 82–3; v. i. 236–7.

I. iii. 155–6. This is probably accidental, but it emphasizes an important statement.

II. ix. 80–1, 82–3 are both gnomic.

33 lines of scene- and act-end rhyme: I. i. 184–5; I. ii. 146–7; I. iii. 179–82; II. i. 45–6; II. iii. 20–1; II. v. 56–7; II. vi. 67–8; II. vii. 78–9; II. ix. 99–101; III. ii. 327–30; III. iv. 83–4; v. i. 302–07.

I. ii. 146–7 are doggerel lines. See Heuser, p. 213.

II. ix. 99–101 is a triplet. *Cf.* Schipper, *A History of English Versification,* p. 217.

III. ii. 327–30 is a quatrain with a lyrical content.

14 lines of exit and cue rhyme: I. i. 111–12; II. v. 42–3, 54–5; II. vi. 58–9; II. vii. 74–7; III. ii. 61–2.

I. i. 111–12 is doggerel for a comic effect.

II. v. 42–3: trochaic tetrameter. *Cf. L. L. L.* IV. iii. 101–20.

II. v. 54–5. For a discussion of the short first line see Heuser, p. 213. Despite Heuser's attempted corrections, the present form of the line must surely be as Shakespeare intended it.

II. vii. 74–5: trochaic tetrameter. The metre is probably inspired by the tetrameter lines in the scroll which Morocco has just read.

49 lines of consecutive rhyme: II. vii. 65–73; II. ix. 63–72, 73–8; III. ii. 108–13, 132–9, 140–9.

II. vii. 65–73; II. ix. 63–72; III. ii. 132–9 are the rhymes in the scrolls. They are in trochaic tetrameter and have a monotonous repetition of the same rhyme sound, which seems to emphasize the artificiality of the whole situation.

II. ix. 73–8. The metre is inspired by the scroll. *Cf.* II. vii. 74–5.

6 lines of unintentional rhyme: II. viii. 38–9; III. ii. 9–10; IV. i. 434–5.

Total lines of rhyme: 132.

THE TAMING OF THE SHREW

24 lines of speech-end rhyme: I. i. 64–5, 166–7, 174–5; I. ii. 34–5, 170–1, 175–6, 192–3, 246–7; III. i. 13–14; IV. iv. 96–7; v. ii. 176–9.

I. i. 166–7. It was not uncommon for the Elizabethan dramatist to rhyme with the English his maxims from another tongue; *cf.* Kyd's *The Spanish Tragedy* III. iv. 83–4; III. xiii. 9–12.

I. ii. 34–5 concludes a prose speech.

IV. iv. 96–7. This is a couplet of doggerel concluding a riddle-like speech.

6 lines of speech-pause couplets: v. ii. 163–4, 167–8, 174–5.

2 lines of speech-beginning rhyme: IV. ii. 44–5.

31 lines of speech-link rhyme: I. ii. 177–9; II. i. 74–5, 227–8, 242–3, 332–3, 339–42; III. i. 71–2; III. ii. 246–7; IV. ii. 9–10; IV. iii. 37–8, 49–50; IV. v. 23–4; V. ii. 180–3.

 I. ii. 178 is an aside. *Cf.* IV. iii. 49–50.
 II. i. 74–5; IV. iii. 37–8; V. ii. 182–3 are doggerel.

10 lines of single-speech rhyme: I. i. 68–9, 70–1; I. ii. 129–30; II. i. 261–2, 328–9.

 I. i. 68–9, 70–1 are probably both spoken in aside. 68–9 may be doggerel.
 I. ii. 129–30 is doggerel for comic effect.
 II. i. 261–2 does not actually fit under any of the present classifications, but is nevertheless a deliberate rhyme.

24 lines of scene- and act-end rhyme: I. ii. 281–2; II. i. 412–13; III. i. 91–2; IV. i. 213–14; IV. ii. 119–20; IV. iv. 107–08; IV. v. 78–9; V. i. 152–5; V. ii. 184–9.

 II. i. 412–13: *wooing-cunning*. Walker, I, 126, recognized this as a couplet but insisted it was not Shakespeare's.
 IV. i. 213–14 contains the title line of the play.
 IV. ii. 119–20 is identical rhyme.
 V. i. 152–5 is doggerel. *Cf.* V. ii. 184–9.

23 lines of exit and cue rhyme: I. ii. 217–18; II. i. 325–6, 404–05; III. ii. 84–8, 149–50; IV. ii. 57–8; IV. iii. 55–60; V. i. 145–6.

 II. i. 325–6: doggerel for comic effect. *Cf.* II. i. 404–05; III. ii. 84–8.
 IV. ii. 57–8: *long-tongue. Cf. along-sung, V. A.* 1093.
 V. i. 145–6: *rest-feast. Cf. R. J.* I. v. 76–7, *feast-guest.*

33 lines of consecutive rhyme: I. i. 244–9; I. ii. 11–14, 16–17, 23–4, 225–7; V. i. 117–20, 122–3.

 I. i. 244–9 are doggerel lines. *Cf.* I. ii. 11–14, 16–17, 23–4, 225–37.
 I. ii. 4–19. Ellis called these lines "all prose, with some mad rhymes stuffed in, without a particle of metre left or intended" (*N. S. S. Trans.* I, 119).

4 lines of unintentional rhyme: induction ii. 120–1; V. ii. 121–2.

Total lines of rhyme: 157.

1 HENRY IV

12 speech-end rhymes: I. iii. 27–8; III. i. 15–16*; IV. i. 122–3*; IV. iii. 36–7; V. iv. 37–8; V. v. 12–13.

IV. i. 122–3 contains a kind of prophecy.

v. iv. 37–8 may be accidental because of the short second line; but it ends a vigorous speech and accompanies action, both of which facts lend it strong justification.

2 lines of single-speech rhyme: v. v. 32–3.

22 lines of scene- and act-end rhyme: I. ii. 239–40; I. iii. 301–02; II. iii. 118–19*; III. ii. 179–80; III. iii. 229–30; IV. i. 131–6; IV. ii. 85–6; v. v. 41–4.

III. iii. 229–30 is a rhyme of Falstaff's. Cf. 2 Hen. IV IV. iii. 88–9.

IV. ii. 85–6: feast-guest. Cf. R. J. I. v. 76–7. This is another of Sir John's couplets, this one in doggerel metre.

12 lines of exit and cue rhyme: III. iii. 227–8; v. i. 113–14; v. iii. 28–9; v. iv. 105–10.

v. i. 113–14: reply-advisedly. Cf. 1 Hen. VI III. ii. 136–7.

4 lines of unintentional rhyme: I. iii. 100–01; III. i. 268–9.

Total lines of rhyme: 52.

2 HENRY IV

10 lines of speech-end rhyme: I. iii. 107–08; III. i. 30–1; IV. iii. 88–9; IV. v. 219–20; v. v. 74–5.*

III. i. 30 is an Alexandrine. See Heuser, p. 233, for his attempted regularization.

IV. iii. 88–9. Falstaff so rarely speaks in verse that Delius printed this three-line speech in prose. But cf. 1 Hen. IV III. iii. 229–30; IV. ii. 85–6.

4 lines of speech-pause couplets: III. i. 54–5; IV. ii. 57–8.

Both of these are open to question. The first seems a parenthetical element in the speech and therefore may intentionally have been set off by rhyme; the second has few surrounding rhymes to support it.

2 lines of single-speech rhyme: IV. ii. 83–4, a popular saying.

26 lines of scene- and act-end rhyme: induction, 39–40; I. i. 214–15; I. iii. 109–10; II. iii. 67–8; III. i. 107–08; IV. ii. 118–23; IV. v. 240–1; v. ii. 144–5; v. iii. 147–8; v. v. 111–14.*

Induction, 39–40: tongues-wrongs. Cf. songs-tongues, V. A. 777.

v. iii. 147–8: they-days. Some modern editions print day in the singular form for the sake of the rhyme, but the *-s* did not destroy the rhyme for the Elizabethan. *Cf. Walker,* i. 143.

8 lines of exit and cue rhyme: iv. v. 46–7, 222–5; v. ii. 12–13.

4 lines of unintentional rhyme: i. i. 152–3; iii. i. 12–13.

Total lines of rhyme: 54.

MUCH ADO ABOUT NOTHING

4 lines of scene- and act-end rhyme: v. iii. 30–3.

6 lines of exit and cue rhyme: iii. i. 105–06; iv. i. 253–6.

    iii. i. 105–06 is spoken in aside.
    iv. i. 253–6 is a quatrain. Pope changed the scene with this couplet, with some justification; for in a play as sparsely scattered with rhyme as this, a quatrain is too strong for merely an exit.

35 lines of consecutive rhyme: iii. i. 107–16; v. iii. 3–8, 9–11, 22–3, 24–7, 30–3; v. iv. 46–51.

    v. iii. 3–8 is an epitaph in trochaic tetrameter, which probably explains the use of this metre in the two following lines as well as in lines 22–3.
    v. iii. 28–9 are unrhymed lines between two quatrains, though 29 rhymes with 25 and 27. Whether rhyme was originally intended or not is merely conjectural.
    v. iv. 48–9: *low-cow.* See Ellis, p. 961.

4 lines of unintentional rhyme: iv. i. 199–200, 217–18.

Total lines of rhyme: 49.

This comedy is usually considered to be in Shakespeare's "second style," the high amount of prose explaining somewhat the low amount of rhyme. See Charles Bathurst, p. 60.

HENRY V

10 lines of speech-end rhyme: i. ii. 295–6*; iii. iii. 42–3; iv. i. 26–7; v. ii. 382–3, 395–6.

    i. ii. 295–6 might be considered an exit couplet, but the rhyme primarily closes the speech. The exit is sufficiently marked by line 297.
    v. ii. 395–6: *Englishmen-Amen. Cf. Rich. III* v. v. 40–1: *again-amen.*

2 lines of speech-pause rhyme: I. ii. 287–8. The couplet is also a kind of prophecy.

2 lines of single-speech rhyme: I. ii. 167–8, a popular saying. *Cf.* 2 *Hen. IV* IV. ii. 83–4.

28 lines of scene- and act-end rhyme: I. ii. 307–10; II. ii. 192–3; III. i. 33–4; III. iii. 57–8; III. v. 67–8; III. vii. 168–9; IV. i. 325–6; IV. ii. 62–3; IV. iii. 131–2; IV. v. 22–3; IV. viii. 130–1; V. i. 93–4; V. ii. 401–02.

III. vii. 168 seems to be an Alexandrine. See Heuser, p. 234. v. i. 93 is an Alexandrine. See Heuser, p. 235.

2 lines of cue rhyme: IV. ii. 36–7.

30 lines of external rhyme: prologue to Act I, 31–4; prologue to Act II, 39–42; prologue to Act III, 34–5; prologue to Act IV, 43–4, 52–3; prologue to Act V, 44–5; epilogue, 1–14.

The epilogue is in sonnet form. *Cf.* prologues in *R. J.*

4 lines of unintentional rhyme: I. i. 17–18; IV. ii. 13–14.

Total lines of rhyme: 78.

JULIUS CAESAR

2 lines of speech-end rhyme: IV. iii. 131–2. Anna Kerrl, p. 120, wrote of this couplet: "Eigentlich sollte dieser Reim für die chronologische Untersuchung ausscheiden, da die Worte des Zynikers auch in Sh.s Quelle reimen." It is taken, of course, directly from North's *Plutarch*.

2 lines of rhyme at the beginning of a speech: I. i. 37–8. This rhyme, though possibly accidental, marks a change in medium from prose to blank verse. Walker, II, 114, removes the rhyme by pronouncing *Rome* as *Room*.

2 lines of single-speech rhyme: II. ii. 10–11.* Although Kerrl, p. 119, lists this as a deliberate rhyme, it is probably unintentional; for the rhyming words are of common occurrence and the lines carry no special weight.

10 lines of scene- and act-end rhyme: I. ii. 325–6; II. iii. 15–16; v. iii. 109–10; v. v. 78–81.

II. iii. 15–16: *live-contrive*. Cf. Ellis, p. 959.

4 lines of cue rhyme: v. iii. 89–90; v. v. 50–1. Both are dying speeches.

4 lines of consecutive rhyme: v. iii. 63–6.

Total lines of rhyme: 24.

AS YOU LIKE IT

12 lines of speech-end rhymes: II. iii. 67–8; II. iv. 86–7; III. v. 61–2*; v. iv. 182–5, 198–9.

v. iv. 182–5 might be construed as a cue for music and dancing to begin.

3 lines of speech-link rhyme: III. iii. 96–8. 97–8 are doggerel.

9 lines of single-speech rhyme: II. iv. 61–2; III. v. 81–2; v. iv. 126–7, 128–30.

II. iv. 61–2. For a discussion of the peculiarities of this rhyme see Heuser, pp. 215–16.
v. iv. 126–7. Cf. II. iv. 61–2 and *L. L. L.* II. i.
v. iv. 128–30 might better be considered repetition than rhyme.

18 lines of scene- and act-end rhyme: I. ii. 299–300*; I. iii. 139–40; II. iv. 99–100; II. vii. 199–200; III. iv. 59–62; III. v. 137–8*; v. iv. 201–04.

III. v. 137–8: *heart-short*. Cf. *L. L. L.* v. ii. 55–6.
v. iv. 201–02: *have-cave*. Cf. *grave-have*, *Rich. II* II. i. 137–8.

6 lines of exit and cue rhyme: III. v. 78–9*; v. iv. 153–6.

112 lines of consecutive rhyme: II. iii. 69–76; III. ii. 1–10, 93–100, 107–18, 133–62; IV. iii. 40–1, 44–5, 47–8, 50–63; v. iv. 114–21, 131–46.

III. ii. 1–10 is a sonnet-like passage which accompanies the pinning of Orlando's verses on the trees.
III. ii. 93–100, 107–18, 133–62 are Orlando's crude verses and Touchstone's parody of them. They are mostly trochaic tetrameter, though

some of the lines are iambic. The poems and situation are paralleled by Sacripant's roundelays in Greene's *Orlando Furioso*.

iv. iii. 40–1, 44–5, 47–8, 50–63 is Phebe's love letter in trochaic tetrameter, lines which Shakespeare obviously thought of as being crude and rustic. As Hartley Coleridge (*Essays and Marginalia* [London, 1851], ii, 144) said, "Phebe is no great poetess. It may be remarked in general that the poetry introduced as such by Shakespeare is seldom better than doggrel."

v. iv. 131–46 is Hymen's speech in appropriate trochaic tetrameter. *Cf. M. N. D.* ii. i.

4 lines of unintentional rhyme: ii. vii. 159–60; iv. iii. 27–8.

Total lines of rhyme: 164.

TWELFTH NIGHT, OR WHAT YOU WILL

10 lines of speech-end rhyme: ii. iv. 39–40, 120–1; iv. i. 62–3; v. i. 169–72.

4 lines of speech-pause rhyme: i. i. 7–8; ii. ii. 32–3.

2 lines of single-speech rhyme: v. i. 135–6; *willingly-die. Cf. die-dignity, S. 94.10.*

30 lines of scene- and act-end rhyme: i. i. 40–1; i. ii. 60–3*; i. iv. 41–2; i. v. 327–30; ii. i. 48–9; ii. ii. 41–2; ii. iv. 126–7; iv. i. 64–9; iv. iii. 32–5; v. i. 396–7.

i. iv. 41–2 is spoken in aside.

20 lines of exit and cue rhyme: i. v. 306–07; ii. iv. 41–2; iii. i. 74–5; iii. iv. 15–16, 236–7, 401–04*; v. i. 98–9, 173–4, 333–4.

46 lines of consecutive rhyme: ii. v. 107–10, 115–18; iii. i. 159–76; iii. iv. 407–10, 414–19; v. i. 138–41, 143–8.

ii. v. 107–10, 115–18 constitute the supposed love note to Malvolio. iii. iv. 407–10, 414–19 may be spoken in aside.

v. i. 138–41, 143–8 are couplets in a passage of paradox and confusion. The rhyme, therefore, is akin to the rhyme used in riddles.

4 lines of unintentional rhyme: i. i. 11–12; iii. iii. 10–11.

Total lines of rhyme: 116.

HAMLET, PRINCE OF DENMARK

12 lines of speech-end rhyme: i. ii. 72–3, 85–6; i. iii. 43–4; iii. i. 100–01*; iii. iii. 22–3; iii. iv. 178–9.*

iii. iv. 178-9. Delius suggests that these lines were spoken in aside.

4 lines of speech-pause rhyme: iii. iv. 209–10, 214–15.

iii. iv. 214–15 might be considered a scene-end rhyme, for Act iii ends after a line and a half. *Cf. M. M.* ii. i. 297–8.

2 lines of single-speech rhyme: iii. iv. 28–9.

26 lines of scene- and act-end rhyme: i. ii. 257–8; i. v. 189–90*; ii. i. 118–19*; ii. ii. 633–4; iii. i. 195–6; iii. ii. 416–17; iii. iii. 97–8; iv. i. 44–5; iv. iii. 69–70; iv. iv. 65–6; iv. v. 217–18*; v. i. 321–2; v. ii. 412–13.*

ii. i. 118-19. The sense here seems to be sacrificed to the rhyme.

iv. iii. 69-70. The Quarto has two couplets in place of this one in the Folio. In general, however, there is slight difference in the number of rhymes in the two versions.

iv. iv. 65-6. See Heuser, p. 260, for the scansion of these lines.

iv. v. 217-18. The Quarto shows two couplets for this one.

18 lines of exit and cue rhyme: i. i. 125–6; i. ii. 254–5; i. iv. 85–6; iii. i. 168–9; iii. ii. 304–05; iii. iii. 95–6; iv. v. 17–20; v. i. 314–15.

i. ii. 254 has only four accents. *Cf. A. W.* ii. iii. 312.

iv. v. 17-20 is spoken in aside.

16 lines of consecutive rhyme: ii. ii. 116–19; iii. ii. 282–5, 292–5; v. i. 236–9.

ii. ii. 116-19 is the childish quatrain of three-stress iambic lines which Hamlet wrote to Ophelia.

iii. ii. 282-5, 292-5 are the two quatrains which the exultant Hamlet recites immediately after his Mouse-trap has been successfully sprung. Actually lines 293 and 295 do not rhyme, thus occasioning Horatio's comment, "You might have rhym'd." In the Quarto of 1603 the rhyme is completed. The lines seem to be a quotation, possibly from some old play. See E. E. Stoll, p. 67, for parallels.

81 lines of external rhyme: iii. ii. 159–61, 165–90, 192–233, 235–8, 266–71.

These lines from the Mouse-trap have an archaic flavor which is intensified by the rhyme, thus making them stand out from the rest of the dialogue. *Cf.* Alvin Thaler, p. 1030; C. M. Ingleby, *Shakespeare, the Man and the Book* (London, 1877), II, 32–3.

10 lines of unintentional rhyme: I. v. 124–5, 179–80; II. i. 56–7; II. ii. 101–02, 154–5.

Total lines of rhyme: 169.

THE MERRY WIVES OF WINDSOR

4 lines of speech-end rhyme: II. ii. 215–16; v. v. 245–6.

II. ii. 215–16. An avowed quotation, this adage closes a prose speech in a prose scene. It is an identical rhyme.
v. v. 245–6 is proverbial.

2 lines of speech-link rhyme: v. v. 251–2.

6 lines of single-speech rhyme: II. ii. 38–9; v. v. 51–2, (179–80).

II. ii. 38–9. See Heuser, pp. 189–90.
(v. v. 179–80). This couplet is not included in the Cambridge edition, but it performs the necessary function of changing the subject and shifting the emotional mood, and thus should be included.

6 lines of scene- and act-end rhymes: IV. iv. 89–90; v. iii. 23–4*; v. v. 258–9.

IV. iv. 89–90: *crave-have*. *Cf. have-cave*, *A. Y. L.* v. iv. 201–02.

6 lines of exit rhyme: I. iii. 92–3; IV. ii. 106–09.

9 lines of consecutive rhyme: I. iii. 105–08; II. i. 15–19.

II. i. 15–19 is the doggerel love poem which Falstaff wrote to Mistress Page.

46 lines of external rhyme: v. v. 41–50, 53–84, 88–91. These lines, exclusive of the ten-line song, constitute the masque which is directed against Falstaff.

v. v. 47–8: *leap-unswept*. *Cf.* Heuser, p. 189.

Total lines of rhyme: 79.

TROILUS AND CRESSIDA

44 lines of speech-end rhyme: I. i. 39–40; I. iii. 136–7, 241–4, 287–90, 300–01, 385–6; II. ii. 49–50, 95–6, 144–5, 161–2; III. ii. 163–4;

III. iii. 48–9; IV. i. 65–6, 73–4; IV. iv. 136–7; IV. v. 85–6, 161–2; V. ii. 186–7; V. iii. 35–6, 111–12.

II. ii. 95–6 may also be a cue for a cry from within.

II. ii. 161–2. The first line of the following speech rhymes with this couplet, but it does not seem to be intentional. *Cf. 3 Hen. VI* IV. iv. 14–16; *C. E.* I. ii. 51–3.

2 lines of speech-pause rhyme: V. x. 21–2.

2 lines of rhyme beginning a speech: III. ii. 178–9. This is a conscious rhyme, for the speaker himself refers to it as such.

2 lines of single-speech rhyme: V. ix. 5–6, a kind of epitaph.

32 lines of scene- and act-end rhyme: I. i. 116–19; I. iii. 391–2; II. ii. 211–12*; II. iii. 274–7; III. ii. 219–20; IV. i. 77–8*; IV, iv. 149–50; IV. v. 292–3; V. iii. 114–15; V. vi. 30–1; V. viii. 19–22; V. ix. 7–10.

V. vi. 30–1. For a discussion of the Alexandrine in line 30 see Heuser, pp. 246–7.

44 lines of exit and cue rhyme: I. i. 114–15; I. iii. 306–09; II. ii. 111–12; III. iii. 212–15; IV. iv. 9–10, 109–10, 138–41; IV. v. 92–3, 275–6; V. i. 48–51*; V. iii. 89–90, 92–3,* 95–6; V. vi. 25–6; V. vii. 7–8; V. viii. 3–4; V. x. 30–1, 33–4.

II. ii. 111–12 is also a prophecy. *Cf.* IV. iv. 138–9.
III. iii. 212–13: *win-him.* For other examples of *-m* rhyming with *-n* see Walker, I, 133.
III. iii. 214–15: *speak-break. Cf.* Ellis, p. 954.
V. ii. 109–12. See Oscar Campbell, *Comicall Satyre and Shakespeare's Troilus and Cressida* (San Marino, California, 1938), p. 216.

68 lines of consecutive rhyme: I. ii. 308–21; IV. iv. 17–18, 20–1; IV. v. 28–31, 33–8, 40–1, 43–6, 49–52; V. ii. 107–14; V. viii. 9–14; V. x. 42–57.

IV. iv. 17–18, 20–1 is a popular quatrain on the pains of love.
V. x. 42–57. Though unseparated from the scene, these lines of Pandarus really form an epilogue to the play. Such critics as Ritson, Steevens, and Delius have doubted the authorship of the lines because of the style.

4 lines of external rhyme: prologue, 28–31. Though the play does not have a specifically designated epilogue, see V. x. 42–57.

4 lines of unintentional rhyme: iv. iv. 102–03; iv. v. 214–15.

Total lines of rhyme: 202.

ALL'S WELL THAT ENDS WELL

34 lines of speech-end rhyme: i. iii. 164–5,* 171–2, 220–3; ii. i.
126–7; ii. iii. 61–2, 308–09, 312–13; iv. ii. 36–7, 62–5; v. iii. 69–
72, 291–4, 301–04.*

ii. iii. 312–13. After an extended discussion of four-foot lines, Heuser, p. 222, concluded, "Fassen wir noch einmal kurz das Ergebniss der
Besprechung zusammen, so lautet es: dass 4-füssige Verse innerhalb
des Blankverses von Shakespeare angewendet werden sind, ist nicht
zu bezweifeln—die angeführten Beispiele lassen es mindestens als
höchst glaubwürdig erscheinen, dass Shakespeare auch im heroischen
Verse 4-Füssler nicht vermied, und dass er sie, wo er sie verwendet,
gern mit dem folgenden Verse als Couplet zusammengefasst an Stellen
anbringt, wo man auch sonst der Verwendung von regelmässigen Couplets häufig begegnet."

v. iii. 291–4, 301–04. These are parallel passages in which the rhyme
is justified by the riddle-like contents. *Cf.* Peele's *Old Wives Tale,* ll.
394 ff.

4 lines of speech-pause rhyme: i. iii. 151–2; iv. iv. 24–5.

4 lines of speech-link rhyme: v. i. 25–8. 25 contains the title-line
of the play.

31 lines of scene- and act-end rhyme: i. iii. 261–2; ii. iii. 314–17; ii.
v. 95–6*; iii. i. 21–2*; iii. ii. 131–2; iii. iii. 10–11; iii. iv. 41–2; iii.
vii. 44–7*; iv. ii. 73–6; iv. iii. 371–5*; iv. iv. 35–6.

iv. iii. 373–5: *live-thrive-alive. Cf. J. C.* ii. iii. 15–16; and Walker, iii.
76: "There is perhaps a line lost after 'found an ass;' something seems
to be wanting; *live-thrive,* too, is a suspicious rhyme for Shakespeare's
age; and triplets are very rare in him, and occur only, I think, under
special circumstances. Perhaps, however, a rhyme is not wanted here."

8 lines of exit and cue rhyme: i. i. 115–16; ii. iii. 189–90; iv. ii.
66–7; v. iii. 295–6.

i. i. 115–16 is unusual in both rhyme and rhythm, but is probably
intentional. The Oxford edition has Parolles make his entrance here.

180 lines of consecutive rhyme: i. i. 231–44; i. iii. 134–41; ii. i. 133–
44, 146–213; ii. iii. 78–83, 86–91, 95–8, 102–03, 109–10, 132–51;
iii. iv. 4–17; iv. iii. 252–9; v. iii. 314–19, 325–34.

II. i. 145. Dr. Johnson conjectured a lost line before this one.

II. i. 184. For a discussion of the irregularities in this line see Heuser, p. 219.

III. iv. 4–17 is a letter in sonnet form. *Cf. L. L. L.* I. i. 80–93.

IV. iii. 252–9 is another rhymed letter. A letter which begins with v. iii. 140, on the other hand, is in prose.

6 lines of external rhyme: epilogue.

Total lines of rhyme: 267.

MEASURE FOR MEASURE

6 lines of speech-end rhyme: II. i. 298–9*; IV. i. 12–13; v. i. 118–19.

One cannot help noticing the curious coincidence that these three speech-end couplets, though scattered throughout the play, all have practically the same rhyme. Two of them end in *so-woe*, the third in *woe-go*. It seems as if the word *woe* put the poet into a rhyming mood.

II. i. 298–9 might well be considered a scene-end rhyme, for the scene closes after the following line and a half. *Cf. Ham.* III. iv. 214–15.

2 lines of speech-pause rhyme: v. i. 415–16. This couplet contains the title-line of the play.

4 lines of speech-beginning rhyme: IV. i. 14–15; v. i. 184–5.

v. i. 184–5: *married-maid.* A poor rhyme, but see Ellis, p. 954. The couplet is justified by the fact that it contains a kind of riddle. *Cf. A. W.* v. iii. 301–04.

16 lines of single-speech rhyme: II. i. 37–40; III. ii. 40–1; IV. ii. 111–16*; IV. iii. 82–5.

II. i. 37–40; IV. ii. 111–16 are gnomic asides. The first is also a cue.

IV. iii. 82–5. Though the rhymes are unusual, they are probably intentional.

20 lines of scene- and act-end rhyme: I. iii. 53–4; II. i. 297–8*; II. ii. 186–7; II. iv. 184–7; IV. i. 73–6; IV. iv. 36–7; v. i. 542–5.

II. ii. 186 has only four accents. See Heuser, pp. 192–3.

IV. i. 73–4: *sin-him. Cf. Rich. III* IV. iv. 416–17.

12 lines of exit and cue rhyme: II. i. 269–70; II. iv. 169–70; III. ii. 196–9*; IV. ii. 64–5, 89–90.

22 lines of consecutive rhyme: III. ii. 275–96. This soliloquy of the Duke is in mixed iambic and trochaic tetrameter. Heuser, p. 192, makes the ingenious suggestion that the metre was chosen to point out the supernatural character of the Duke as executor of the divine order.

Total lines of rhyme: 82.

OTHELLO, THE MOOR OF VENICE

6 lines of speech-end rhyme: I. iii. 290–1; III. iii. 379–80; IV. iii. 103–04.

2 lines of rhyme beginning a speech: I. ii. 88–9. This couplet may be unintentional, though it does emphasize its content.

4 lines of single-speech rhyme: V. ii. 124–5, 358–9. Both are dying speeches. *Cf. A. W.* II. iii. 312–13.

14 lines of scene- and act-end rhyme: I. ii. 98–9; I. iii. 409–10; II. i. 320–1; II. iii. 393–4; IV. iii. 105–06; V. i. 128–9; V. ii. 370–1.

v. i. 128–9 is spoken in aside.

12 lines of exit and cue rhyme: I. iii. 293–4; II. iii. 9–10,* 64–5, 257–8; III. iii. 298–9; V. i. 35–6.

II. iii. 64–5. The Cambridge text has the entrance immediately before this couplet, though in the Oxford text it follows. The lines are not addressed on stage to those who enter and thus might logically be considered an entrance cue.

40 lines of consecutive rhyme: I. iii. 202–19; II. i. 115–16, 130–1, 133–4, 137–8, 142–3, 148–59, 161.

4 lines of unintentional rhyme: III. iii. 218–19; V. ii. 341–2.

Total lines of rhyme: 82.

MACBETH

10 lines of speech-end rhyme: I. iv. 20–1; I. v. 70–1; II. ii. 42–3; III. i. 35–6; IV. iii. 209–10.

II. ii. 42–3. Although not listed by Heuser or D. L. Chambers this seems definitely a rhyme, and a deliberate one. These words of supernatural foreboding are included within the two-line unit and gain emphasis through the rhyme. For the rhyme *cf. Rich. III* I. i. 136–7.

2 lines of speech-pause rhyme: IV. i. 153–4. The scene closes after the following line and a half. *Cf. M. M.* II. i. 297–8. For a discussion of the metre of line 153 see Heuser, p. 260.

8 lines of speech-beginning rhyme: II. iii. 59–60; III. iv. 69–70, 99–100; v. viii. 51–2.

D. L. Chambers, p. 17, considers II. iii. 59–60 accidental; Heuser, inexplicable. Also III. iv. 69–70.

2 lines of single-speech rhyme: I. iii. 146–7, an aside.

50 lines of scene- and act-end rhyme: I. ii. 64–7; I. v. 72–3*; I. vii. 81–2; II. i. 63–4; II. iii. 151–2; II. iv. 37–(41); III. i. 141–2; III. ii. 52–5*; III. iv. 142–3*; IV. iii. 239–40; v. i. 85–6*; v. ii. 29–30*; v. iii. 61–2; v. iv. 17–20*; v. v. 47–52; v. vi. 7–10; v. viii. 72–5.

I. ii. 64–7. Line 66 consists of only two accents. *Cf.* Heuser, pp. 259–60.

II. iv. 37–8, 40–1. A short line separates the two couplets which, nevertheless, are used as a double tag at an act-end.

v. iii. 61–2 is listed as an aside in the Cambridge edition, but since the speaker is the only one left on stage, there is no need for such a stage direction.

Fleay ("On Two Plays of Shakspere's, The Versions of Which as We Have Them Are the Results of Alterations by Other Hands," *N. S. S. Trans.* I, 357) called attention to the fact that this play has a higher number of scenes ending in rhyme than any other of Shakespeare's plays.

24 lines of exit and cue rhyme: I. iv. 48–53; II. i. 60–1; III. ii. 4–7; IV. i. 133–4*; v. iii. 9–10, 59–60; v. vii. 3–4, 12–13; v. viii. 33–4.

I. iv. 48–9: *step-leap. Cf. V. A.* 277.

IV. i. 133–4: *hour-calendar.* Though there are no parallels for this rhyme, it seems to be demanded here.

v. iii. 9–10: *bear-fear. Cf. M. N. D.* II. ii. 27–34.

v. iii. 59–60. The stage cue is missing in the Cambridge text, though it does seem appropriate to have the Doctor remain alone on the stage to finish the scene.

v. vii. 3–4. The three-stress line (l. 4) is unusual. *Cf. Hen. VIII* I. ii. 213–14.

152 lines of consecutive rhyme: I. i. 1–12; I. iii. 8–9, 11–12, 13–14, 15–16, 18–25, 28–31, 32–3, 35–6; III. iv. 135–40; III. v. 2–35; IV. i. 4–42, 44–7, 64–8, 69–72, 79–80, 90–101, 110–11, 125–32.

I. i; I. iii; III. v; IV. i contain the rhymes of the witches, mostly in trochaic tetrameter. *Cf.* Abbott, sec. 504; D. L. Chambers, pp. 11–14.

2 lines of unintentional rhyme: I. iii. 104–05.

Total lines of rhyme: 250.

KING LEAR

8 lines of speech-end rhyme: I. i. 276–7,* 281–2; I. iii. 19–20*; IV. vi. 284–5.

I. i. 276–7. Heuser, p. 263, conjectures that these lines were spoken in an aside, but despite the fact that this would give the rhyme a double reason for existing, there seems no necessity for such a conjecture.

IV. vi. 284–5. This speech might well end with "Of the death-practised duke"; for the couplet, the only one in this scene, adds nothing to the meaning of the speech. Capell, to be sure, has a stage direction here, "Exit Edgar, dragging out the Body," and R. G. White, "Buries Oswald." The couplet would seem to justify some such stage direction, since other strong reasons for its use are lacking.

4 lines of rhyme at the beginning of speeches: IV. v. 28–9; IV. vi. 225–6. Because of the general lack of rhyme in these scenes, both couplets may be accidental.

4 lines of single-speech rhyme: I. i. 283–4*; I. iv. 368–9.

I. iv. 368–9 is printed as prose in the Quarto. It might be considered a scene-end couplet, since the action closes after two short lines.

14 lines of scene- and act-end rhyme: I. ii. 199–200; I. v. 55–6; II. iii. 20–1; III. iii. 25–6; IV. iv. 27–8*; IV. vii. 97–8; V. i. 68–9.

I. v. 55–6 is doggerel. For the rhyme *departure-shorter,* see Ellis, p. 954.
II. iii. 20–1: *Tom-am.* See Ellis, p. 954.

58 lines of consecutive rhyme: I. i. 183–90, 257–68; III. ii. 81–94; III. vi. 109–20; V. ii. 319–26; V. iii. 3–6.

III. ii. 81–94. This prophecy, absent from the 1608 edition, has caused much concern. A possible imitation of Chaucer, it has been considered as an interpolation (White, Cowden Clarke), as a garbled combination of two prophecies written by Shakespeare (Warburton, Capell), and, by some, as a pair of rhymes original and correct in its present form.

III. vi. 119–20: *defile thee-reconciles thee*. Cf. *2 Hen. IV* v. iii. 147–8. For a discussion of Edgar's monologue see N. Delius, "On the Quarto and Folio of *King Lear*," *N. S. S. Trans.* III–IV (1875–76), p. 143.

Total lines of rhyme: 88.

ANTONY AND CLEOPATRA

2 lines of speech-end rhyme: I. iii. 64–5. For a discussion of the scansion of line 64 see Heuser, p. 264.

2 lines of speech-link rhyme: II. vii. 99–100. These two iambic lines of three feet each are paralleled in *L. L. L., Rich. III*, and *R. J.*

2 lines of speech-pause rhyme: I. ii. 130–1, elegiac lines over the dead Octavia.

18 lines of scene- and act-end rhyme: I. iii. 103–04*; II. i. 50–1*; III. xi. 73–4; IV. iv. 36–7*; IV. x. 6–9; IV. xv. 90–1; v. ii. 366–9.

IV. x. 6–9. These lines have been hopelessly spoiled.

4 lines of exit and cue rhyme: I. iii. 11–12; v. ii. 189–90.

I. iii. 11–12: *forbear-fear*. Cf. *M. N. D.* II. ii. 30–4.

4 lines of unintentional rhyme: IV. viii. 21–2; IV. xiv. 58–9.

Total lines of rhyme: 32.

CORIOLANUS

2 lines of single-speech rhyme: v. iii. 129–30.*

8 lines of act-end rhyme: IV. vii. 54–7; v. vi. 151–2, 154–5.*

v. vi. 151–5 forms the *aabcc* pattern which appears frequently in the later plays. Cf. *Tim.* v. iv. 80–4.

2 lines of cue rhyme: II. i. 177–8. For a discussion of this rhyme see Heuser, p. 247. M. A. Bayfield, p. 193, wrote: "Surely the

author of this wretched bombast was not Shakespeare?" But the couplet serves a strong rhetorical emphasis and is certainly intentional.

12 lines of consecutive rhyme: ii. iii. 120–31.

6 lines of unintentional rhyme: i. ix. 85–6; iii. ii. 84–5; iv. ii. 44–5.

Total lines of rhyme: 30.

TIMON OF ATHENS

28 lines of speech-end rhyme: i. ii. 12–13, 52–3, 61–2, 132–3; iii. iv. 55–6; iii. v. 22–3, 36–7, 73–4, 84–5, 87–8, 94–5*; iv. iii. 492–3, 528–9, 538–9.*

i. ii. 12–13. For a discussion of the various attempted improvements of these lines see Heuser, pp. 256–7.

i. ii. 52–3 and i. ii. 61–2 both conclude prose speeches of Apemantus. The second, while not strictly a speech-end actually concludes the body of Apemantus' discourse. His "Grace" follows.

iv. iii. 528–9: *wealth-yourself.* Though this is an unusual rhyme for Shakespeare, the lines definitely form a couplet. Walker, i, 132, moreover, cites the following lines from Beaumont and Fletcher:

> Though thou diedst not possess'd of that same pelf,
> That nobler souls call dirt, the city, wealth.

iv. iii. 538–9: *woods-bloods. Cf. L. C.* 47: *blood-good; V. A.* 742: *blood-wood.*

20 lines of speech-pause rhyme: i. ii. 17–18, 45–6, 145–6; ii. ii. 5–6; (iv. i. 35–6); iv. ii. 31–2, 38–41; iv. iii. 380–1, 520–1; v. iii. 3–4.

i. ii. 45–6. This couplet, plus a blank-verse line, divides two halves of a prose speech, an unusual usage.

(iv. i. 35–6) Since this is the first of three couplets to end the scene, it is counted as a scene-end couplet. Actually, however, it performs one of the functions of the speech-pause couplet. Thus, Sykes (*Sidelights on Elizabethan Drama* [London, 1924], pp. 41–2) denies that lines 37–40 are part of the speech in date of composition. For a discussion of the various theories of authorship of this play see K. Deighton, *Timon of Athens* (London, 1905).

iv. iii. 380–1 contains an epitaph. *Cf.* v. iii. 3–4.

2 lines of rhyme at the beginning of a speech: iii. iv. 21–2. Heuser, p. 255, attempts to regularize these lines, but it seems scarcely necessary to regularize individual lines in this very uneven text.

8 lines of single-speech rhyme: III. iv. 26–7; III. v. 38–9; v. i. 44–5, 47–8.*

III. v. 38–9: *clear-bear*. See Ellis, p. 964.

v. i. 44–5, 47–8. Although these have a short line before and after, they are really single units.

35 lines of scene- and act-end rhyme: I. ii. 255–7; II. ii. 239–42; III. i. 65–6; III. ii. 93–4; III. iv. 118–19; III. v. 116–17; III. vi. 130–1; IV. i. 35–40*; IV. ii. 49–50; IV. iii. 542–3; v. ii. 16–17; v. iii. 9–10; v. iv. 80–1, 83–4.*

I. ii. 255–7 is a triplet. *Cf. M. V.* II. ix. 99–101. Heuser, p. 257, discusses the metrical difficulties and suggests abandoning the rhyme altogether.

II. ii. 239–42. Sykes, p. 36, doubts the authorship of the rhymes; but, for that matter, Shakespeare has been absolved by one critic or another of nearly every rhyme in the play.

IV. iii. 542–3. See Heuser, p. 254.

v. iv. 80–4 is another example of the *aabcc* pattern. *Cf. Cor.* v. vi. 151–5.

24 lines of exit and cue rhyme: I. i. 37–8; I. ii. 149–50, 167–70, 209–10*; III. ii. 68–9; III. iii. 25–6; III. vi. 112–15; IV. ii. 28–9; v. i. 223–6.

I. ii. 167–70 are spoken in aside. *Cf.* I. ii. 209–10.

III. vi. 112–13: *feast-guest. Cf. R. J.* I. v. 76–7.

20 lines of consecutive rhyme: I. ii. 237–40; III. v. 52–7; IV. iii. 470–5; v. iv. 70–3.

v. iv. 70–3. Timon's epitaph is taken directly from North's *Plutarch*.

4 lines of unintentional rhyme: III. iii. 36–7; v. iv. 9–10.

Total lines of rhyme: 141.

PERICLES, PRINCE OF TYRE

56 lines of speech-end rhyme: I. i. 37–40, 57–8, 84–5,* 148–9*; I. ii. 46–7, 99–100, 109–10; I. iv. 8–9, 18–19, 28–31, 48–9,* 95–6; II. i. 54–5,* 137–40, 148–9; II. iii. 18–19, 25–6, 46–7, 68–9; II. iv. 11–12, 14–15, 38–9; II. v. 63–4, 86–7*; v. i. 96–7.

I. i. 148–9. Though this rhyme might be considered an entrance cue, the short half line which follows is the actual cue; the rhyme is an organic part of the speech.

II. i. 54–5; II. iii. 46–7; v. i. 96–7: all are speech-ends in asides.

50 lines of speech-pause rhyme: I. i. 32–3, 45–6, 50–1, 76–7, 79–80, 117–18, 132–3, 135–8; I. ii. 42–3, 61–2, 78–9, 84–5, 92–3; I. iv. 5–6, 45–6; II. i. 6–7, 54–5, 134–5; II. ii. 12–13; II. iii. 15–16, 43–4, 62–3; II. iv. 43–4; II. v. 16–17.

I. i. 76–7 and I. i. 79–80 are separated by a blank-verse line, thus forming a kind of stanza: *aabcc. Cf.* I. i. 132–3; I. iv. 5–6, 45–6; II. iii. 15–16, 43–4; II. iv. 11–12.

I. i. 117–18. Although there is an exit two lines later, this couplet is correctly listed here.

I. i. 135–8: two couplets of gnomic content.

I. ii. 61–2. See Heuser, p. 268, for a discussion of the metrical difficulties in these lines.

II. iii. 43–4 is part of an aside.

II. iii. 62–3: *gnats-at.* See Bernard, p. 6.

8 lines of speech-beginning rhyme: I. i. 12–13; I. iv. 74–5; II. ii. 56–7; II. iv. 1–2.

II. iv. 1–2. The awkward inversion in line 2 shows that this is a deliberate couplet.

2 lines of speech-link rhyme: II. iii. 35–6: spoken in aside.

16 lines of single-speech rhyme: I. i. 57–8; I. ii. 113–14; II. ii. 8–9, 34–5, 54–5; II. iii. 21–2; II. v. 71–2; IV. ii. 159–60.*

I. i. 57–8: *prosperous-happiness,* a very poor rhyme, but probably intentional.

II. v. 71–2. This short first line is a favorite device of Dekker. See F. E. Pierce, *Collaboration of Webster and Dekker* (New York, 1909), pp. 141–2.

26 lines of scene- and act-end rhyme: I. i. 170–1; I. ii. 120–1, 123–4; I. iii. 39–40; I. iv. 107–08; II. i. 171–2; II. iii. 115–16; II. iv. 57–8; II. v. 92–3; III. iv. 17–18; IV. i. 102–03; IV. iii. 50–1; V. ii. 83–4.

I. ii. 120–4 shows the *aabcc* pattern common in the late plays. *Cf.* I. i. 76–7.

II. v. 92–3 are doggerel lines. *Cf. T. S.* v. i. 152–5.

III. iv. 17–18. Heuser, p. 269, calls the short first line of this couplet a "Silbenpausler."

IV. iii. 50–1. Walker, III, 338, declared that rhyme was out of place here and tried to rearrange the lines. Rhyme, on the contrary, is perfectly fitting here, for it marks an exit and possibly also gives a cue to Gower who enters immediately.

v. ii. 83–4. This is listed as an act-end rhyme, though Gower enters and closes the play with a prologue growing out of the action.

18 lines of exit and cue rhyme: I. i. 141–2, 148–9*; I. ii. 32–3; I. iv. 54–5, 83–4; II. i. 10–11; II. ii. 6–7; II. iii. 97–8; III. ii. 85–6.

I. iv. 54–5: *tears-theirs*. Cf. Viëtor, p. 172.
III. ii. 85–6. For a discussion of these uneven lines see Heuser, p. 269.

24 lines of consecutive rhyme: I. i. 64–71, 98–9, 103–08; III. ii. 68–75.

I. i. 64–71 is Antiochus' riddle. Cf. *T. N.* v. i. 138–41.
III. ii. 68–75 is a scroll in iambic tetrameter, with the first and third lines in trochaic. Cf. *M. V.* II. vii. 65–73.

315 lines of external rhyme: I. Gower. 1–42; II. Gower. 1–40; III. Gower. 1–60; IV. i. Gower. 1–52; IV. iv. Gower. 1–32, 34–51; v. Gower. 1–24; v. i. 241–9; v. ii. Gower. 1–20; v. iii. Gower. 85–102.

Gower's speeches, many of which are in trochaic metre with very eccentric rhymes, are used to mark the transitions in the play and to condense the action of many years into the brief compass of a "two hours' traffic." The lines have a distinctly archaic flavor similar to that of the play within the play in *Hamlet*.
v. i. 241–9 is the supernatural message of Diana. Lines 242 and 244 do not rhyme, but are included here because they fit into the rhymed pattern and cannot be conveniently dissociated.

8 lines of unintentional rhyme: I. iv. 13–14; II. v. 25–6, 52–3; v. iii. 59–60.

Total lines of rhyme: 523.

CYMBELINE

4 lines of speech-end rhyme: IV. ii. 357–8*; v. iii. 57–8.

v. iii. 57–8 is within quotation marks and cannot be considered as an organic part of the dramatic medium.

8 lines of speech-pause rhyme: IV. ii. 286–7; v. i. 29–30; v. ii. 6–7; v. iv. 125–6.

With the exception of v. iv. 125–6 all these couplets are separated from a following couplet by a blank-verse line. Cf. *Per.* I. i. 76–7.

6 lines of rhyme at the beginning of speeches: IV. ii. 3–4, 380–1; v. iii. 64–5.

v. iii. 64–5. Walker, III, 328, accepts these lines as rhyme, but Furness (*The New Variorum Shakespeare: Cymbeline* [Philadelphia, 1913], pp. 365–6) stoutly rejects them.

2 lines of speech-link rhyme: IV. ii. 228–9. This is probably accidental, though the lyrical mood makes rhyme acceptable.

16 lines of single-speech rhyme: III. v. 104–05; IV. ii. 26–9, 33–6; v. iii. 59–62*; v. v. 106–07.*

IV. ii. 26–9, 33–6 are spoken in aside. The Folio has IV. ii. 26–9 within quotation marks, and many critics have rejected the passage as spurious. The marks can have little significance in determining the validity of the lines, however, since in many early plays all gnomic passages were so punctuated.

31 lines of scene- and act-end rhyme: I. v. 85–7; II. i. 69–70; II. ii. 49–50*; II. v. 33–4*; III. ii. 83–4; III. v. 163–8; IV. ii. 400–03; IV. iii. 45–6; IV. iv. 51–4; v. i. 32–3; v. v. 484–5.

II. ii. 49–50 may also be the cue for ringing a bell off-stage.
IV. iv. 53–4 is spoken in aside.
v. i. 29–33 is another example of the *aabcc* pattern.

16 lines of exit and cue rhyme: III. v. 64–5, 68–9; IV. ii. 59–60,* 193–4, 289–90; v. ii. 9–10; v. iii. 80–3.

III. v. 68–9 is to be spoken in aside.
IV. ii. 193–4 is rejected by both Pope and Furness as spurious. It is, of course, a poor couplet, but that does not necessarily mean it is un-Shakespearian.
IV. ii. 289–90. See IV. ii. 286–7. *Cf.* v. ii. 9–10.

4 lines of consecutive rhyme: v. iv. 129–32.

86 lines of external rhyme: v. iv. 30–92, 93–113, 121–2.

All these rhymes are in Leonatus Posthumus' Vision. The lines from 30 to 92 are not all rhymed, but since it is impossible conveniently to separate the rhymed from the unrhymed, the precedent of Fleay ("Metrical Tests Applied to Shakespeare," in Ingleby, p. 123) has been followed and the total has been listed under this classification. The authorship of this Vision is, of course, a matter of considerable dispute. *Cf.* Furness, *The New Variorum Shakespeare: Cymbeline*, pp. 374–9;

and G. Wilson Knight, "The Vision of Jupiter in *Cymbeline,*" *London Times Literary Supplement* (Nov. 21, 1936), p. 958.

6 lines of unintentional rhyme: II. iv. 144–5; III. ii. 10–11; IV. ii. 72–3.

Total lines of rhyme: 179.

THE WINTER'S TALE

2 lines of speech-link rhyme: IV. iv. 770–1. The absence of rhyme in the play must cast doubt upon this one, despite the fact that it achieves a comic effect common in Shakespeare's earlier plays.

32 lines of external rhyme: IV. i. 1–32, a chorus in which Time covers a gap of sixteen years. *Cf.* the Gower speeches in *Pericles.* The authenticity of these lines has been seriously doubted, though they perform a function essential to the whole plan of the play.

27–8: *daughter-after. Cf. T. S.* I. i. 244–5.

4 lines of unintentional rhyme: II. iii. 168–9; IV. iv. 140–1.

Total lines of rhyme: 38.

THE TEMPEST

2 lines of scene-end rhyme: II. i. 326–7. It is probably spoken in aside.

5 lines of consecutive rhyme: IV. i. 44–8. Although it is not so indicated, this passage may have been intended as a song. Its general lyricism and the fact that it is spoken by the musical Ariel, both point in that direction.

77 lines of external rhyme: IV. i. 60–105, 128–38; epilogue, 1–20.

IV. i. 60–105, 128–38, with the addition of twelve lines in trochaic tetrameter, constitute the masque. See Heuser, p. 181; Abbott, sec. 504; Schipper, *Englische·Metrik,* II, 120; König, p. 116. For discussions of the validity of the masque see the following: Henry David Gray, "Some Indications that 'The Tempest' was Revised," *Studies in Philology* XVIII (1921), 129–40; J. M. Robertson, "Shakespeare and Chap-

man," *London Times Literary Supplement* (March 31, 1921), p. 210;
E. K. Chambers, "The Integrity of *The Tempest*," *Review of English
Studies* I (1925), 129–50.

2 lines of unintentional rhyme: II. i. 219–20.

Total lines of rhyme: 124.

HENRY VIII

4 lines of speech-pause rhyme: II. iii. 84–5; IV. ii. 22–3. The general absence of rhyme in the play, however, must cast the shadow of doubt upon these two couplets.

10 lines of scene- and act-end rhyme: I. ii. 213–14; III. i. 183–4; III. ii. 458–9; v. iii. 181–2; v. v. 76–7.

I. ii. 213–14. The short second line is very unusual in Shakespeare.

2 lines of cue rhyme: III. ii. 105–06.

46 lines of external rhyme: prologue, 1–32; epilogue, 1–14. Both passages show some eccentricities in the rhyme, but since both are consecutive passages of rhyme the sound-likeness is not to be questioned. Parallels for most can be found elsewhere in Shakespeare. *Cf.* Heuser, p. 244; Dodge, p. 177.

The epilogue is a series of couplets and not a sonnet.

2 lines of unintentional rhyme: I. i. 5–6.

Total lines of rhyme: 64.

Appendix C. Tables of Shakespeare's Couplet Rhetoric

	a	b	c	d	e	f	g	h	i	j	k	l	m	n	o	p	q
1 Hen. VI	6	29		2	3		1	2			2	5	1	2	5	3	62
2 Hen. VI	2	28		2	3		1	2			2	7	5	2	2	3	64
3 Hen. VI	1	27		1	4				2		3	4	4	3	1	3	80
Rich. III	2	18	1	2	5			2	2		9	4	4	2	1	3	76
T. A.	3	20		1	4						3	1		4	1	4	44
C. E.	3	20		1	1		3				1	1		2		5	51
T. G.	5	10		1	3		3				4	2		2	2	2	46
L. L. L.		2			2		2			2	2	4	1	1		3	35
R. J.	2	32		1	4		1	2		2	4	3	4	5	4	14	129
Rich. II	6	39	2	6	7		1	2		4	13	5	6	8	4	15	202
M. N. D.		9		1	1						1	2	2	1	1	2	41
John	3	23		3	3	1		2			2	6	2	1	1	4	71
M. V.	3	18		7	5		2				4	1		4	1	5	65
T. S.		13	1	2			2	8	4	10	1			1	1	5	73
1 Hen. IV	4	20		3	3	1	1				3	1	2	1	1	4	46
2 Hen. IV		17		3	3	1	2				3	3	2	3	3	0	44
M. A.	1	9			1						1					1	26
Hen. V		14		3	3						3	2	2	4			40
J. C.		4			1						1	2		1			16
A. Y. L.		18	1	6	1		3	6		4	1			2	1		44
T. N.	3	16		1	5		1	2		2	5	2	2	2		4	60
Ham.	2	20		9	3				2		6	4		4	1	3	56
M. W.		8					4		2		1	1					16
T. C.	2	45	2	8	11		3	6		4	9	5	6	7	5	8	144
A. W.		17		11	9		3				12	3	2	2	1	3	81
M. M.	1	7	1	2	6		1	2		2	3	4	1				38
Oth.	1	15		4	4		1	2		2	6	2	2	1	1	2	32
Mac.	3	31		8	9		2				8	7	2	4	1	4	84
Lear	1	10		4	3		1				3	5	2	3		1	50
A. C.		8	1	3	6		4	2		2	3			1			24
Cor.		2		1	1						2						10
Tim.	4	27		11	10		5	4	2	4	14	18	4	7		3	86
Per.	2	46		2	2		2	4		6	11	13	6	5	2	2	92
Cy.	2	14		6	8	1					2	7	6	4		1	53
W. T.																	0
Tp.		1														1	2
Hen. VIII		3	2		1						1	1		1		1	12

a. Variant caesura
b. No caesura
c. Weak ending
d. First line divided syntactically between couplet and previous lines
e. Enjambed line
f. Enjambed couplet
g. Irregular metre
h. Double rhyme
i. Masculine rhyming with feminine ending
j. Feminine rhyming with feminine ending
k. Balance and parallelism
l. Line antithesis
m. Couplet antithesis
n. Inversion
o. Repetition
p. Alliteration and word play
q. Total lines of rhyme

All figures refer to the number of lines, even where the rhetorical feature depends on the couplet rather than the single line.

List of Works Cited

The Complete Dramatic and Poetic Works of William Shakespeare: Edited from the Text of the Early Quartos and the First Folio, ed. William Allan Neilson, New York, 1906.

The New Variorum Edition of Shakespeare, ed. H. H. Furness, Philadelphia, 1871–1936, vols. I–XXI.

The Works of William Shakespeare Gathered into One Volume, Oxford University Press, New York, 1938.

ABBOTT, EDWIN A., *A Shakespearian Grammar: An Attempt to Illustrate Some of the Differences Between Elizabethan and Modern English*, London, 1874.

ADDISON, JOSEPH, *The Spectator*, ed. G. Gregory Smith, New York, 1930.

ALDEN, RAYMOND M., *English Verse*, New York, 1903.

ASCHAM, ROGER, *The Scholemaster*, in *Elizabethan Critical Essays*, ed. G. Gregory Smith, Oxford, 1904, I, 1–45.

BATHURST, CHARLES, *Remarks on the Differences in Shakespeare's Versification in Different Periods of his Life, and on the Like Points of Difference in Poetry Generally*, London, 1857.

BAYFIELD, M. A., *A Study of Shakespeare's Versification with an Inquiry into the Trustworthiness of the Early Texts*, etc., Cambridge, 1920.

BERNARD, JULES E., *The Prosody of the Tudor Interlude*, New Haven, 1939.

BONE, GAVIN, "The Clue of Pronunciation," *London Times Literary Supplement* (March 21, 1929), p. 241.

BORDUKAT, GERTRUD, *Die Abgrenzung zwischen vers und prosa in den dramen Shakespeares*, Königsberg, 1918.

BOYLE, R., "Beaumont, Fletcher, and Massinger," *Englische Studien* v (1882), 74–96.

——, "Pericles," *Englische Studien* v (1882), 363–9.

——, "Blank Verse and Metrical Tests," *Englische Studien* XVI (1892), 440–8.

BRADBROOK, M. C., *Elizabethan Stage Conditions*, Cambridge, 1932.

BRIGHT, JAMES W., "The Rhetoric of Verse in Chaucer," *Publications of the Modern Language Association* XVI (1901), xl–xliii.

BROOKE, C. F. TUCKER, "Marlowe's Versification and Style," *Studies in Philology* XIX (1922), 186–205.

—— and PARADISE, N. B., *English Drama 1580–1642*, New York, 1933.

CALDECOTT, THOMAS, quoted in *The New Variorum Edition of Shakespeare: Hamlet*, ed. H. H. Furness, Philadelphia, 1877, I, 129.

CAMPBELL, OSCAR JAMES, *Comicall Satyre and Shakespeare's Troilus and Cressida*, San Marino, California, 1938.

CAMPION, THOMAS, *Observations in the Art of English Poesie*, in *Ancient Critical Essays upon English Poets and Poësy*, ed. Joseph Haslewood, London, 1815, II, 159–89.

CHAMBERS, DAVID LAURANCE, *The Metre of Macbeth: Its Relation to Shakespeare's Earlier and Later Work*, Princeton, 1903.

CHAMBERS, SIR EDMUND K., *The Elizabethan Stage*, Oxford, 1923, 4 vols.

——, "The Integrity of The Tempest," *Review of English Studies* I (1925), 129–50.

——, *William Shakespeare: A Study of Facts and Problems*, Oxford, 1930, 2 vols.

CHELLI, MAURICE, *Étude sur la collaboration de Massinger avec Fletcher et son groupe*, Paris, 1926.

CLARKE, CHARLES COWDEN and MARY COWDEN, *The Shakespeare Key: Unlocking the Treasures of his Style, Elucidating the Peculiarities of his Construction, and Displaying the Beauties of his Expression*, etc., London, 1879.

COLERIDGE, HARTLEY, *Essays and Marginalia*, London, 1851.

COLLIER, JOHN PAYNE, *The History of English Dramatic Poetry to the Time of Shakespeare: and Annals of the Stage to the Restoration*, London, 1831, vol. III.

CORSON, HIRAM, *An Introduction to the Study of Shakespeare*, Boston, 1889.

CRAIG, HARDIN, *Shakespeare: A Historical and Critical Study with Annotated Texts of Twenty-one Plays*, New York, 1935.

CREIZENACH, WILHELM, *The English Drama in the Age of Shakespeare*, tr. Cécile Hugon, London, 1916.

CROLL, MORRIS W., *The Works of Fulke Greville*, Philadelphia, 1903.

CROMWELL, OTELIA, *Thomas Heywood: A Study in the Elizabethan Drama of Everyday Life*, New Haven, 1928.

CUNLIFFE, JOHN W., "Gascoigne and Shakspere," *Modern Language Review* IV (1909), 231–3.

DANIEL, SAMUEL, *A Defence of Ryme. Against a Pamphlet entituled: "Obseruations in the Art of English Poesie,"* in *Ancient Critical Essays upon English Poets and Poësy*, ed. Joseph Haslewood, London, 1815, II, 191–219.

DAVID, RICHARD, *The Janus of Poets: Being an Essay on the Dramatic Value of Shakspere's Poetry Both Good and Bad*, Cambridge, 1935.

DEANE, CECIL VICTOR, *Dramatic Theory and the Rhymed Heroic Play*, London, 1931.

DEIGHTON, K., *Timon of Athens*, London, 1905.

DELIUS, N., "On the Quarto and Folio of *King Lear*," *New Shakspere Society's Transactions* III–IV (1875–76), 125–47.

DODGE, R. E. NEIL, "An Obsolete Elizabethan Mode of Rhyming," *University of Wisconsin Shakespeare Studies*, Madison, Wisconsin, 1916, pp. 174–200.

DOWDEN, EDWARD, *Shakspere,* Cincinnati, "Literary Primers," n.d.

DRAPER, JOHN W., "King James and Shakespeare's Literary Style," *Archiv für das studium der neueren sprachen,* vol. 171 (1937), pp. 36–48.

DUNN, E. C., *Ben Jonson's Art,* Northampton, Mass., 1925.

EDWARDS, THOMAS, *Canons of Criticism,* London, 1750.

EKWALL, EILERT, "Die Shakespeare Chronologie," *Germanisch-Romanische Monatsschrift* III (1911), 90–108.

ELLIS, ALEXANDER J., *On Early English Pronunciation, With Especial Reference to Shakespere and Chaucer,* etc., London, 1871, vol. III.

——, "On the Metre of *The Shrew,*" *New Shakspere Society's Transactions* I (1874), 116–19.

ELTON, OLIVER, *Style in Shakespeare,* London, 1936.

ELZE, KARL, "Nachträgliche bemerkungen zu 'Mucedorus' und 'Fair Em,'" *Jahrbuch* XV (1880), 339–52.

FLEAY, FREDERICK G., "On Metrical Tests as Applied to Dramatic Poetry," *New Shakspere Society's Transactions* I (1874), 1–16, 51–73.

——, "On Two Plays of Shakspere's, The Versions of Which as We Have Them are the Results of Alterations by Other Hands," *New Shakspere Society's Transactions* I (1874), 339–66.

——, "The Authorship of the *Taming of the Shrew,*" *New Shakspere Society's Transactions* I (1874), 85–98.

——, "On Metrical Tests Applied to Shakespeare," in C. M. Ingleby, *Shakespeare, the Man and the Book,* London, 1877, II, 50–141.

——, *A Chronicle History of the Life and Work of William Shakespeare, Player, Poet, and Playmaker,* London, 1886.

FURNIVALL, FREDERICK J., "The Succession of Shakspere's Works and the Use of Metrical Tests in Settling It," Introduction to G. G. Gervinus, *Shakespeare Commentaries,* London, 1874.

——, Comments in *New Shakspere Society's Transactions* I (1874), 31–5.

GASCOIGNE, GEORGE, *Certayne Notes of Instruction Concerning the making of Verse or Ryme in English,* in *Ancient Critical Essays upon English Poets and Poësy,* ed. Joseph Haslewood, London, 1815, II, 1–12.

GAW, ALLISON, "Evolution of 'The Comedy of Errors,'" *Publications of the Modern Language Association* V (1926), 620–66.

GERVINUS, GEORG G., *Shakespeare Commentaries,* tr. F. E. Bunnètt, London, 1903.

GOSSON, STEPHEN, quoted in J. P. Collier, *The History of English Dramatic Poetry to the Time of Shakespeare,* London, 1831, III, 108.

GRANVILLE-BARKER, HARLEY, *Prefaces to Shakespeare,* London, 1927.

GRAY, HENRY DAVID, "Some Indications that 'The Tempest' was Revised," *Studies in Philology* XVIII (1921), 129–40.

GREG, W. W., "Act-Divisions in Shakespeare," *Review of English Studies* IV (1928), 152–8.

GUEST, EDWIN, A History of English Rhythms, ed. W. W. Skeat, London, 1882.

HALES, J. W., Comments in New Shakspere Society's Transactions I (1874), 21–6.

HAMELIUS, P., Was dachte Sh. über poesie?, 1889.

HARINGTON, SIR JOHN, An Apologie of Poetrie. Prefixed to Orlando Furioso in English Heroical Verse, in Ancient Critical Essays upon English Poets and Poësy, ed. Joseph Haslewood, London, 1815, II, 117–46.

HARRISON, J., GOODLET, J., and BOYLE, R., "Report of the Tests Committee of the St. Petersburg Shakspere Circle," Englische Studien III (1880), 473–503.

HASLEWOOD, JOSEPH, Ancient Critical Essays upon English Poets and Poësy, London, 1811–15, 2 vols.

HAZLITT, WILLIAM CAREW, English Proverbs and Proverbial Phrases, Collected from the Most Authentic Sources, etc., London, 1907.

HERTZBERG, W., Introduction to Cymbeline, Ausgabe der deutschen Shakespeare-gesellschaft, 1871.

——, "Metrisches, grammatisches, chronologisches zu Shakespeare's dramen," Jahrbuch XIII (1878), 248–66.

HEUSER, JULIUS, "Der Coupletreim in Shakespeare's dramen," Jahrbuch XXVIII (1893), 177–272.

HEWLETT, JAMES H., "The Influence of Seneca's Epistulae Morales on Elizabethan Tragedy," Abstracts of Theses. The University of Chicago Humanistic Series IX (1930–32), 455–9.

HEYWOOD, THOMAS, The Royal King, and Loyal Subject. A Woman Killed with Kindness, ed. J. P. Collier, London, 1850.

——, The Royall King and Loyall Subject, ed. K. W. Tibbals, Philadelphia, 1906.

HUBBARD, F. G., "Repetition and Parallelism in the Earlier Elizabethan Drama," Publications of the Modern Language Association XX (1905), 360–79.

HUNTER, SIR MARK, "Act- and Scene-Division in the Plays of Shakespeare," Review of English Studies II (1926), 295–310.

INGLEBY, CLEMENT MANSFIELD, Shakespeare, the Man and the Book: Being a Collection of Occasional Papers on the Bard and his Writing, London, 1877, 2 vols.

INGRAM, JOHN K., "On the 'Weak Endings' of Shakspere, with Some Account of the History of Verse-tests in General," New Shakspere Society's Transactions I (1874), 442–64.

ISAAC, HERMANN, "Die Hamlet-periode in Shaksperes leben," Archiv für das studium der neueren sprachen unde literaturen LXXIV (1885), 45–59.

JAMES, KING, A treatis of the airt of Scottis Poësie, in Ancient Critical Essays upon English Poets and Poësy, ed. Joseph Haslewood, London, 1815, II, 97–117.

JENTE, RICHARD, "The Proverbs of Shakespeare with Early and Contemporary Parallels," *Washington University Studies* XIII (1925–26), 391–444.

JONSON, BEN, *The Works of Ben Jonson*, ed. W. Gifford, London, 1875.

KENNEDY, MILTON B., "The Oration in Shakespeare," *University of Virginia Abstracts of Dissertations*, Charlottesville, Virginia, 1937, pp. 16–18.

KERRL, ANNA, *Die metrischen Unterschiede von Shakespeares King John und Julius Caesar: eine chronologische untersuchung*, Bonn, 1913.

KLEIN, DAVID, *Literary Criticism from the Elizabethan Dramatists: Repertory and Synthesis*, etc., New York, 1910.

KNIGHT, G. WILSON, "The Vision of Jupiter in *Cymbeline*," *London Times Literary Supplement* (Nov. 21, 1936), p. 958.

KÖNIG, GOSWIN, "Der Vers in Shaksperes dramen," *Quellen und forschungen*, vols. 61–4 (1888).

KRAMER, GUSTAV, *Über Stichomythie und gleichklang in den dramen Shakespeares*, Duisburg, 1889.

KRUMM, H., *Die Verwendung des reimes in dem blankverse des englischen dramas zur zeit Shakspere's (1561–1616)*, Kiel, 1889.

LANIER, SIDNEY, *The Science of English Verse*, New York, 1880.

——, *Shakspere and his Forerunners: Studies in Elizabethan Poetry and its Development from Early English*, New York, 1902, 2 vols.

LANZ, HENRY, *The Physical Basis of Rime. An Essay on the Aesthetics of Sound*, Stanford University, California, 1931.

LETTSOM, WILLIAM N., editor's note in W. Walker, *A Critical Examination of the Text of Shakespeare*, London, 1860.

LEVER, KATHERINE, "Proverbs and *Sententiae* in the Plays of Shakspere," *Shakespeare Association Bulletin* XIII (1938), 173–83, 224–39.

MALONE, EDMOND, "An Attempt to Ascertain the Order in which the Plays of Shakspeare were Written," in *The Plays of William Shakspeare*, ed. George Steevens, London, 1793, I, 472–617.

MARLOWE, CHRISTOPHER, *Tamburlaine*, in *English Drama 1580–1642*, ed. C. F. Tucker Brooke and N. B. Paradise, New York, 1933.

MAYNADIER, HOWARD, "The Areopagus of Sidney and Spenser," *Modern Language Review* IV (1909), 239–301.

MAYOR, JOSEPH B., *Chapters on English Metre*, London, 1886.

MEINERS, MARTIN, *Metrische Untersuchungen über den dramatiker John Webster*, Halle, 1893.

MIDDLETON, THOMAS, *The Works of Thomas Middleton*, ed. A. H. Bullen, London, 1885.

MOODY, DOROTHY, *Shakespeare's Stage Directions: An Examination for Bibliographical and Literary Evidence*, unpublished dissertation, Yale University, 1938.

NASHE, THOMAS, *The Works of Thomas Nashe*, ed. R. B. McKerrow, London, 1904–1910, 5 vols.

NEILSON, WILLIAM ALLAN, ed., *The Complete Dramatic and Poetic*

Works of William Shakespeare: Edited from the Text of the Early Quartos and the First Folio, New York, 1906.

—— and THORNDIKE, A. H., *The Facts about Shakespeare*, New York, 1933.

NICHOLSON, B., comments in *New Shakspere Society's Transactions* I (1874), 36–7.

NICOLL, ALLARDYCE, *The English Theatre: A Short History*, New York, 1936.

NOBLE, RICHMOND, "Shakespeare's 'Curtains,'" *London Times Literary Supplement* (May 3, 1928), p. 334.

OLIPHANT, E. H. C., "Shakspere's Plays: an Examination," *Modern Language Review* IV (1909), 190–9, 342–51.

OMOND, THOMAS S., *English Metrists: Being a Sketch of English Prosodical Criticism from Elizabethan Times to the Present Day*, Oxford, 1921.

PARROT, T. M., *William Shakespeare: A Handbook*, New York, 1934.

PIERCE, F. E., *Collaboration of Webster and Dekker*, New York, 1909.

POLLARD, A. W., Introduction to Peter Alexander, *Shakespeare's Henry VI and Richard III*, Cambridge, 1929.

POPE, E. F., "Critical Background of Spenserian Stanza," *Modern Philology* XXIV (1926–27), 31–53.

PULLING, FREDERICK S., "The 'Speech-Ending Test' Applied to Twenty of Shakspere's Plays," *New Shakspere Society's Transactions* V–VII (1877–79), 457–8.

PUTTENHAM, GEORGE, *The Arte of English Poesie*, in *Ancient Critical Essays upon English Poets and Poësy*, ed. Joseph Haslewood, London, 1811, vol. I.

REYHER, PAUL, *Essai sur le doggerel*, Bordeaux, 1909.

REYNOLDS, GEORGE F., *Some Principles of Elizabethan Staging*, Chicago, 1905.

——, *The Staging of Elizabethan Plays at the Red Bull Theater, 1605–1625*, New York, 1940.

RICHARDSON, CHARLES F., *A Study of English Rhyme*, Hanover, New Hampshire, 1909.

ROBERTSON, JOHN M., *Did Shakespeare Write "Titus Andronicus"?*, London, 1905.

——, "Shakespeare and Chapman," *London Times Literary Supplement* (March 31, 1921), p. 210.

RUSHTON, WILLIAM L., *Shakespeare and 'The Arte of English Poesie,'* Liverpool, 1909.

RYLANDS, GEORGE, "The Early and the Mature Shakespearian Manner," in *Shakespeare Criticism, 1919–1935*, ed. Anne Bradby, London, 1936, pp. 372–88.

SAINTSBURY, GEORGE, *A History of English Prosody from the Twelfth Century to the Present Day*, London, 1906–10, vols. I, II.

SCHELLING, FELIX, *Poetic and Verse Criticism of the Reign of Elizabeth*, Philadelphia, 1891.

——, "Ben Jonson and the Classical School," *Publications of the Modern Language Association* XIII (1898), 221–49.

SCHIPPER, JAKOB, *De Versv Marlovii*, Bonn, 1867.

——, *Englische Metrik in historischer und systematischer entwickelung dargestellt*, Bonn, 1881–88, 3 vols.

——, *A History of English Versification*, Oxford, 1910.

SCHRÖER, ARNOLD, "Über die anfänge des blankverses in England," *Anglia* IV (1881), 1–72.

A Series of Papers on Shakespeare and the Theatre, together with Papers on Edward Alleyn and Early Records Illustrating the Personal Life of Shakespeare, by Members of the Shakespeare Association, London, 1927.

SIDNEY, SIR PHILIP, *Apologie for Poetrie*, in *Elizabethan Critical Essays*, ed. George Gregory Smith, Oxford, 1904, I, 148–207.

SMITH, G. C. MOORE, "The Use of an Unstressed Extra-Metrical Syllable to Carry the Rime," *Modern Language Review* XV (1920), 300–03.

SMITH, GEORGE GREGORY, *Elizabethan Critical Essays*, Oxford, 1904, 2 vols.

SPENSER, EDMUND, *The Shepherd's Calendar*, ed. W. L. Renwick, London, 1930.

——, *Three Proper and Wittie, Familiar Letters*, in *Ancient Critical Essays upon English Poets and Poësy*, ed. Joseph Haslewood, London, 1815, II, 255–83.

STOLL, ELMER EDGAR, *John Webster: The Periods of his Work as Determined by his Relations to the Drama of his Day*, Boston, 1905.

SWINBURNE, ALGERNON CHARLES, quoted by Oliver Elton, *Style in Shakespeare*, London, 1936.

SYKES, HENRY DUGDALE, *Sidelights on Elizabethan Drama: A Series of Studies Dealing with the Authorship of Sixteenth and Seventeenth Century Plays*, London, 1924.

THALER, ALVIN, "Shakespeare on Style, Imagination, and Poetry," *Publications of the Modern Language Association* LIII (1938), 1019–36.

UHLAND, MAUDE, "A Study of Samuel Daniel," *Cornell University Abstracts of Theses*, Ithaca, N. Y., 1938, pp. 40–2.

VERRIER, PAUL, *Essai sur les principes de la metrique anglaise*, Paris, 1909, 3 vols.

VIËTOR, WILHELM, *A Shakespeare Phonology, With a Rime-Index to the Poems as a Pronouncing Vocabulary*, London, 1906.

WALKER, WILLIAM SIDNEY, *A Critical Examination of the Text of Shakespeare, with Remarks on his Language and That of his Contemporaries, together with Notes on his Plays and Poems*, London, 1860, 3 vols.

WALLERSTEIN, RUTH C., "The Development of the Rhetoric and Metre of the Heroic Couplet, Especially in 1625–1645," *Publications of the Modern Language Association* L (1935), 172–81.

WARD, SIR ALDOLPHUS W., *A History of English Dramatic Literature to the Death of Queen Anne*, London, 1899, vol. II.

WEBBE, WILLIAM, *A Discourse of English Poetrie. Together with the Authors iudgment, touching the reformation of our English Verse*, in *Ancient Critical Essays upon English Poets and Poësy*, ed. Joseph Haslewood, London, 1815, II, 13–95.

WELLS, HENRY W., *A Chronological List of Extant Plays Produced in or about London 1581–1642*, New York, 1940.

WHITE, RICHARD GRANT, *Studies in Shakespeare*, New York, 1886.

WILDE, OSCAR, "The Critic as Artist," *Intentions*, New York, 1907.

WILKE, W., "Anwendung der rhyme-test und double-endings-test auf Ben Jonson's dramen," *Anglia* x (1888), 512–21.

WILLCOCK, GLADYS D., *Shakespeare as Critic of Language*, London, 1934.

WILLIAMSON, GEORGE, "The Rhetorical Pattern of Neo-classical Wit," *Modern Philology* XXXIII (1935–36), 55–81.

WILSON, J. DOVER, "Act- and Scene-Division in the Plays of Shakespeare: A Rejoinder to Sir Mark Hunter," *Review of English Studies* III (1927), 385–97.

WITHERSPOON, ALEXANDER M., *The Influence of Robert Garnier on Elizabethan Drama*, New Haven, 1924.

WYLD, HENRY CECIL, *Studies in English Rhymes from Surrey to Pope: A Chapter in the History of English*, London, 1923.

YOUNG, SIR GEORGE, *An English Prosody on Inductive Lines*, Cambridge, 1928.

Index

THIS selective index does not include the modern critics. Their names and the titles of their works are to be found in the List of Works Cited. Also, since the material in the Appendices is presented under lists of plays arranged chronologically, it has not been included in this index.